Preventing Adolescent Depression

Preventing Adolescent Depression

Interpersonal Psychotherapy –
Adolescent Skills Training

Jami F. Young
Laura Mufson
Christie M. Schueler

OXFORD
UNIVERSITY PRESS

OXFORD
UNIVERSITY PRESS

Oxford University Press is a department of the University of Oxford. It furthers
the University's objective of excellence in research, scholarship, and education
by publishing worldwide. Oxford is a registered trade mark of Oxford University
Press in the UK and certain other countries.

Published in the United States of America by Oxford University Press
198 Madison Avenue, New York, NY 10016, United States of America.

A copy of this book's Catalog-in-Publication Data is on file with the Library of Congress
ISBN 978–0–19–024318–0

9 8 7 6 5 4 3 2 1

Printed by Webcom, Inc., Canada

Contents

Preface   ix

1.   Importance of Depression Prevention   1
    Depression Is a Public Health Issue   1
    Adolescence Is a Prime Time for Depression Prevention 2
    Why Develop a Prevention Program Focusing on Interpersonal Relationships? 3
    How Is IPT-AST Similar to or Different From Other Prevention Programs? 4
    For Whom Is IPT-AST Appropriate?   5
    Implementing Prevention Programs in Diverse Settings   7
2.   IPT-AST Overview   9
    What Is IPT-AST?   9
    Course of IPT-AST   10
    Key IPT-AST Intervention Components   11
    The Leader's Role in IPT-AST   15
3.   Selecting Adolescents to Participate in IPT-AST   16
    Conducting a Clinical Interview   17
    Considerations for Group Composition   22
4.   IPT-AST Pre-Group Sessions   24
    Pre-Group Session 1   25
    Pre-Group Session 2   33
    Summary of the Pre-Group Sessions   38
5.   IPT-AST Initial Phase   39
    Group Session 1   39
    Group Session 2   49
    Group Session 3   56
    Summary of the Initial Phase   69

6. IPT-AST Middle Phase 70
   Group Session 4 72
   Group Sessions 5 and 6 89
   Summary of the Middle Phase 95
7. IPT-AST Mid-Group Session 96
   Mid-Group Session 96
   Opening Tasks for All Mid-Group Sessions 97
   Middle Tasks for Mid-Group Sessions When Parents Are Present 99
   Middle Tasks for Mid-Group Sessions When Parents Are Not Present 104
   Closing Task for All Mid-Group Sessions 105
   Summary of the Mid-Group Session 106
8. IPT-AST Termination Phase 108
   Group Session 7 109
   Group Session 8 114
   Summary of the Termination Phase 124
9. IPT-AST Booster Sessions 125
   Booster Sessions 126
   Summary of the Booster Sessions 135
10. Conducting IPT-AST in Schools 136
    The Advantages of School-Based Prevention Programs 136
    Obtaining Agreement From Key Stakeholders 137
    Assessing Capacity to Implement IPT-AST 139
    Identifying Adolescents to Participate 140
    Discussing IPT-AST With Adolescents and Parents 141
    Logistical Concerns for Implementation 142
11. IPT-AST With Different Populations and in Diverse Settings 144
    Conducting IPT-AST With Adolescents at Varying Levels of Risk 144
    Implementation of IPT-AST in Diverse Settings 147
    Logistical Concerns for Implementation 149
    Funding 150
12. Common Clinical Issues 151
    Missed Sessions 151
    Engaging Reluctant Teens 153
    Difficult or Defiant Adolescents 154
    Breaches to Confidentiality 157
    Challenging Family Situations 158
    Sensitive Topics 159
    Self-Harm and Suicidality 161
    Suspected Abuse 162
13. Review of Empirical Evidence for IPT-AST 164
    Efficacy Research 164
    For Whom Is IPT-AST Effective? 169

Satisfaction and Attendance 170
IPT-AST Adaptations 171
Current and Future Directions 172

Appendix 175
   Pre-Group Session 1 Outline 177
   Pre-Group Session 2 Outline 178
   Group Session 1 Outline 179
   Group Session 2 Outline 180
   Group Session 3 Outline 181
   Group Session 4 Outline 182
   Mid-Group Session With Parent(s) Outline 183
   Mid-Group Session Without Parents Outline 184
   Group Session 5 Outline 185
   Group Session 6 Outline 186
   Group Session 7 Outline 187
   Group Session 8 Outline 188
   Booster Session Outline 189
   Closeness Circle 190
   Interpersonal Inventory: How to Query About Relationships 191
   Depression Checklist 192
   Depression Vignettes 193
   Communication Notecards 198
   Interpersonal Scenario Notecards 204
   Communication Strategy Cue Cards 215
   Communication Strategy Descriptions 225
   Certificate of Participation 226

References 227
About the Authors 231
Index 233

Preface

The idea for developing a prevention program for adolescent depression stemmed from our experiences conducting treatment with depressed adolescents who had been referred to mental health clinics. Many of these adolescents had been depressed for a considerable period of time before initiating care. Because of their depression, these youth experienced significant disruptions in their social and academic functioning. Although many of these adolescents improved with short-term treatment, others required more intensive and long-term treatment because of the chronicity of their depression and the related impairments. We began to think about whether early identification and intervention may have mitigated these difficulties.

This led to our interest in developing and studying a depression prevention program for youth who are experiencing depressive symptoms but do not yet qualify for a diagnosis of depression. The impetus for developing Interpersonal Psychotherapy – Adolescent Skills Training (IPT-AST) specifically was our positive experiences utilizing Interpersonal Psychotherapy for Depressed Adolescents (IPT-A) as a treatment approach. We believed that the interpersonal problem-solving and communication strategies taught in IPT-A would be helpful for most adolescents, not just those suffering from depression. Our hope was that teaching these strategies in a prevention program would make adolescents better equipped to handle current interpersonal problems and future stressors, and that this might prevent them from developing depression.

We spent the past 12 years developing, evaluating, refining, and implementing the IPT-AST program in schools and other settings. During this process, we have been struck by the number of adolescents who experience elevated depressive symptoms. The terms *elevated depressive symptoms* and *subthreshold depression* describe individuals who experience depressive symptoms, such as feeling sad, having difficulty concentrating, or losing interest or pleasure in activities, but who do not report enough symptoms to meet criteria for a depression diagnosis. In our studies, a quarter to a third of adolescents that we have screened exhibited elevated scores on the depression screening measure. Some of these youth were known to school personnel, but many of them were suffering quietly; teachers and parents were unaware that these youth were distressed.

Our experiences have persuaded us of the importance of identifying youth who would benefit from prevention programs and the benefits of providing these interventions in schools where youth are most likely to receive mental health services. Our work has also demonstrated the power of IPT-AST to improve adolescents' depressive symptoms, interpersonal relationships, and overall functioning. There is research and policy to support the necessity and importance of implementing mental health prevention programs. Ultimately, however, it has been our clinical experiences, first working with depressed adolescents and subsequently implementing IPT-AST, that convinced us of the importance of disseminating evidence-based prevention programs such as IPT-AST.

As a semistructured preventive intervention, IPT-AST can be delivered in schools, mental health settings, primary care offices, and community centers. Although to date IPT-AST has been delivered by clinical psychologists and graduate students in clinical and school psychology, our hope is that this book will allow professionals from diverse backgrounds to deliver this program, thereby reaching more adolescents who could benefit from a preventive intervention. This includes school counselors; clinical, school, and counseling psychologists; social workers; and child psychiatry residents. We believe that those best equipped to deliver IPT-AST will have some training and experience providing counseling to adolescents. Those who have knowledge about providing group-based counseling will be best prepared, although prior group experience is not necessary. For those who wish to deliver IPT-AST but have not had experience running groups, we recommend gaining expertise via supervision, training, or self-study.

We believe that group leaders who will implement IPT-AST as well as those who oversee organizations that provide services to adolescents will benefit from reading this book. The book begins with a chapter on the importance of depression prevention, followed by an overview of the IPT-AST program. Chapter 3 provides information on how to determine whether an adolescent is appropriate for IPT-AST. Chapters 4 through 9 outline each phase of the intervention (pre-group sessions, initial phase, middle phase, mid-group session, termination phase, and booster sessions), with separate sections within each chapter devoted to each of the individual and group sessions. In Chapters 10 through 13, we discuss the implementation of IPT-AST in schools and other settings, address common clinical issues, and summarize the research on IPT-AST.

We recommend that the group leader read through the book in its entirety before starting an IPT-AST group. Then, prior to each session, the leader should read the corresponding section of the book to remember the session tasks, to determine if any materials are needed, and to reread the examples provided. For each session, there is a box that provides a session checklist and a list of needed materials. This is followed by a detailed description of the different topics that should be covered in the session. Throughout each chapter, there are examples of how a given topic might be discussed. We have chosen examples that are representative of the IPT-AST groups we have run and that reflect the types of adolescents that are appropriate for a prevention program. These examples are meant to help leaders find their own words for implementing core IPT-AST techniques. They are not meant to be read verbatim in the sessions. We think the group will be much more engaging for all involved if IPT-AST leaders adapt these examples based on their own style and utilize examples and language that are relevant to the adolescents in the group.

In the Appendix, we provide materials to help leaders run an IPT-AST group. These reproducible materials are also available online. To download and print the materials in the Appendix, please visit http://www.oxfordclinicalpsych.com/, search for the book's title, and click on the Appendix section. The Appendix includes an outline of each session for the leader's reference. There are also materials that can be printed or copied for use in the pre-group sessions and the group sessions, such as the closeness circle for the pre-group sessions, depression scenarios for session 1, and notecards with communication statements and interpersonal scenarios for sessions 2 and 3. Finally, there is material in the Appendix that is meant to be placed in individual binders for each of the group members. Specifically, each binder should include eight copies of the depression checklist so group members can complete the symptom checklist and mood rating at the beginning of each IPT-AST group. In addition, each binder should have a large copy of each of the communication strategies, the one-page description of the communication strategies, and notecards with each of the communication strategies. The leader will hold on to the binders in between sessions so everyone has them at each group. At the end of the group, teens can take the binders home as a reminder of the work that was accomplished in the group.

Preventing Adolescent Depression

Importance of Depression Prevention

Depression Is a Public Health Issue

Depression is a common and debilitating illness. According to the World Health Organization (2008), depression is the number one cause of disability and will be the most important disorder in terms of disease burden by 2030. This means that depression has a significant cost to individuals and society in terms of financial expenses, impact on quality of life, and its association with other medical and mental health conditions. As such, there is a pressing need to address this significant public health problem. Although a number of effective depression treatments have been identified and studied, estimates suggest that current treatments can only reduce a third of the burden associated with depression, given the large number of new cases and the delays in accessing treatment (Andrews, Sanderson, Corry, & Lapsley, 2000). Community studies demonstrate that a large number of individuals with depression never receive treatment. Furthermore, even in research studies, in which highly trained mental health professionals deliver psychotherapeutic or pharmacologic interventions that have demonstrated efficacy, a significant proportion of depressed individuals do not experience notable improvements in their symptoms or levels of functioning. Preventive interventions have been suggested as a possible and necessary way to reduce the burden of depression (Muñoz, Cuijpers, Smit, Barrera, & Leykin, 2010). Prevention programs can reach a larger proportion of the population than traditional treatment approaches and, if efficacious, can prevent the onset of a depression diagnosis and its associated impairments. Furthermore, given the link between depression and various medical, emotional, and academic problems, efforts aimed at preventing depression have the potential to prevent problems in other domains as well.

Despite the significant impairments associated with depression, relatively little attention has been paid to developing, studying, and disseminating depression prevention programs. This is in contrast to other public health initiatives for commonly occurring and debilitating medical problems, such as cardiovascular disease. The initiatives to address cardiovascular disease have included population-based efforts to reduce sodium intake, regular assessment of core risk factors such as high cholesterol and hypertension, education about healthy lifestyle choices, and the provision of interventions (e.g., statins) to select populations with key risk factors. Given how common and impairing depression is, why have there not been similar initiatives to prevent depression?

Over the past 25 years, the emphasis on mental health prevention has vacillated. Although reducing youth mental health problems was one of the broad objectives of Healthy People 2000, this was not included in Healthy People 2010. In the most recent initiative, Healthy People 2020, mental health improvement is again a core objective, with a specific focus on reducing the proportion of adolescents who experience a major depressive episode (US Department of Health and Human Services, 2010). Thus, there is increasing recognition of the need to prioritize depression prevention, particularly among adolescents. Two related goals of Healthy People 2020 relevant to depression prevention are to decrease the number of adolescents who make suicide attempts and increase the number of adolescents who are regularly screened for depression. Thus, it is an opportune time to conduct depression screenings, as long as there are systems in place to handle youth who are identified as depressed and to initiate prevention efforts with adolescents before their symptoms become more severe.

The good news is that there are effective depression prevention programs available to address this public health concern. Two recent reviews concluded that 22% to 38% of major depressive episodes could be prevented if currently existing depression prevention programs, such as Interpersonal Psychotherapy – Adolescent Skills Training (IPT-AST), were implemented (Cuijpers, Muñoz, Clarke, & Lewinsohn, 2009; Cuijpers, van Straten, Smit, Mihalopoulos, & Beekman, 2008). This would have a substantial impact at the individual and societal levels. Further, there is mounting evidence that screening youth for depression and then providing evidence-based depression prevention programs to at-risk youth is a cost-effective way to reduce the morbidity and mortality associated with depression (Mihalopoulos, Vos, Pirkis, & Carter, 2012). According to the Centers for Disease Control and Prevention, the preventive and intervention efforts that have been implemented to reduce hypertension and high cholesterol have resulted in a significant decrease in the number of deaths related to coronary heart disease and stroke. We now need to do the same thing with individuals who are at risk for depression: disseminate evidence-based depression prevention programs so there can be a substantial reduction in the number of individuals who experience a major depressive episode.

Adolescence Is a Prime Time for Depression Prevention

Depressive symptoms and disorders rise dramatically during adolescence. Although estimates vary from study to study, approximately 15% of individuals will experience a depressive episode during their teenage years (Merikangas et al., 2010). An even larger number of adolescents will experience elevated depressive symptoms without meeting criteria for a major depressive disorder. Contrary to popular beliefs about adolescence being a time of fluctuating moods, these elevations in depressive symptoms are not fleeting. Rather, depressive symptoms persist over time and place adolescents at considerable risk for developing a depressive episode later in life (Keenan et al., 2008; Tram & Cole, 2006). Adolescents with elevated depressive symptoms also experience significant impairment across multiple domains, including interpersonal difficulties and impaired school functioning, similar to the impairment experienced by adolescents who have a depression diagnosis (Lewinsohn, Solomon, Seeley, & Zeiss, 2000). Finally, adolescent depression, at both the symptom and disorder levels, greatly increases the risk for substance abuse, adult depression, and suicide (Fergusson, Horwood, Ridder, & Beautrais, 2005). Given that depressive symptoms and disorders rise dramatically during adolescence and adolescent-onset depression increases risk for continuity and recurrence of depression in adulthood, adolescence is an opportune time to provide interventions aimed at preventing depression.

Why Develop a Prevention Program Focusing on Interpersonal Relationships?

The rationale for developing an interpersonally focused prevention program came from three related lines of study: interpersonal risk factors for depression, empirical studies of interpersonal psychotherapy (IPT), and the burgeoning literature on depression prevention programs. Interpersonal theories of depression, as outlined by Joiner and Coyne (1999), posit that certain individuals behave in ways that lead to impairments in their interpersonal relationships, placing them at risk for the development of depression. Consistent with these theories, a large number of studies have found that ineffective interpersonal problem-solving, high levels of conflict in family and peer relationships, and low levels of perceived support are associated with subsequent increases in depressive symptoms during adolescence. This research suggests that an intervention that helps teens to develop interpersonal skills to address problematic relationships and promote positive relationships may be particularly effective at decreasing their risk for depression.

Interpersonal psychotherapy was developed in the late 1970s for the treatment of adult depression. The focus of treatment is on the patient's depressive symptoms and the interpersonal context in which these symptoms occur (Weissman, Markowitz, & Klerman, 2000). A large number of studies have demonstrated the efficacy of IPT with depressed adults (see Cuijpers et al., 2011, for a meta-analysis of these studies). Based on the positive findings in adults, Mufson and colleagues adapted IPT for adolescent depression (Interpersonal Psychotherapy for Depressed Adolescents, IPT-A) in the 1990s (Mufson et al., 1994; Mufson, Weissman, Moreau, & Garfinkel, 1999). Studies demonstrate that IPT-A is an acceptable and efficacious treatment for adolescent depression, resulting in improvements in depressive symptoms, anxiety symptoms, social functioning, and overall functioning. Furthermore, IPT-A is unique in that it has been shown to be an effective treatment for adolescent depression when delivered by school-based mental health clinicians who received a brief training in IPT-A and weekly supervision (Mufson, Dorta, Wickramaratne, et al., 2004). This study demonstrates that interventions based on IPT are easy to learn and implement successfully. Given the empirical support for IPT and IPT-A, high client satisfaction with the treatment approach, and the ease of training clinicians in this model, we believed there was a strong rationale for developing a prevention program based on IPT. In addition, we believed that an interpersonally oriented program would resonate well with adolescents and the kinds of difficulties they encounter on a day-to-day basis. This has been confirmed in the past decade, during which we conducted IPT-AST groups.

Given the high incidence of depression and the impairments associated with the disorder, there has been a call in the past two decades for depression prevention initiatives, particularly during high-risk developmental periods such as adolescence. This led to the creation of a number of depression prevention programs for youth based primarily on cognitive-behavioral approaches. Some of these programs are universal prevention interventions that are delivered to an entire population regardless of their risk for developing depression. Others are selective prevention programs that were designed specifically for youth with a known risk factor for developing depression, such as the death of a parent or a depressed parent. Finally, others are indicated prevention programs for youth experiencing elevated depressive symptoms. Recent reviews support the efficacy of selective and indicated prevention programs for depression, with less empirical support for universal prevention programs. However, the effects of these selective and indicated programs are generally small to moderate (Horowitz & Garber, 2006; Merry et al., 2011; Stice, Shaw, Bohon, Marti, & Rohde, 2009). As such, we wanted to develop a novel prevention approach that addresses distinct risk factors for depression (i.e., interpersonal risk factors rather than cognitive risk factors) and is based on an effective treatment model for depression.

How Is IPT-AST Similar to or Different From Other Prevention Programs?

Interpersonal Psychotherapy – Adolescent Skills Training offers an alternative, and perhaps a complement, to existing cognitive-behavioral prevention programs to help decrease the disease burden associated with depression. IPT-AST is both similar to and different from existing cognitive-behavioral depression prevention programs, such as Coping With Stress (CWS; Clarke & Lewinsohn, 1995) and the Penn Resiliency Program (PRP; Jaycox, Reivich, Gillham, & Seligman, 1994). The primary similarities are that (a) all are manualized group interventions that have been researched in several studies; (b) all have been implemented in school settings and other contexts; and (c) all include psychoeducation, problem-solving, and skill-building components. The primary difference between IPT-AST and these cognitive-behavioral programs is the target of the skill building. IPT-AST emphasizes interpersonal skill building to address communication problems in relationships that contribute to depression, whereas the other two programs primarily emphasize the detection, evaluation, and challenging of negative or inaccurate thoughts that have an impact on mood and behavior. Another difference is that PRP has been primarily implemented with younger children (Grades 5 and 6), whereas CWS and IPT-AST have been predominantly studied in adolescents. All of these depression prevention programs have been shown to be effective, so implementing any of these programs is likely to be beneficial for many youth. At this point, we do not know which adolescents would benefit most from a specific prevention program. This is something we are investigating in our current research. However, at this point, we feel confident that IPT-AST is an appropriate prevention program for many different types of adolescents (e.g., from different racial and ethnic backgrounds, with varying depressive symptoms) that can be delivered in a diversity of settings, as discussed further in this chapter.

For Whom Is IPT-AST Appropriate?

Interpersonal Psychotherapy – Adolescent Skills Training can be delivered to adolescents of various ages. To date, IPT-AST has primarily been tested with adolescents aged 12 to 16, in the 7th to 10th grades. We have focused on teens in this age range because depressive symptoms and disorders rise dramatically during the transition from preadolescence to adolescence. We have chosen not to test this program with younger children given that IPT-AST is a verbal intervention that requires insight into one's relationships and interpersonal patterns, and this may be challenging for children younger than 12. We have generally not focused on older adolescents because they have already passed through the window of greatest risk for depression, and many will have already experienced a first depressive episode. As such, these adolescents would more likely benefit from treatment, rather than a preventive intervention. That said, we have included 17-year-olds who are in the 11th grade in some of our IPT-AST groups, and they have responded favorably to the program. While IPT-AST is appropriate for adolescents aged 12 to 17, we recommend grouping adolescents according to age so 12-year-olds are not in the same group as 16- or 17-year-olds, given the large developmental changes that occur during adolescence.

Interpersonal Psychotherapy – Adolescent Skills Training is an appropriate program for adolescents with different levels of risk for developing depression. As discussed previously, there are three categories of prevention programs appropriate for people along a spectrum of risk: universal, selective, and indicated. Given the risks and impairments associated with elevated depressive symptoms, IPT-AST was initially developed as an indicated prevention program for youth with elevated symptoms of depression. To date, we have conducted three studies of IPT-AST as an indicated intervention. IPT-AST also has been tested as a universal intervention with all ninth graders in a particular school district, with positive results (Horowitz, Garber, Ciesla, Young, & Mufson, 2007). Currently, we are examining the benefits of IPT-AST in a selective sample of youth who are at risk for depression by virtue of having cognitive or interpersonal vulnerabilities for depression. Based on these various studies (see Chapter 13 for a review of empirical evidence), we believe that IPT-AST is appropriate for universal, indicated, and selective prevention populations. However, there is the most evidence to support using IPT-AST as an indicated intervention with youth with elevated symptoms. While leaders may choose to implement IPT-AST with a universal population (e.g., with all seventh-grade students), they should be aware that empirical reviews of the depression prevention literature suggest limited benefits of universal depression prevention (Horowitz & Garber, 2006; Merry et al., 2011; Stice et al., 2009). Relatedly, while we believe IPT-AST would be appropriate for a selective population (e.g., with teens who have a depressed parent), we have no data at this point on the effects of IPT-AST when delivered as a selective prevention program. In Chapter 11, we provide more detailed information about conducting IPT-AST with different populations, including alternate sample scripts that may be more appropriate for a particular group (i.e., adolescents endorsing no symptoms, those with a shared risk factor such as a depressed parent).

Finally, based on our experiences conducting IPT-AST with adolescents from diverse ethnic and racial backgrounds, from varying socioeconomic levels, and in urban and rural settings, we think that IPT-AST is an appropriate program for a wide variety of adolescents. Because adolescents are encouraged to apply communication strategies in a way that feels comfortable to them, there is inherent flexibility in the program. For example, teens learn the skill *I Statements*, which involves expressing a feeling without blaming the other person. In cultures or families where adolescents are expected to defer to adults rather than state their own opinions, leaders can help teens to apply this strategy sensitively, expressing feelings in ways that feel appropriate for their own culture and their own family. Some teens might feel that attempting to negotiate is not appropriate, given that it is accepted in their culture or their family that adults make the rules and children cannot argue with those rules. However, they may be able to use other communication strategies to make a parent aware of how a particular rule is affecting them (e.g., "I understand that I am not allowed to visit friends' houses because I have responsibilities here, but sometimes I feel sad when I hear about other friends having fun together on the weekend, and I feel left out").

Interpersonal Psychotherapy – Adolescent Skills Training leaders should be alert to situations for which certain ways of communicating that may be appropriate from the stance of a Western worldview would not be appropriate in other cultures. In these instances, it is important to listen to the adolescents, as they are the experts on their families. This does not mean, however, that considering new ways of communicating might not be helpful. For example, a teen might say that he cannot ask to go out with friends after school, even though this might improve his mood and reduce his social isolation. However, he may be able to ask to invite a friend over to his home so his parents are able to meet his friend. This may lead his parents to begin to feel more comfortable, which might increase his independence over time.

We have also had experiences where adolescents were convinced that a particular interpersonal situation could not change but were able to make small changes that had a significant impact on their mood. For example, a teen might feel like she cannot ask a parent to reduce her babysitting responsibilities for her younger siblings because the parent works full time and there is no money to pay an outside sitter. With help from the group, the teen is able to negotiate with her parent one afternoon a week when she can spend time with friends instead of watching her siblings. This improves her peer relationships, decreases her resentment, and ameliorates her mood. Thus, it is important to be aware of the familial, cultural, and socioeconomic context of each teen in the group to make the program most effective and appropriate for each adolescent while encouraging group members to consider new ways of interacting with those around them.

Implementing Prevention Programs in Diverse Settings

Prevention programs offer an opportunity to provide mental health services to adolescents who might not otherwise seek or receive services. This is particularly true because preventive interventions, such as IPT-AST, can be delivered in nontraditional settings such as schools, primary care offices, and community centers. Over the past several years, we have provided IPT-AST workshops and trainings to clinical psychologists, social workers, child psychiatry residents, graduate students in clinical and school psychology, and school counselors with diverse educational backgrounds. These clinicians and counselors worked in a variety of settings, including schools, outpatient clinics, and private practice. The majority of people we trained have felt positively about the program. In particular, they liked the focus on teaching communication skills and interpersonal problem-solving to improve relationships and believed IPT-AST would be beneficial for the adolescents that they work with in these various settings.

We believe that schools are a particularly opportune setting to provide IPT-AST. Because adolescents spend the majority of their time in school, schools offer an opportunity to reach a majority of youth (Masia-Warner, Nangle, & Hansen, 2006). This is particularly important for group-based prevention programs, which require that a number of adolescents participate in a group at the same time. Furthermore, the delivery of prevention programs in schools allows school counselors to identify and address the emotional problems of adolescents who were previously unidentified. Many of these teens will be appropriate for IPT-AST, and there will be others who are identified as part of the screening process who would benefit from more intensive services. These more intensive services can be provided at the school or in a community mental health setting. The hope is that by investing time and effort in identifying underserved adolescents and delivering IPT-AST, there will be a positive impact on the school system over time.

From our experiences working in schools, we know that many school counselors are forced to deal with one crisis after another. This takes up considerable time and resources and makes it difficult to imagine allocating time and resources to deliver a prevention program. As we discuss in Chapter 13, our research shows that IPT-AST has sustained effects on depressive and anxiety symptoms, overall functioning, and school retention. Thus, adolescents who participate in IPT-AST groups may be less likely to experience crises over time, eventually decreasing the burden on school counselors and the larger school system. Because we believe schools provide an ideal setting for depression prevention, we have a separate chapter (Chapter 10) devoted to issues regarding implementing IPT-AST in schools, including getting school administrators to recognize the benefits for individual students as well as the school, addressing scheduling issues, and identifying appropriate youth in a school setting.

Although much of our work has focused on delivering IPT-AST in schools, there are other opportune settings for prevention delivery. Our group and others have had success providing prevention groups in primary care offices and in community settings. The provision of prevention services in these types of environments promotes access to mental health services and may decrease the stigma associated with more traditional mental health settings. There is a growing movement toward co-locating mental health services in primary care settings to promote ease of access and decrease stigma. There are also a number of recent recommendations to increase depression screenings during medical visits, such as in Healthy People 2020. These two movements make the delivery of prevention programs in primary care offices feasible while addressing the concern that screenings only take place in settings where there are resources available to manage the identified youth in need.

Other groups (e.g., Clarke et al., 2001) have conducted depression prevention groups within the context of a large health maintenance organization (HMO), which allowed them to identify adolescents who had a parent receiving treatment for depression. If feasible, this would be an ideal way to identify youth who are at risk for developing depression based on a known risk factor (the model of selective prevention).

Finally, afterschool programs, community centers, and religious organizations all offer possibilities for prevention programming, particularly universal prevention programs, given the large number of children and adolescents served in these settings. In Chapter 11, we discuss issues related to conducting IPT-AST in these diverse settings, as well as adaptations that can be made when utilizing IPT-AST as a universal or selective prevention program.

2

IPT-AST Overview

What Is IPT-AST?

Interpersonal Psychotherapy – Adolescent Skills Training (IPT-AST) is an adolescent depression prevention program that teaches communication and interpersonal problem-solving skills to improve relationships with the goal of preventing depression. IPT-AST is based on interpersonal psychotherapy (IPT), an evidence-based treatment for adolescent and adult depression (Mufson, Dorta, Moreau, & Weissman, 2004; Weissman et al., 2000). IPT-AST consists of two individual pre-group sessions (45 minutes each); eight group sessions (60 to 90 minutes each); and an individual mid-group session (45 minutes each). When possible, parents are invited to attend part of the first pre-group session and part of the mid-group session. Following completion of the IPT-AST group, individual booster sessions (45 minutes each) can be provided to enhance the long-term effects of the program. Certain modifications to the frequency and duration of sessions may be necessary depending on the setting in which IPT-AST will be delivered. These modifications are discussed in Chapters 10 and 11.

We developed IPT-AST as a group intervention because group is often the modality of choice for preventive interventions due to its cost-effectiveness. In addition, group is an ideal place to work on interpersonal skills with adolescents because participants can practice newly acquired skills with peers in the group. For instance, adolescents can role play different communication strategies, such as expressing their feelings, offering solutions, and empathizing with another person's point of view. Group members can use the sessions to discuss problems they are having with family and friends and can learn whether their situation differs from other adolescents. Teens often report feeling comforted by the fact that others in the group have had similar experiences and difficulties and find that other group members are a good source of support. Together, the group members can generate solutions to an interpersonal problem and can discuss how to apply and adapt communication and problem-solving skills to different situations or relationships.

Course of IPT-AST

Like IPT and its adaptations, IPT-AST is broken up into three phases: initial phase (pre-group sessions and group sessions 1–3); middle phase (group sessions 4–6 and mid-group session); and termination phase (group sessions 7 and 8). The phases of IPT-AST are briefly described next.

Initial phase: The initial phase of IPT-AST begins with two pre-group sessions (45 minutes each). Depending on the setting and the preferences of the leader, parents can be invited to attend part of the first pre-group session so both the teen and parent can learn about depression, the concept of prevention, and the focus of the IPT-AST program. The purpose of these sessions is to build rapport with the adolescent and prepare the adolescent for the group program. Most of the time in the pre-group sessions is spent conducting an interpersonal inventory of the adolescent's significant relationships to identify interpersonal goals for the group.

Group sessions 1–3 provide a chance for adolescents to get to know each other before they begin to disclose more personal information in later sessions. In these sessions, adolescents review the concept of prevention and learn about depression, including symptoms of depression and the interpersonal factors that contribute to or maintain depression. Adolescents are educated regarding the effects of mood on relationships as well as the effects of relationships on mood. They also learn about communication, particularly the impact of what you say and how you say it on people's perceptions and responses. In group session 3, adolescents learn six communication strategies and practice applying these skills in hypothetical situations.

Middle phase: The majority of the skill building takes place during the middle phase of IPT-AST. The focus of the group shifts from learning interpersonal skills to applying these strategies to specific situations important to the group members. It is often helpful to use the communication strategies that are taught in the group to address the interpersonal issues that group members bring in, but the leader should also encourage adolescents to find other solutions if needed. Teens are encouraged to practice communication and interpersonal problem-solving strategies outside group, with work at home assigned when appropriate. While general tasks of the middle phase sessions are described in Chapter 6, specific topics discussed will vary based on the needs and priorities of group members. The group leader takes on a collaborative coaching role as adolescents work to address their interpersonal goals.

Between sessions 4 and 6, each adolescent in the group has a mid-group session (45 minutes in length) with the leader. The mid-group session is described in Chapter 7. The purpose of the mid-group session is to discuss how the group is progressing for the adolescent and to give the teen an opportunity to apply the interpersonal skills to a current relationship difficulty. Ideally, one or both parents are invited to attend part of the mid-group session. Parent involvement in the mid-group session provides an opportunity for the adolescent to utilize the strategies with live coaching from the leader. Because parent involvement is not always feasible, Chapter 7 provides topics and scripts for mid-group sessions with and without parents.

Termination phase: In the last two sessions, the group focuses on helping members establish a sense of competence, with attention paid to reviewing what has been learned and accomplished. The group leader helps adolescents consider how they will continue to apply what they have learned after the group ends. Group members are encouraged to use the communication skills learned in group, to continue working on any interpersonal goals that are still relevant, and to apply interpersonal problem-solving and communication strategies to novel situations they encounter in the future. In addition, the group discusses how each adolescent can determine if his or her depressive symptoms are becoming worse and what the adolescent can do if these symptoms persist over time. This discussion emphasizes the importance of continued monitoring and implementation of the strategies to prevent the development of depression.

Booster sessions: Booster sessions refer to sessions that occur after completion of the acute intervention in order to help maintain the gains made during the group. Booster sessions typically occur less frequently than the initial intervention. In our two initial studies of IPT-AST, we did not include booster sessions. The short-term effects of IPT-AST were strong, but the effects dissipated around 6 months to 1 year following the intervention. Thus, we are including individual booster sessions (45 minutes in length) in our current research studies to enhance the long-term effects of IPT-AST. This parallels the inclusion of booster sessions in other depression prevention interventions. The number of booster sessions is flexible; we have included three or four booster sessions in our recent studies. The booster sessions should occur in the 6 months following group and are flexibly timed to fit with the adolescent's needs and, if necessary, with the school calendar. They are used to monitor the adolescent's depressive symptoms and to discuss the application of the interpersonal strategies to current life stressors. These sessions are meant to solidify the adolescent's interpersonal skills and to address current interpersonal problems before they result in worsening depression.

Key IPT-AST Intervention Components

Many techniques from IPT and IPT-A (Interpersonal Psychotherapy for Depressed Adolescents) are included in IPT-AST. Other components of IPT-AST are unique to the prevention model. More information about these techniques can be found in the intervention chapters and in books on IPT and IPT-A (Mufson, Dorta, Moreau, et al., 2004; Weissman et al., 2000). Next, we provide a brief description of the core IPT-AST components.

Psychoeducation. Providing education to adolescents (and parents if they are included in the first pre-group session) about depression, prevention, and the interpersonal model of depression is an important component of IPT-AST, particularly in the initial phase of the program. The education begins in the pre-group sessions when the adolescent is introduced to the concept of prevention and the core IPT-AST model, which describes how relationships affect mood and mood affects relationships. In the first group session, adolescents learn about the symptoms of depression and the difference between experiencing symptoms of depression and being depressed. In group session 2, the leader educates group members about the link between interpersonal relationships and mood. Much of this session is spent in various activities that illustrate how one person's communication (words, tone of voice, facial expression) has an impact on how the other person feels and then responds and the eventual outcome of the interaction. Finally, in group session 3, the group leader teaches communication and interpersonal problem-solving strategies that form the basis of the interpersonal skill building that comprises much of the middle phase of IPT-AST.

Monitoring depressive symptoms. Throughout the course of IPT-AST, the group leader monitors the adolescents' depressive symptoms. In the individual sessions (pre-group, mid-group and booster), the leader conducts a brief verbal assessment of the teen's symptoms during the previous week and asks the teen to rate his or her mood on a 1–10 scale, with 1 being the best mood and 10 being the most depressed. The leader also asks the teen to identify times when his or her mood was better or worse during the week and helps the teen to link changes in mood to specific interpersonal events. In the group sessions, adolescents complete a brief depression checklist (see Appendix) about their symptoms and complete a mood rating for the week. The leader reviews these checklists throughout the course of the group.

Monitoring depressive symptoms serves several purposes. First, it familiarizes the group members with the common symptoms of depression, which contributes to psycho-education about depression. Second, it allows the leader to assess for worsening of symptoms, which might indicate that an adolescent would benefit from more intensive services. Third, in the middle phase of group, teens verbally report on changes in their mood ratings. This helps the leader reinforce the link between mood and interpersonal relationships and informs the leader's decision about what to work on in a given session.

Interpersonal inventory. The interpersonal inventory, a core strategy of IPT, occurs during the pre-group sessions. In IPT-AST, the inventory is more abbreviated than it is in the original treatment model. The interpersonal inventory is an assessment of the important relationships in the adolescent's life, with the goal of identifying relationships or interpersonal patterns that can be improved during the group. During the interpersonal inventory, the leader asks the adolescent to identify important people in his or her life using a closeness circle, which is a visual diagram of the adolescent's relationships (Mufson, Dorta, Moreau, et al., 2004). The leader then asks detailed questions about these relationships to understand positive and negative aspects of the relationships, how these relationships have changed over time, and how they have an impact on the adolescent's mood. On the basis of the interpersonal inventory, the group leader identifies problems in specific relationships (e.g., the adolescent does not get to spend one-on-one time with his father) or patterns that cut across various relationships (e.g., the adolescent does not communicate when she is upset because she thinks people should know her feelings without her telling them) that may be contributing to the adolescent's negative mood.

Individual goal setting. At the completion of the interpersonal inventory, the leader and adolescent collaboratively decide on two individualized goals for the group. It is helpful to set two goals, rather than one, so that there is flexibility to help the adolescent work on whichever goal is most relevant over time. In many cases, one goal will be most salient at the start of the group, but as priorities shift, a different goal might be most relevant later in the group. These goals are focused on improving the adolescent's relationships with the hope that this will improve the adolescent's mood and prevent the likelihood of a future depressive episode.

While IPT-AST does not select one of the original IPT problem areas (grief, role transitions, interpersonal role disputes, and interpersonal deficits; Mufson, Dorta, Moreau, et al., 2004; Weissman et al., 2000), the identified goals typically relate to one of these problem areas. Goals can be focused on particular relationships, such as arguing less with parents about chores, or can be more general, such as talking more to people about how the adolescent feels in order to obtain support. Often, the goals are focused on addressing a problematic relationship or interpersonal pattern. However, it is also appropriate to have goals related to strengthening positive relationships in the adolescent's life. It is important that the goal setting be collaborative so the adolescent is invested in working on the identified goals during the course of the group. In addition, the goals are individualized for each adolescent based on the detailed information that the leader obtains during the interpersonal inventory.

Communication analysis. A communication analysis is a detailed analysis of a conversation that examines the verbal exchange line by line as well as the context of the interaction. The goal is to help adolescents recognize the impact of their words on others, the feelings they conveyed verbally and nonverbally, the feelings generated by the interaction, and how modifying the communication might have an impact on the outcome of the interaction and the adolescents' feelings. In IPT-AST, communication analysis is introduced in group session 2 during a communication activity. Group members act out different hypothetical scenarios, such as talking to a friend who did not include the teen in an activity or asking a parent for permission to go to a party. The group then dissects the interaction by obtaining detailed information about the conversation, such as the following: How did it start? What exactly did the adolescent say? What did the person say back? How did that make the adolescent feel? What happened next? Is that the outcome the adolescent wanted?

Introducing communication analysis in the initial phase of group orients the adolescents to the types of questions the leader will ask in the middle phase of IPT-AST when an adolescent brings in an interpersonal issue to work on. Communication analysis remains an important technique in the middle phase of IPT-AST. It helps the leader and other group members understand what occurred in a previous interaction (negative or positive) before deciding what the next steps may be to solve a particular interpersonal problem or to improve a specific relationship.

Interpersonal skill building. In group session 3, group members are taught six communication strategies that form the basis of the interpersonal skill-building work that occurs in the middle phase of IPT-AST. The six strategies, described in more detail in Chapter 5, are as follows: ***Strike while the iron is cold; I statements; Be specific; Put yourself in their shoes; Have a few solutions in mind and remember to compromise; and Don't give up***. Although these strategies are similar to those included in IPT-A and other interventions, IPT-AST is unique in its explicit focus on improving interpersonal skills across multiple situations and relationships. Because this is a group preventive intervention, we felt it was important to have an explicit language for the communication strategies to increase the long-term use of these skills and to emphasize the generalizability across a variety of situations.

Each strategy is listed on a cue card that is included in the group members' binders and has an associated label to help the adolescents remember the strategy (see the Appendix for the cue cards and a brief description of each strategy). After the skills are taught in group session 3, they are applied throughout the middle phase of IPT-AST to address the different interpersonal situations that group members bring in to work on. Not every strategy applies to every situation, and these strategies are not meant to be exhaustive. Rather, the strategies provide a starting point to help adolescents communicate more effectively in their relationships and to help achieve their goals for a specific conversation.

Decision analysis. Decision analysis closely resembles problem-solving techniques in other interventions but focuses specifically on addressing interpersonal problems. Although much of the middle phase is spent applying the communication strategies to different situations, first it may be necessary to conduct a decision analysis to help determine the best course of action. Decision analysis includes defining and clarifying the problem, encouraging the adolescent and other group members to generate solutions, evaluating the pros and cons of each solution, and selecting a solution to try. If the chosen solution involves an interaction with another person, it is then helpful to discuss how the communication strategies might be useful to explain the solution to the other person and to script and role play the interaction. There are also times when the chosen solution does not require an interaction, such as deciding to complete homework right after school to avoid conflict with a parent. In these cases, a decision analysis may be the only strategy needed to initially address the problem. In subsequent group sessions, the leader should check with the adolescent to see if the chosen solution has been helpful and to discuss any necessary follow-up.

Role playing. Role playing is used throughout the group sessions. In the initial phase of group, adolescents act out different hypothetical situations. This gives them a fun introduction to role playing without the pressure of worrying about how to say things effectively. In the middle phase of IPT-AST, role playing is used to practice specific conversations that the adolescents would like to have outside group. Role plays provide an excellent opportunity for group members to practice interpersonal interactions so they feel more comfortable utilizing the strategies in real life.

Before the role plays, it is important to think about the goal of the interaction and then script the conversation so the adolescent is prepared to act out the interaction with another group member acting as the other person. Detailed scripting is a unique feature of role plays within IPT-AST and other IPT-based interventions. This scripting might include discussing and outlining different ways of starting the conversation or thinking of the best way to express a feeling and then anticipating how the other person will respond. After the role play, the adolescent can obtain feedback from the other group members about how the various statements came across, and the group can discuss and practice possible modifications. It is important to role play outcomes that are most likely for a given situation, as well as less successful interactions, to prepare adolescents for the variety of responses that may occur when the strategies are utilized outside the group.

Work at home. Work at home refers to the interpersonal work that adolescents are asked to do outside group. These assignments typically follow the interpersonal work that occurred in the group sessions. IPT-AST differs from other prevention programs in that homework is not given every week, and the same work is not assigned to every adolescent in the group. Rather, work at home is individualized based on the discussion in group. In the initial phase of group, there are no formal assignments given. Rather, group members are asked to pay attention to events that happen in their relationships and how these events have an impact on their mood. This prepares them for the middle phase of IPT-AST.

In the middle phase, adolescents are given a work-at-home assignment if they have discussed an interpersonal situation during the group. This typically involves asking adolescents to have a conversation that was scripted and role played in group so they can report back to the group on how it went. Work at home might also involve thinking more about an interpersonal problem so the group can focus in on a particular solution or interaction in a subsequent group session. Regardless of the assignment given, it is important for the leader to follow up with group members about the work at home so they realize that this outside work is highly valued and essential.

The Leader's Role in IPT-AST

For indicated and selective IPT-AST groups, we think it is important for group leaders to have some mental health background and training in responding to crises, such as suicidal ideation or suspected abuse, as these problems can arise when working with adolescents at increased risk for depression. For universal groups, a mental health or counseling background, while beneficial, may not be necessary. To date, we have only studied IPT-AST when delivered by psychologists, social workers, psychiatrists, or trainees from these disciplines. We have also trained school counselors in IPT-AST and think they are optimally suited to deliver the program in schools. At this point, we do not know how effective IPT-AST is when delivered by leaders from other diverse fields. We know that other prevention programs have been delivered successfully by school counselors, teachers, and school nurses and hope the same is true for IPT-AST. This is something we plan to study in future research projects.

One or two leaders can conduct IPT-AST. In settings where coleaders are possible, this is preferable to provide teens with multiple perspectives and to ensure that groups run smoothly. We have utilized coleaders in our own work but recognize that, in many settings, it may only be feasible to have one group leader. For simplicity, the term *leader* in the singular is used throughout the remainder of the book. Of note, this is not meant to discourage the use of coleaders, which can greatly facilitate the successful implementation of IPT-AST.

Whether a single leader or coleaders, it is important to maintain a semistructured focus to the groups. There will be specific topics and skills that the leader will cover and the sessions will follow a specific structure, but the discussions will flow from the material brought in by the adolescents themselves. There is some pressure to keep the group moving and to work on specific tasks, but the leader generally works in a supportive, collaborative, educational way with the adolescent group members. While the teens can receive feedback about within-group behavior in IPT-AST, there is less emphasis on interpretation of group process than one would ordinarily see in an open-ended interactional group. Group behavior is discussed as it relates to the member's interpersonal difficulties and is viewed as representing a microcosm of some of the difficulties the teen is experiencing outside the group.

Selecting Adolescents
to Participate in IPT-AST

3

Before beginning an Interpersonal Psychotherapy – Adolescent Skills Training (IPT-AST) group, the leader needs to identify adolescents who would be appropriate for and benefit from the program. The process through which the leader identifies appropriate group members will differ depending on the setting and the number of groups that can be offered at a given time. For our indicated prevention groups in schools, we have identified adolescents through a two-stage process. First, we screened large numbers of adolescents, using a self-report measure of depression. In our own work, we have utilized the Center for Epidemiological Studies Depression Scale (CES-D; Radloff, 1977). The CES-D is in the public domain, so it is available at no cost. Other self-report depression questionnaires, such as the Children's Depression Inventory (Kovacs, 2003) or the Reynolds Adolescent Depression Scale (Reynolds, 2002), are also appropriate screening tools. In the second stage, we invited adolescents with elevated scores on the self-report measure to complete a more in-depth diagnostic assessment to determine whether they were appropriate for a prevention program or required more intensive services.

The benefit of the first stage is that it allows us to identify adolescents who might otherwise go undetected, creating a larger pool of youth to enroll in groups. The second stage provides important additional information to determine suitability for prevention groups. However, a larger screening followed by a diagnostic interview may not be feasible in certain settings and may not be the best approach if the goal is to identify a limited number of adolescents.

For universal and selective groups that occur outside school settings, we have invited families from the community to participate without any knowledge of their level of risk. The benefit of this process, as opposed to the one described previously, is that these families are interested in prevention, so less work needs to be done to persuade them of the possible benefits of participating. In these situations, we conduct a diagnostic assessment before group to make sure the adolescent is not currently depressed or does not have another emotional problem that would make the adolescent inappropriate for group. This process would translate well to settings that serve a particular community, where all youth could be invited to participate. IPT-AST groups could be implemented with adolescents who are interested in participating and who are deemed appropriate for prevention based on a clinical interview. It would be important to have other services available on site or referrals for outside services if families are interested in participating in an IPT-AST group but the clinical interview determines that the adolescent would benefit from more intensive services.

Conducting a Clinical Interview

As discussed, screening measures can be helpful to determine youth who may benefit from a prevention group. However, even if using a screening measure, it is important to conduct a clinical interview to determine whether a particular adolescent would be appropriate for a prevention group. This interview should include a thorough assessment of depression symptoms as well as a brief review of other mental health problems to determine if a prevention program is appropriate or if the adolescent requires more intensive services. For indicated or selective groups, leaders should look for adolescents who are experiencing elevated depressive symptoms or who share a common stressor that puts them at risk for depression. If IPT-AST is being used as a stand-alone prevention program, adolescents who need more intensive services should not be included.

Prior to initiating the clinical interview, the leader should review the limits of confidentiality with both the teen and parent(s). The review should include psychoeducation about confidentiality, explaining to them that most of what the teen discusses with the leader is confidential between the two of them unless the leader feels that the teen may be a danger to self or someone else or when the teen is in danger. In those situations, the leader is obligated to break confidentiality and share these concerns with a parent or other authority. Importantly, in such instances, the leader will discuss with the teen the need to break confidentiality due to these reasons before speaking with the parent. The leader also explains to the teen that there may be other times when the leader feels that something they have discussed would be beneficial to share with the parent to improve the teen's mood or situation; the leader will discuss that with the teen first and obtain permission to share it before doing so. Situations like this may come up in the initial clinical interview as well as during the mid-group session when parent and teen are together to discuss progress in group and to address specific interpersonal issues.

The leader should conduct a verbal assessment of the symptoms of depression, described further in this section, as part of an initial interview. The adolescent must endorse at least five symptoms, and these symptoms would have to persist for at least 2 weeks to meet criteria for a diagnosis of depression. For each of the symptoms of depression, the leader should ask one or two questions to determine whether the adolescent is experiencing this symptom and how often. It is also helpful to assess whether any depressive symptoms are impairing the teen's functioning at home, school, or with peers. To be included in a prevention program such as IPT-AST, it is acceptable for a teen to endorse several symptoms. However, if a teen reports that he or she is experiencing five or more of these symptoms, and they occur every day and last the majority of the day for 2 weeks or more, the teen likely would benefit from more intensive services. Typically, teens in an indicated or selective program may endorse some sad mood or irritability or anhedonia, some sleep difficulties, and one or two more symptoms intermittently. The following are common symptoms of depression and questions that the leader can ask to assess each of these symptoms:

Depressed or irritable mood. One of the core symptoms of depression is sad mood. Unlike adults, adolescents may experience their mood as irritable, rather than feeling sad. Helpful questions include the following: How has your mood been the past few weeks? Do you feel sad or bored or blah? Are you more irritable toward people, or do you get bothered by little things a lot more than usual? How often do you feel sad or irritable? How long do these feelings last?

Loss of interest or pleasure in activities. Many adolescents with depressive symptoms or a depression diagnosis report anhedonia, which refers to a loss of interest or pleasure in activities that they usually enjoy. Normative changes in interests (e.g., "I don't like dance anymore, but I started playing softball") should not be considered signs of anhedonia. The leader can ask: What kinds of things do you enjoy doing when you are not in school? Has your interest in or motivation to do these things decreased lately? If you push yourself to do that activity, do you find it enjoyable?

Difficulties with sleep. Sleep disturbances can include trouble falling asleep (early insomnia), waking up in the middle of the night (middle insomnia), waking up earlier in the morning than necessary and being unable to fall back to sleep (late insomnia), or sleeping too much (hypersomnia). To assess difficulties with sleep, the leader can ask: How has your sleep been in the past 2 weeks? Do you have trouble falling asleep or staying asleep or waking up too early? Are you sleeping more than you used to?

Fatigue or low energy. Feeling tired or having little energy is another symptom that teens may experience. Questions to ask include the following: Do you feel more tired than usual? How does it feel when you go to do things like getting up for school? Does it feel like everything takes a lot of effort? When did you start feeling this way? How long have you been feeling this way?

Feeling slowed down or restless. Some teens may feel either slowed down or more agitated than usual. To be considered a symptom of depression, teens should exhibit behavioral changes rather than only subjective feelings of psychomotor retardation or agitation. To assess feeling slowed down, the leader can ask: Have you noticed that you are not moving as fast as before? Have you noticed that your speech is slowed down? Have others noticed these changes? Questions to ask about agitation include the following: Have you found it more difficult than usual to sit still or noticed that you feel restless? Do you find that you are fidgeting more than usual? Have others noticed these changes?

Change in appetite. Appetite changes can include either loss of appetite or an increase in appetite that may be accompanied by weight loss or gain, respectively. The leader can ask: Have your eating habits changed so that you are eating more or less than usual? Have you felt less or more hungry than usual? Have you lost or gained weight? Could this be related to feeling sad or down, or are you purposefully trying to lose or gain weight?

Concentration difficulties or indecision. Having trouble concentrating can be a symptom of depression. It is also a symptom of other common mental health problems. It is helpful to determine whether the concentration difficulties began at the same time as the depressed or irritable mood. The following are questions to assess concentration difficulties: How are you doing in school? Are you having trouble concentrating, or have your grades gone down in the past few weeks since you have been feeling sad or down? Indecision is a related symptom of depression, particularly difficulty making decisions about small choices, such as what to wear or what to do after school. To assess indecision, the leader might ask: Is it hard to make decisions? Big decisions can be hard for anyone; how difficult is it to make little decisions like what to do after school or what to wear? Has this become more difficult since you have been feeling sad?

Feelings of guilt or low self-worth. All people experience feelings of guilt at some point in their lives, particularly when they have done something wrong. It is considered a symptom of depression when an adolescent reports feelings of guilt that are out of proportion to the trigger. The following questions assess feelings of guilt: Do you feel guilty for things that you have done; do you feel guiltier than others might feel in a similar situation? How long do these feelings last? A related symptom of depression is worthlessness, or feeling inadequate. To assess self-worth, the leader might ask: How are you feeling about yourself lately? Do you like most things about yourself or often wish you were different? How often do you feel badly about yourself in general compared to your peers?

Thoughts of death or suicidal ideation/behavior. Having thoughts of death or thoughts of wanting to hurt oneself is a symptom of depression, although these thoughts also occur with other mental health issues. The assessment of suicidal ideation or behavior is important in evaluating whether a teen is appropriate for the prevention group. Even if the teen does not endorse a lot of other symptoms, it is still necessary to assess suicidality because it can be present even when significant depression symptoms are not reported. A leader needs to assess for several aspects of suicidality and should ask: Do you have any thoughts about life not being worth living? The leader is looking for information about whether these thoughts are passive, such as "Sometimes I wish I wouldn't wake up in the morning," or active, "I am thinking about taking some pills."

If the teen endorses thoughts of suicide, the leader should ask additional questions to gather information about the frequency and extent of the suicidal thoughts, any planning that may have occurred, and any prior suicide attempts. These questions include the following: How often do you have these thoughts? How long do they last? Can you make these thoughts go away, and if so, how do you do that? Have you thought of a plan to kill yourself, and do you have access to carry out this plan? When is the last time you had these thoughts? How close have you ever come to acting on these thoughts? Do you feel you want to act on these thoughts? Have you told anyone about these thoughts? Have you ever tried to hurt yourself in the past?

If an adolescent has had suicidal ideation in the past but not currently, or if the individual reports fleeting and infrequent thoughts of wanting to be dead without intent, the leader can decide on a case-by-case basis whether to include the teen in the prevention group if he or she does not meet criteria for a depression diagnosis. If the teen is included in IPT-AST, it will be important for the leader to monitor the teen's suicidal ideation closely, verbally assessing current suicidal thoughts in the individual sessions (pre-group, mid-group, and booster) and checking the suicidal ideation item on the depression checklist during each group session. If an adolescent endorses having current active thoughts of harming him- or herself with intent to die, the adolescent is in need of a formal psychiatric evaluation, and the leader should refer the teen for more intensive services.

Assessing nonsuicidal self-injury. Similarly, the leader should assess for nonsuicidal self-injury (NSSI), which refers to self-harm that is not accompanied by thoughts of wanting to die when engaging in the behavior. While a prior history of a suicide attempt is a strong predictor of future suicide attempts, recent findings also point to the significant role of NSSI as a risk factor for suicidal behavior (Brent et al., 2013). Moreover, research suggests that adolescents are often uncertain of their intent when engaging in self-harming behaviors, which contributes to NSSI being considered a significant risk factor for suicide attempts and to the importance of thoroughly assessing self-harming behavior. To find out about NSSI, the leader should ask questions such as these: Have you ever had thoughts of harming yourself? If so, what were those thoughts? How often do they occur? Have you ever tried to harm yourself? What did you do? When was the last time you injured yourself? Have you ever received medical attention for an injury? When you were doing that, were you having any thoughts of wanting to die or be dead? If so, what stopped you from continuing to harm yourself? What were you feeling or thinking when you were engaging in these behaviors?

There is a continuum of severity for behaviors that are considered as NSSI, and these behaviors can range from scratching oneself with a paper clip or picking at skin until it bleeds to burning oneself with a cigarette or cutting one's arm or wrist with a knife. Typically, if an adolescent reports any percentage of his or her thoughts at the time of self-harm as hoping to die or wanting to be dead, it is no longer considered NSSI but rather suicidal behavior. However, as stated previously, teens have a difficult time describing their thoughts and feelings in these situations, so it is better to err on the side of caution if the leader is unsure and to refer for a second evaluation. In addition, NSSI not only is found in conjunction with depression but also can be manifest with other disorders, such as anxiety or other mood disorders.

For the purposes of the prevention program, the leader can decide to include the adolescent if the leader concludes that the NSSI is superficial and infrequent. If such adolescents are included in the groups, it is important to closely monitor the NSSI behaviors and refer for more intensive services if the behavior becomes more frequent or high risk. In these cases, NSSI can be assessed during the individual sessions and can be incorporated into the depression checklist as an additional symptom to assess weekly during the group. Alternatively, the leader can arrange to check in individually with the teen before or after the group sessions to monitor NSSI.

Assessing other mental health problems. Often, adolescents at risk for depression due to subsyndromal depression symptoms may have symptoms of other disorders or may have a comorbid disorder. The most common comorbid disorders are an anxiety disorder and attention deficit hyperactivity disorder (ADHD). Comorbid anxiety symptoms are common among adolescents with depression or elevated depression symptoms as they are often a precursor to the depression. Our studies have shown that the anxiety symptoms tend to remit with the depression symptoms as an outcome of participation in the prevention groups.

While anxiety symptoms or even an anxiety disorder would not necessarily prevent the adolescent from participating in the prevention group, it is important to assess whether an anxiety disorder is impairing enough that it should be treated first or whether the teen should be receiving additional treatment for the comorbid disorder. Specifically, the leader needs to assess whether enough anxiety symptoms are present to suggest the presence of an anxiety disorder and whether the depression symptoms are a result of the impact of the anxiety on functioning. If the leader finds either of these situations to be the case, it would suggest that the anxiety disorder is the primary diagnosis leading to the adolescent's difficulties. In these situations, the leader should refer that teen for treatment for anxiety as the first intervention.

For an adolescent who is really struggling in the classroom with untreated ADHD symptoms, an evaluation of the ADHD behaviors would be recommended to determine whether the adolescent would benefit from medication or another type of intervention for the ADHD-related impairments. If the ADHD is being treated through medication or through another intervention, IPT-AST may be helpful to address any current depressive symptoms or to prevent future depression.

In addition, the leader may want to briefly assess other mental health difficulties and exposure to stressful life events, as this may have an impact on the decision about whether IPT-AST is the most appropriate intervention. This includes an assessment of substance abuse and other risky behaviors, as well as exposure to traumatic events, physical or sexual abuse, and bullying. If the adolescent is abusing substances or has significant symptoms related to trauma, IPT-AST may not be the most appropriate intervention. The group leader may also want to consider excluding youth who would be very anxious or uncomfortable in group, be significantly disruptive to the group process, or would have a difficult time relating to other adolescents. In particular, the leader should be alert to the possibility of any iatrogenic effects for other group members. This can occur when an adolescent has significant behavioral or conduct problems or engages in significant high-risk behaviors that may negatively influence or impact other group members. Similarly, adolescents who meet criteria for autism spectrum disorders may not be appropriate for the group because they are likely to require an intervention with a longer duration to be able to effectively incorporate the strategies into their repertoire. Teens with autism spectrum disorders also may not be able to relate to the other interpersonal situations being discussed in group, which could exacerbate feelings of social isolation or not fitting in. However, some high-functioning teens with autism spectrum diagnoses may benefit from IPT-AST.

Assessing interpersonal relationships. Another issue to consider when deciding whether IPT-AST is the best fit for an adolescent is whether the teen is experiencing any interpersonal difficulties. IPT-AST may feel less relevant for adolescents with universally strong and positive relationships or those with well-developed communication and interpersonal problem-solving skills. On the other hand, IPT-AST may be particularly beneficial for youth with current relationship difficulties. Interpersonal psychotherapy posits that most individuals with depression can be classified into one of four interpersonal problem areas: role disputes, role transitions, interpersonal deficits, and grief (Mufson, Dorta, Moreau, et al., 2004; Weissman et al., 2000). The interpersonal skills taught in IPT-AST are particularly relevant for adolescents with interpersonal conflicts (role disputes), for teens with recent life changes that have affected their relationships (role transitions), or for teens who have difficulty making and maintaining close relationships (interpersonal deficits). The strategies may also be relevant for adolescents who have depressive symptoms in response to a death (grief), although grief is not explicitly addressed in group sessions.

It is important to note that IPT-AST was not specifically developed to address bereavement. Thus, it is up to the leader to decide whether IPT-AST is the most appropriate intervention for an adolescent who has recently lost someone close to him or her. In making this decision, the leader should determine whether there are other interpersonal goals that an adolescent can work on in group. In addition, the leader should consider how it would feel for the grieving adolescent to listen to other youth discussing interpersonal problems with their relatives when the teen is grieving the loss of a significant relationship. From our experiences, this is particularly an issue with the loss of a parent but is less of a concern with the loss of other relatives or friends. Therefore, we typically only include youth who have lost a more distant relative or friend or where grief is secondary to other relationship challenges.

Based on this clinical interview, the leader will have a good understanding of the adolescent's baseline depression symptoms and other mental health concerns, as well as a preliminary idea of the teen's interpersonal relationships. This information will inform the decision of whether a given adolescent will benefit from participating in IPT-AST and the appropriate level of prevention. Furthermore, this information will be valuable as the intervention progresses. Given this knowledge, the leader can be alert to significant increases in depression symptoms or other mental health problems during the course of IPT-AST that might indicate that an adolescent would benefit from more intensive services. In addition, the preliminary assessment of the adolescent's interpersonal relationships during the clinical interview informs the interpersonal inventory that will be conducted in the pre-group sessions.

Considerations for Group Composition

Aside from considerations related to each individual group member, group composition issues are also important to consider. The first issue to consider is the age and gender makeup of the group. As discussed in Chapter 1, we recommend that groups comprise similarly aged adolescents, given the large developmental differences that occur between ages 12 and 17. Given the higher rates of depression in female adolescents, some prevention and intervention programs have been developed specifically for girls. IPT-AST, on the other hand, is designed for girls and boys. We have run both single-sex and mixed-gender IPT-AST groups. When we implemented IPT-AST in single-sex parochial schools, the groups naturally consisted of all boys or all girls, and these groups ran smoothly. We have also run successful mixed-gender groups. Groups composed of boys and girls allow teens to gain multiple and diverse perspectives from other group members, which can be particularly helpful when discussing peer issues. If the leader decides to run a mixed-gender group, we recommend that the group composition be relatively balanced between boys and girls. Although we have had groups with only one boy or one girl, teens are often more comfortable when the gender composition is relatively balanced.

Another thing to consider is whether potential group members have close positive or negative relationships with each other, particularly in settings where individuals are likely to know each other (e.g., schools). Typically, it is not realistic to exclude adolescents who know each other outside the group. However, we think it is important to ensure that siblings and others with close family relationships (e.g., cousins, etc.) are in separate groups. This is because adolescents are asked to discuss problems in relationships with the group, and often these include problems in relationships with parents, siblings, or other family members. When siblings are in the same group, they may be reluctant to discuss issues in their family relationships, which may limit their ability to benefit from the intervention. Those who are close friends or romantically involved may similarly be unable to discuss difficulties in that relationship with the group. This may be more or less problematic for the adolescents, depending on whether the relationship becomes a target of change. The presence of close friends or couples in the group may influence the group dynamic more generally if two individuals remain aligned with each other and do not connect as well to the rest of the group.

Therefore, the leader may want to consider the pros and cons of having close friends or couples in the same group. In our own work, we have permitted these dyads to be in the same group and remained alert to any issues that may arise for specific group members and the larger group dynamic. However, we feel more strongly about not including individuals with intensely negative relationships (such as between a bully and a victim) in the same group. The presence of a bully in the group is likely to inhibit someone who has been victimized by that person from participating, which would reduce the benefit to the teen and possibly be harmful if it increases his or her exposure to bullying.

For these reasons, it is advisable to pay close attention to information gathered from adolescents about their relationships in the clinical interview and the pre-group sessions. This way, the leader can be alerted to potential issues and make decisions about group composition on a case-by-case basis. If issues related to group members' relationships arise later in the group, these issues can often be addressed individually or in the context of the group. However, the leader may in rare cases decide to remove someone from the group (e.g., if a bully in the group is aggressive toward other group members and strategies to manage aggressive behavior are unsuccessful). This is discussed in greater detail in the chapter on common clinical issues (Chapter 12).

4

IPT-AST Pre-Group Sessions

The two pre-group sessions serve a number of functions. The goals of these sessions are to get to know the adolescent better and build rapport; assess for depression symptoms over the past week; provide psychoeducation about depression; explain the structure of Interpersonal Psychotherapy – Adolescent Skills Training (IPT-AST); conduct an interpersonal inventory; and help the teen to set two interpersonal goals to work on throughout the group. As described in the previous chapter, we recommend conducting a clinical interview with the adolescent and parent prior to the pre-group sessions so these sessions can be spent conducting tasks that are specific to IPT-AST. It is helpful to draw on basic information gathered during the clinical interview to inform the questions the leader asks in the pre-group sessions (e.g., if the mom is remarried and a stepfather lives in the home, the leader will make note that this relationship should be covered in the interpersonal inventory).

When there are coleaders, the same leader should meet with the teen for the pre-group sessions, the mid-group session, and booster sessions (if provided). It is preferable to conduct two 45-minute pre-group sessions; consequently, we describe the pre-group component utilizing a two-session format. This allows the leader time to reflect on relationships that were discussed in the first pre-group session and to brainstorm a few ideas for interpersonal goals to suggest at the end of the second pre-group session. If it is not feasible for teens to come in for two separate sessions, a single 90-minute pre-group session can be offered instead.

When possible, it is helpful for parents to attend the first pre-group session to learn about the focus and structure of IPT-AST. When this is not feasible (e.g., in school settings when parents might have difficulty coming during the school day), the leader can reach out to parents by phone. Spending time with parents in the pre-group session or speaking briefly by phone provides an opportunity for the leader to get to know parents, to encourage a collaborative working relationship, and to discuss what the adolescent will be learning in IPT-AST. In addition, time should be set aside before the start of, or during, pre-group session 1 to explain policies regarding limits to confidentiality and how information will or will not be shared with parents. It is recommended that information not be shared with parents unless the teen presents an imminent risk of harm to self or to another (identified) person, reports suspected or known child abuse, or if the teen agrees that information should be shared. However, whatever the leader's policy is, this should be shared with the teen prior to the start of pre-group sessions.

Pre-Group Session 1

Pre-Group Session 1 Checklist:

☐ Introduce concept of prevention and provide a rationale for the group intervention

☐ Orient adolescent and parent(s) to the group program

☐ Assess for depression symptoms in the past week

☐ Introduce and complete mood rating

☐ Complete a closeness circle

☐ Begin the interpersonal inventory

☐ Closing tasks: summarize and prepare teen for next session

Materials Needed:

☐ Copy of depression checklist for leader's reference (see Appendix)

☐ Closeness circle (see Appendix)

☐ List of questions to ask during interpersonal inventory for leader's reference (see Appendix)

Session goals and tasks. The first pre-group session is a chance to explain the prevention program to the teen and his or her parent. This is also an opportunity to build rapport with the adolescent and help the teen begin to feel comfortable with the leader before entering the group. During this session, the teen is introduced to key concepts that will be reiterated throughout the group, such as the value of monitoring mood, connections between mood and interpersonal relationships, and the concept of prevention. The group leader also begins to assess the teen's relationships through the interpersonal inventory.

Introduce the concept of prevention and provide a rationale for the group intervention. After providing an orientation to the policies and procedures in place in the setting, the leader's first task is to provide an overview of the purpose and preventive nature of the group. If one or both parents can attend the first pre-group session, it is best to provide this overview to the adolescent and parent together. When parents cannot be present, the leader can reach out by phone to provide a brief overview of the group program. Session tasks where we believe parents should be included are described as if a parent is present. However, these tasks can be approached in a similar manner if the adolescent attends the pre-group session alone.

The introduction should engage the teen and the parent, and should be conversational rather than didactic. This is the leader's opportunity to engage both the parent and the teen in the prevention program, helping them to feel connected to the leader through a shared understanding of how this group program could be beneficial to them. It is helpful to give an example from everyday life that the teen and parent are likely to understand. One way to explain the concept of prevention is to use the example of brushing one's teeth every day as a way to prevent cavities. This does not mean that all people who brush their teeth every day never get cavities, but that people who brush their teeth every day are less likely to get cavities than people who do not brush. This helps teens and parents to understand the concept of preventing a worsening of symptoms preemptively rather than waiting for symptoms to appear or to become problematic. This emphasizes that it is hoped that teenagers who participate in this program will be less likely to become depressed later than teenagers who do not participate in these groups.

Once the leader feels that the teen and parent understand the concept of prevention, the next step is to explain the interpersonal focus of group and its rationale. The primary framework for the group is that depression occurs in an interpersonal context. Although problems with peers or family are not necessarily the cause of depression, they can make these problems worse. This is the first of many opportunities to help the adolescent and his or her parent understand the connections between mood and relationships. The leader explains that relationships affect mood (e.g., arguments or lack of contact with people might bring mood down, while positive interactions with people tend to improve mood) and in turn mood affects relationships (e.g., when people feel down, they sometimes withdraw or become irritable, and this can have a negative impact on relationships). People may have more difficulty with the concept that mood affects relationships, but tend to understand that events in relationships affect mood. It is helpful to have the adolescent and parent individually identify times when each of their moods affected how they acted toward others, as well as times when their relationship with others affected their moods. It is okay if the teen does not initially accept the link between mood and relationships. There will be opportunities to make these connections later in the session during the mood check-in and interpersonal inventory, as well as during group sessions. If the teen or parent has difficulty generating personal examples, provide hypothetical examples to illustrate the concepts. Last, connect this idea with the goals of the group, explaining that learning new skills to help the teen cope better with the people in his or her life will help the teen avoid developing more serious depression.

Example: Introduction to interpersonal framework of IPT-AST

LEADER: *We don't know exactly what causes depression for any one person. But we do know that when we feel sad, it affects how we act toward other people. Some people who are sad don't want to be around other people. Others argue more when they feel down. So how we feel affects our relationships. Have you noticed ways that your mood has affected your relationships?*

JESSICA: *Yeah, I notice that when I am in a bad mood I get more annoyed with my brother.*

LEADER: *That is a great example, Jessica. Our relationships also affect how we feel. If we have a bad fight with someone or are having a hard time making friends, it can make us feel sad. On the other hand, if something positive happens in our relationships, we often feel happier. Ms. Garcia, do you have an example of a recent time when your relationships affected your mood?*

MS. GARCIA: *Yes, my boss at work has been giving me a hard time lately, and that has made me stressed out and moody.*

LEADER: *Great example. What about you, Jessica?*

JESSICA: *I feel happier when I get to spend time with my friends.*

LEADER: *Those are both examples of how our relationships affect how we feel. The purpose of the group is to work on improving your relationships, how you can communicate better in these relationships, and your ability to solve problems that come up in relationships, with the hope that this will make you feel better, and, if you keep working on your relationships after group ends, it may prevent you from becoming depressed in the future. Does this make sense?*

JESSICA: *Yeah.*

LEADER: *Great. So, what we are going to do this week is spend time talking about the important relationships in your life and see how they have an impact on your mood.*

Orient adolescent and parent(s) to the group program. Before asking the parent to leave so the leader can meet with the adolescent alone, the leader orients the parent and teen to the group schedule (one additional pre-group session, eight group sessions, mid-group session, and booster sessions, if applicable). This is also a good opportunity to let the parent know that the teen will be attempting new ways of communicating and behaving in relationships over the course of the group and to encourage the parent to be open to and supportive of these changes. If parents will be invited to the mid-group session, it is also important to let the teen and the teen's parent know that the leader will be meeting with them together again between group sessions 4 and 6 to give the teenager an opportunity to practice the skills the teen will be learning in group. When parents and teens expect this from the beginning, they are more likely to be open to the idea of another joint session. In our experience, teens sometimes become resistant to having a parent come in for this mid-group session when it is optional or not explicitly stated as an expectation. In the meantime, the leader informs the parent that the program will primarily involve the adolescent alone, but the parent can contact the group leader as needed with questions or concerns.

Assess for depression symptoms in the past week (with the adolescent alone). The adolescent should be informed that because this program is meant to prevent depression, time will be spent each session checking in about any symptoms of depression the teenager might have experienced in the past week. The leader takes note of any symptoms that the teen endorses and asks follow-up questions about any areas of concern (e.g., if the teen says that he or she has thoughts of death). As this check-in is not a diagnostic evaluation, it is not necessary to ask detailed questions about each symptom area. This should take no longer than 5–10 minutes to complete unless a particular area of concern (i.e., suicidal thoughts) comes up. The leader can use the depression checklist (see Appendix) as a guide for assessing symptoms or can ask about the following core symptoms of depression:

- Feeling sad, bored, or irritable most of the time
- Not being interested in things you used to like doing
- Difficulty sleeping or sleeping too much
- Feeling slowed down or restless

- Increase or decrease in appetite
- Feeling tired
- Difficulty concentrating or making decisions
- Feeling worthless or guilty
- Thoughts of death

Introduce and complete mood rating. The mood rating will be used throughout the program to help the adolescent learn to monitor his or her own mood and facilitate an understanding of how mood is related to events in relationships. As this is the first time the teen encounters the mood rating, the leader takes time to explain the purpose of rating one's mood: To make connections between mood and relationships, it is necessary to learn to label mood as well as identify fluctuations in mood. Next, the leader explains the scale that will be used, with 1 being the best or happiest the teen has ever felt and 10 being the worst or most depressed. After the adolescent rates his or her mood on average for the past week, it is helpful to assess whether the mood varied over the course of the week. Was there a time when the mood was worse than the number given? Better? This is particularly useful for teens who give a global rating that is highly influenced by one negative or positive event. If the teen reports fluctuations in mood over the course of the week, briefly ask about what might have influenced the mood during those times, focusing particularly on events or issues in relationships. The mood rating provides the leader with information about the adolescent's mood over the past week. It also provides another opportunity for the group leader to help the adolescent make connections between mood and events in relationships. It is helpful to explain that the teen will complete this scale each week to monitor his or her mood over the course of the intervention.

Example: Mood rating

LEADER: Jessica, you told me that you feel sad sometimes, about twice a week for several hours. You also report difficulty concentrating in school, especially in math class, and difficulty falling asleep a couple of days a week. As we discussed, these are all symptoms of depression, and I hope they will improve during the group. In addition to the specific symptoms, I find it helpful to have a general sense of how sad you are feeling each week. Can you think of a 1-to-10 scale, with 1 being the best or happiest you have ever felt or can imagine feeling and 10 being the worst or saddest? How would you rate your mood this past week on that 1–10 scale?

JESSICA: A 6.

LEADER: Was there a time this week when you felt better than a 6?

JESSICA: Yeah, I was in a really good mood on Saturday because I hung out at a friend's house and we listened to music. That was probably a 3.

LEADER: What about a time when you felt worse than a 6?

JESSICA: Well, I got in trouble on Sunday because my mom found out I didn't finish my homework for Monday. She yelled at me and told me I wouldn't be able to see my friends next weekend if it wasn't turned in on time. Then, my mood was probably an 8.

LEADER: So, it sounds like you noticed that when you were spending time with friends, your mood really improved, but when you got into trouble and had an argument with your mom, it made your mood worse. In this program, we are going to talk a lot about how our relationships and interactions with people affect our mood. We will also talk about how our mood affects our relationships, so I will be asking you to do these mood ratings each week.

Complete a closeness circle. The closeness circle (see Appendix) allows the leader to create a visual diagram of important people in the adolescent's life to discuss in more detail in the interpersonal inventory. The interpersonal inventory is a detailed, interview-based assessment of the adolescent's significant relationships. It allows the leader to assess relationships that currently affect the teen's mood in either a positive or a negative way. The difficulties or themes that are revealed during the inventory form the basis for individual goal setting.

Before beginning the closeness circle, the leader provides a rationale for this activity, explaining that because this group is going to focus on improving relationships, the first step is getting to know who the important people are in the teen's life. It is not necessary to label it as a closeness circle, as some teenagers might react negatively to this term, particularly those who are uncomfortable talking about relationships or feelings. Rather, it can be referred to simply as a visual diagram used to identify the main people in the teen's life. The leader should explain that the next step after identifying these people will be to discuss several of these relationships in greater detail, and that, by the end of the pre-group sessions, the goal will be to identify one or two relationships to work on during the course of the group.

Completing the closeness circle should be an interactive exercise, with the leader filling in names as the teen explains where to put them on the circle. First, the leader draws a series of concentric circles (or uses the blank closeness circle included in the Appendix), puts the teen's name in the innermost circle, and asks the teen to give names of people with whom he or she has significant relationships. The leader explains that the inner circle represents the people with whom the teen feels the strongest connection, even if these connections are not always positive. The next circle is for people who are less important to the teenager or to whom the teen feels less close. The outermost circle is for people for whom the connection is felt to be weaker or more negative (i.e., an estranged father). As the leader adds names to each circle, it is useful to ask a brief question or two about some identifying information (i.e., How old is your brother? Is Eva a friend from school or somewhere else?). More detailed questions should be reserved for the interpersonal inventory. It is also useful to ask the teen if there is anyone he or she does not feel close to but who affects how the teen feels. These people can be added to the circle. The leader can also ask about any people who are clearly missing from the circle, based on the leader's previous knowledge of the teen. For instance, a teen may choose not to put a stepparent on the closeness circle, when the leader knows that a stepparent lives in the home. In such instances, the leader can ask the teen if he or she is willing to talk about that person as well.

Example: Introduction to the closeness circle (see Figure 4.1)

LEADER: Because we are going to focus on improving relationships in this group, I want to spend the rest of today learning about the important people in your life and what those relationships are like. The reason we are doing this is so that we can work together to decide on one or two relationships that you want to work on in the group. Does that sound okay?

JESSICA: Yeah.

LEADER: To do that, we are going to start by making a diagram of the relationships in your life. So, this picture is going to include all the people who are currently important in your life. I am going to put your name in the middle. I'd like you to put people who are most important to you in the innermost circle. They are people you feel the closest to. The next circle will be for people who are less important or who you feel less close to. The final circle can include people who are still important in your life but you feel less connected with. People who affect your mood in both a positive and a negative way can be placed in these circles. Once we have finished filling in this picture, we are going to start talking in more detail about some of the relationships that are most important to you. Does that make sense?

JESSICA: Yeah.

LEADER: Great. Whom would you put in the circle closest to you here?

JESSICA: I guess my mom and my sister, Carla. [Leader writes this in]

LEADER: Would anyone else go in that circle?

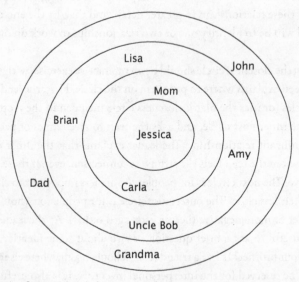

FIGURE 4.1 Example of a completed closeness circle.

Begin the interpersonal inventory. Using the closeness circle as a guide, the leader asks detailed questions about important relationships in the adolescent's life. The interpersonal inventory is an opportunity to ask questions about each relationship that the adolescent might not be asked in other settings. Many teens appreciate this opportunity to discuss relationships in this level of depth, given that relationships are often important and salient to them at this developmental stage. For each relationship, the goal is to assess interactions, expectations, positive and negative aspects of the relationship, how the teen's mood has an impact on the relationship, how the relationship has an impact on the teen's mood, and desired changes in the relationship (see Mufson, Dorta, Moreau, et al., 2004, for more details on conducting an interpersonal inventory). The leader should direct the teen to focus on one relationship at a time to improve clarity and depth for each relationship. If the adolescent brings up another relationship, this should be noted and returned to after inquiry about the current relationship is complete. It should take between 5 and 15 minutes to adequately address each relationship, depending on the importance or complexity of the relationship and the level of detail the teen provides.

The goal is to complete an inventory on four to six people over the course of both pre-group sessions, and it is most important to discuss any relationships that have a substantial impact on the adolescent's mood. When an adolescent has a lot of people on the closeness circle, it may be necessary to limit discussion to the relationships that have the most impact on the teen's mood, in a good or bad way. It is important to spend sufficient time discussing the adolescent's key relationships. This should be prioritized over superficially covering a larger number of less important people on the circle. If it is not possible to cover everyone on the teen's closeness circle, it is most important to cover the teen's main family relationships (e.g., parents) and at least two peer relationships. Although both positive and negative relationships are helpful to discuss, it is essential to discuss problematic relationships that influence mood, as these will form the basis for goals that the teen will work on throughout the group. A discussion of positive relationships can help the leader understand where the adolescent may obtain support to work on other more problematic relationships.

To build rapport and provide the adolescent with some agency in the session, the teen should be invited to choose the first person to talk about. This can be someone the teen thinks is most important to talk about or who the teen most wants to discuss with the group leader. Then, the leader should help guide the teen to discuss the most relevant relationships. If the adolescent has a lot of people on the closeness circle, the leader can ask the teen to identify which relationships would be most important to review. The more conversational the inventory, the better it will feel for the adolescent, so the leader should follow the adolescent's lead as long as the teen provides useful information about his or her relationships.

It is important to collect specific information about the quality of the relationships and types of interactions that occur in each relationship. Most teens will start by making global, general statements, so it is the leader's job to elicit the details. The questions located in the Appendix are helpful to elicit specific information and are recommended for assessing most relationships. It is not necessary to ask every question about each relationship or ask the questions in any particular order. Additional questions should be asked if needed to better understand the adolescent's relationships. It is helpful for the leader to take notes about each relationship during the interpersonal inventory. This can be explained at the start of the interpersonal inventory so that the adolescent understands why the leader is taking notes (e.g., "I am going to take notes so that I make sure to remember what we talk about today"). The leader should take care to note issues that might be important to address during the group as well as which relationships might be a source of support for the adolescent. This will help the leader to facilitate personal goal setting. The following example illustrates how the questions listed in the Appendix, as well as additional follow-up questions, can be used to elicit details about a relationship with a parent.

Example: Parent interpersonal inventory inquiry

LEADER: Jessica, we are going to spend the rest of today talking about the people you've put in your circle. Which relationship do you think would be most important to talk about first?

JESSICA: My mom, I guess.

LEADER: I am going to ask you lots of questions about your relationship with your mom. If it's okay with you, I am going to take notes while we talk today so I can remember what you tell me about your relationships. That will help me to really understand the important people in your life. Can you tell me about your relationship with your mom?

JESSICA: She's okay. I guess. . . . I don't know what to say.

LEADER: What do you like about your mom?

JESSICA: I like that she's not as strict as some of my friend's moms. I mean she lets me go out with friends after school and stuff, and I can talk to her about boys . . . sometimes.

LEADER: So, you can talk to her about boys sometimes. When are the times that it is harder to talk about boys?

JESSICA: I can talk to my mom about boys in general, but I'm worried that if I tell her I have a crush on someone she will ask a lot of questions and maybe say something to my dad about it. Whenever my dad hears about things like that, he says something embarrassing.

LEADER: Are there other things that are difficult to talk to your mom about?

JESSICA: Not really.

LEADER: What about your feelings? Are you able to tell your mom when you are feeling sad?

JESSICA: No, I don't have to tell her. She just knows. She can tell by how I am acting, and she just stays away.

LEADER: Do you want her to stay away when you are upset?

JESSICA: Sometimes I do, but sometimes I wish she would ask me what was wrong.

LEADER: How would you feel if she asked?

JESSICA: I might be annoyed at first, but then I think I would feel good. I would think that she cared about me.

LEADER: There are times you wish your mom would ask you what was wrong because it would show she cared. Are there other things about your relationship that you don't like so much?

JESSICA: Sometimes, she is so busy with other stuff, I feel like she forgets that I am there. And, when my brother and I fight, she yells at me more than at him.

LEADER: Can you tell me more about how your mom responds when you and your brother fight?

JESSICA: We'll be fighting over something stupid like who gets to choose what to watch on television. We start yelling at each other, and then my mom will come in and say, "Jessica, stop fighting with your brother!"

LEADER: How do you feel when that happens?

JESSICA: Mad. It's not fair.

LEADER: How do you feel when your mom is really busy and you feel like she forgets about you?

JESSICA: Sad, I guess.

LEADER: *So, sometimes your mom doesn't have time for you and that makes you feel sad. Other times, she favors your brother and that makes you mad. Jessica, since you've been feeling sad, have you noticed any changes in your relationship with your mom?*

JESSICA: *I guess we don't talk as much. She's busy and I am quieter, so there can be days when we don't talk at all. Also, because my brother and I are fighting more, I feel like she yells more than she used to.*

LEADER: *Would you like to spend more time with your mom?*

JESSICA: *I guess so.*

LEADER: *What about being able to talk to her more about how you are feeling?*

JESSICA: *It would be nice to be able to talk to her more, but I'm not sure; it might feel kind of weird.*

Closing tasks: summarize and prepare teen for next session. Before ending the session, the leader should briefly summarize what was accomplished in the session and preview what will happen in the next pre-group session. The leader can thank the teen for engaging in this process to continue to build rapport.

Example: Summary of session

LEADER: *Thanks for sharing all of that with me today. It was helpful to get to know a bit about your relationship with your mom, dad, and brother, Brian. Next time, we are going to talk about a few more relationships, and then we will decide together which relationships are most important for you to focus on in group.*

Pre-Group Session 2

Session goals and tasks. In the second pre-group session, the leader continues to build rapport with the adolescent while assessing important relationships in the teen's life. The majority of this session is spent completing the interpersonal inventory that was started during the first pre-group session. Toward the end of the session, the leader reviews important relationship issues and helps the teen set goals to work on during the group. Last, this session provides an opportunity to address any questions or concerns the teen has about the group before it begins.

Assess for depression symptoms in the past week and complete a mood rating. At the start of the session, the leader should briefly assess depression symptoms in the past week and ask the teen to complete a mood rating on the same scale, with 1 being the best the teen could feel and 10 being the worst or most depressed. Again, the leader asks for times when the teen's mood was better or worse than the average and helps the teen to link any fluctuations in mood to interpersonal events if possible. This should take approximately 5–10 minutes.

Complete the interpersonal inventory. Most of this session should be spent continuing to assess relationships that the adolescent identified on the closeness circle in the previous session, using the same type of inquiry described in the section on pre-group session 1. An example of a peer-related interpersonal inventory inquiry is provided next:

Pre-Group Session 2 Checklist:

☐ Assess for depression symptoms in the past week and complete a mood rating

☐ Complete the interpersonal inventory

☐ Provide a summary and feedback about the interpersonal inventory

☐ Collaboratively set two goals for teen to work on based on the interpersonal inventory

☐ Introduce teen to the group program

☐ Closing tasks: address concerns about the group

Materials Needed:

☐ List of depression symptoms for leader's reference

☐ Completed closeness circle from pre-group session 1

☐ List of questions to ask during interpersonal inventory for leader's reference (see Appendix)

☐ Written group schedule to give to teen at end of session

Example: Peer interpersonal inventory inquiry

LEADER: Let's talk next about your friend, Amy. Tell me what things are like with her.

JESSICA: I don't know, okay, I guess. We've been friends since third grade.

LEADER: What do you like about her?

JESSICA: She's nice and funny. We always laugh when we hang out together.

LEADER: That's great. How often do you see her?

JESSICA: Every day at school, and we sit together at lunch sometimes. I used to see her on the weekends, but we haven't done that much lately.

LEADER: Is there any reason you've seen her less recently?

JESSICA: I don't know; I guess I haven't felt like doing much lately.

LEADER: Okay. Are there any things that you don't like or that bother you about Amy?

JESSICA: Well, sometimes she acts differently when other people are around, like she isn't really my friend. That makes me mad.

LEADER: What does she do when other people are around that makes you mad?

JESSICA: Well, she kind of ignores me when certain people are there, like she won't even say hi. And, she starts acting really fake.

LEADER: What do you usually do when that happens?

JESSICA: I just ignore her back. Sometimes, I walk away or try to find someone else to talk to. Our other friend, Lisa, notices it, too, I think, but we don't really talk about it.

LEADER: Have you ever talked to Amy about it?

JESSICA: No.

LEADER: What stops you?

JESSICA: I worry that she will think I am making a big deal out of it.

LEADER: How does it affect your mood when that happens with Amy?

JESSICA: Well, I feel bad about it sometimes for the rest of the day, but then I get over it.

LEADER: How often does this happen?

JESSICA: It happens a few times a week, usually during lunch or in the hallway.

LEADER: Have you noticed changes in your friendship with Amy since you've been feeling down?

JESSICA: Yeah, I guess we haven't hung out as much, and I'm quieter even when I do see her.

LEADER: Is your relationship with Amy something you might want to work on in group? In particular, finding ways to handle it when Amy ignores you, maybe even talking to her about how it makes you feel?

JESSICA: I'm not sure I want her to know how I feel, but she used to be a really good friend, and I'd like for us to spend more time together like we used to.

Some teenagers might have difficulty providing information related to their relationships and mood. For teenagers who either have little insight into interpersonal difficulties or who do not report difficulties in relationships, it might be necessary for the leader to ask some additional questions. These questions can be interspersed into the inventory. For instance, the leader can ask questions probing for difficulties making friends or sustaining positive relationships with others. It is also sometimes helpful to ask teens what affects their mood or makes them feel upset if this has not been possible to find out during the interpersonal inventory. Examples of additional questions include the following:

- What tends to affect your mood the most?
- Can you give me an example in the past few weeks when you felt upset?
- Do you have difficulty making friends? In what way?
- How do you feel about meeting new people?
- How do you feel in new social situations?
- Can you confide in anyone? Who?
- Have there been any changes in your family recently?
- Have you noticed changes in your friendships? How has this affected your mood?
- Have you had to adapt to anything new, like a new school or new neighborhood?
- What has been difficult about the change(s)?
- Are there people at school who bother you or pick on you? How does it affect your mood when that happens?

Provide a summary and feedback about the interpersonal inventory. Throughout the inventory, the leader should pay attention to information that will inform individual goal setting: Which relationships or interactions affect the adolescent's mood the most? What happens when the adolescent communicates within the relationship? How does the adolescent tend to solve problems in relationships? What changes can be made in the relationships? What relationships or interactions are associated with improvements in mood? Can the adolescent strengthen these positive relationships or increase the interactions that lead to improvements in mood? By the time the inventory is complete, the leader should have several hypotheses about how the teen's relationships are affecting his or her mood, as well as how the teen's mood affects his or her relationships. The leader should also have a few ideas about changes that the teen might want to work toward in personal relationships to improve his or her mood.

After completing the inventory, it is helpful to elicit the adolescent's thoughts about what he or she has learned from the inventory before moving on to collaboratively set goals for the group. The leader can ask the adolescent what he or she has noticed about the relationships that were discussed in the inventory. Did any particular relationships or communication patterns stand out? The leader can also share observations or feedback with the teen at this point. To continue to build rapport, it is best to ask permission to share feedback (e.g., "Would it be okay with you if I shared some things that I noticed as we were talking today and last week?"). An example of how to lead this discussion is provided next.

Example: Interpersonal inventory summary and feedback

LEADER: *Jessica, we've talked about a lot of your relationships. Have you learned anything new from what we've talked about?*

JESSICA: *Yeah, I see that I haven't wanted to hang out with friends as much as I used to.*

LEADER: *That's right. You mentioned not spending as much time with your friends Lisa and Amy. You also mentioned that Amy has been acting differently, particularly when she is around other kids at the high school.*

JESSICA: *Yeah. That has been really bothering me. Amy, Lisa, and I used to hang out all the time, and now with Amy acting so weird, I don't talk to either of them much anymore.*

LEADER: *That sounds really hard. Those experiences, coupled with feeling sad and down, have made you withdraw somewhat from these friends, which ends up making you feel even worse. What else has changed?*

JESSICA: *I have been fighting more with my brother.*

LEADER: *You did say you've been more irritable with him. You've also been talking less to your mom since you've been feeling sad. Does that sound right?*

Collaboratively set two goals for teen to work on based on the interpersonal inventory. It is important for goal-setting to be collaborative between the leader and the adolescent, so that the adolescent takes ownership of the goals as much as possible but is also guided to choose goals that the leader believes will be most helpful. Goals should be specific, focused both on a particular relationship and on a particular issue to address within that relationship. The leader provides possible goals as options for the adolescent based on the interpersonal inventory and also asks for additional input and ideas from the adolescent. While some teenagers will have a clear idea of what they want to work on in the group, many will require considerable direction from the leader. If an adolescent chooses a goal that the leader does not see as particularly helpful, it might be necessary to compromise by keeping the adolescent's goal while adding a second or third goal that the leader thinks would be more useful. For example, if a teen chooses to focus on spending more time with friends and is reluctant to address frequent arguments with a parent, the leader might suggest working on reducing those arguments as a secondary goal. An example of this type of negotiation is provided in the next script. It is recommended that the leader and teen identify two goals rather than one so that there is more flexibility for the leader to choose targets for intervention and practice of communication skills. Given that teens' priorities often change over the course of the group, having two goals also makes it more likely that at least one will remain a priority for the adolescent. Some examples of goals include the following:

- I want to learn to express my feelings better to my father.
- I want to figure out the best way to negotiate with my mom about more freedom to go out with friends.
- I want to talk to my parents to better understand their divorce and figure out how to talk to them about how I am feeling about it.
- I want to find ways to argue less with my mom about homework.
- I want to spend more time with Teresa [a friend].
- I want to find ways to handle it when certain peers tease or bother me.
- I want to argue less with my brother about sharing use of the family computer, television, and other things at home.

Example: Goal setting

LEADER: *Jessica, based on what we have talked about, what do you think you would like to work on in terms of your relationships?*

JESSICA: *Well, I do miss hanging out with my friends. Maybe I could work on trying to see them more often.*

LEADER: *That's a good idea. You also mentioned that you were not happy with the way Amy has been treating you lately. It seems like a goal for group would be to let her know how you feel when she ignores you around other people.*

JESSICA: *I don't know if I want to tell her how I feel.*

LEADER: *What do you think is the worst thing that would happen if you told her how you feel?*

JESSICA: *I don't think she would understand. And, I worry she would keep doing it and then I would feel even worse.*

LEADER: *It sounds like right now you are not ready to commit to talking to Amy about how you feel. Maybe one goal could be to decide whether you want to work on that friendship, and in the meantime we can talk about ways to be closer to some of your other friends, like Lisa?*

JESSICA: *That sounds good.*

LEADER: *I am also wondering if you would be interested in talking to your mom about how you have been feeling. By talking to her about how you have been feeling, you would be giving her a chance to help you. How do those two goals sound to you?*

JESSICA: *That sounds okay.*

LEADER: *Great. I hope that as you work on your friendships and your relationship with your mom, you will notice improvements in your mood as well.*

Introduce teen to the group program. At the end of the second pre-group session, the leader introduces the group as an interpersonal lab where teens can experiment with new approaches to interacting with people. This includes an explanation that group members will first learn about new ways of interacting with others before being asked to apply these skills to their own relationships. Adolescents are often relieved to learn that, in these initial sessions, they will not be asked to share any personal information. Then, in later group sessions as people feel comfortable, group members will bring in information about problems that have arisen in their own relationships so they can practice better ways of communicating with others. The leader should explain that in the group the teen will learn (a) how to tell people how he or she feels; (b) how to understand another person's point of view; (c) how to problem-solve in relationships; (d) how to compromise; and (e) how to establish new relationships. The leader also outlines the overall structure of the program, reminding the teen that there will be eight weekly group sessions, a mid-group session that parents will attend (depending on the setting and the leader's plans for parent involvement), and booster sessions. Finally, it is important to provide the teen with a schedule for group sessions and discuss the importance of regular attendance for getting the most benefit from the group program.

Closing tasks: address concerns about the group. The end of pre-group session 2 is a good time for the leader to ask if the teen has any concerns about participating in the group so that the concerns can be addressed. For a teen who is anxious about the group setting, it can be helpful to emphasize that he or she will never be required to share any personal information if the teen is not comfortable. The leader may also mention that the group will establish rules to make the group feel safe, and this will include keeping confidential what is said in the group. If a teen is worried about information being shared with parents, it is helpful for the leader to remind the teen of the policy about what information will or will not be shared with parents.

Summary of the Pre-Group Sessions

By the end of the two pre-group sessions, the teen should have a good sense of the format and goals of IPT-AST and will feel more comfortable going into the first group meeting after getting to know the leader. The parent will also be familiar with the purpose and structure of the intervention from the discussion. By conducting the interpersonal inventory, the leader will have gained an understanding of the interpersonal issues that the teenager faces. Working collaboratively, the adolescent and leader will have set interpersonal goals to work on during the course of the program. It will be useful for the leader to keep each group member's interpersonal goals in mind during the remainder of the group, as this will help the leader to guide group discussions in the most productive direction. The leader will also be able to identify common themes across group members' interpersonal goals. This knowledge can inform the hypothetical situations that the leader chooses to discuss as a group, as the leader can pick interpersonal scenarios that are particularly relevant for the adolescents in the group.

5

IPT-AST Initial Phase

The initial phase of Interpersonal Psychotherapy – Adolescent Skills Training (IPT-AST) provides an opportunity for group members to get to know each other and feel comfortable in the group setting. These sessions are educational in tone and do not require adolescents to disclose much personal information. In session 1, the group members introduce themselves, establish group rules, learn about the purpose of the group, and talk about symptoms of depression and interpersonal issues that are common in adolescence. In session 2, the leader uses activities to illustrate issues in communication, and group members act out hypothetical interpersonal situations to illustrate the technique of communication analysis. In session 3, the group leader teaches adolescents the communication strategies and continues to use hypothetical interpersonal situations to illustrate how they can be used. In the less likely event that adolescents are eager to share interpersonal situations from their own lives, the leader can apply the communication strategies to the adolescents' real-life examples. The initial phase sessions should be interactive and fun to engage teens in the program. While it is important to accomplish the tasks described, it is equally important that teens have a positive experience in the group and are comfortable enough in the group to move into the middle phase, where they will be asked to share personal information about their relationships to work on their interpersonal goals.

Group Session 1

Session goals and tasks. Group session 1 provides teens with an opportunity to get to know each other, start to feel comfortable with the group, and work together to set group rules. This session should be a fun introduction to the IPT-AST group. Teens learn what the group will be like and receive education about depression. Group session 1 closes with a discussion of common issues and problems that teenagers face.

   Distribute binders. We have found it useful to distribute binders to each of the group members at the start of each group session. The binders contain a depression checklist to be filled out each week, a pen for filling out the weekly checklists, a description of the communication strategies taught in group session 3, and cue cards to be used for the role plays (see Appendix for these materials). The leader should explain the purpose of the binders

---

Group Session 1 Checklist:

☐ Distribute binders

☐ Have adolescents complete depression checklist and mood rating

☐ Conduct group introductions and icebreaker activity

☐ Collaboratively establish group rules

☐ Discuss purpose of group, role of group members, and role of the group leader

☐ Discuss signs and symptoms of depression using depression vignettes

☐ Discuss issues and problems that teenagers face

☐ Closing task: encourage consistent attendance

Materials Needed:

☐ Binders and pens

☐ Materials for icebreaker activity (e.g., candy)

☐ Printed depression vignettes (see Appendix)

☐ Written group schedule to give to teens (optional)

(filling out depressive symptoms, description of some communication strategies that will be discussed in a later group) and explain that he or she will keep the binders during the course of the group. Teens will take the binders home at the end of the group as a reminder of the work done during the program.

Have adolescents complete depression checklist and mood rating. At the beginning of each group session, teens complete the depression checklist and 1–10 mood rating on their own to help them self-monitor their mood and symptoms without forcing them to share this personal information with the group. The leader looks over each group member's depression checklist briefly at the beginning of the session, paying particular attention to items 14 and 15, which ask about wishing to disappear and thoughts about harming oneself, respectively. If an adolescent answers yes to either of these items, the leader should meet with the teen after the group to assess for safety (see Chapter 3 for more detailed information about conducting a suicide risk assessment). The leader is encouraged to pay attention to changes in the number of symptoms and changes in mood ratings from week to week to monitor teens' progress during the group.

Group introductions and icebreaker activity. Teens should briefly introduce themselves. Next, it is helpful to do an icebreaker activity so the teens can get to know each other and can begin to feel more comfortable in the group setting. The leader can decide to spend more or less time on the icebreaker activity depending on how comfortable the group members seem to feel with each other. Less time is often needed when group members know each other already. The icebreaker activity we typically use involves a bag of multicolored candy. Give each group member and group leader several pieces of candy of different colors. For each color, pick a category that every person with that color candy needs to answer. Examples of categories include favorite dessert, favorite subject in school, something they do for fun, favorite television show, least favorite vegetable, place they would like to visit, and things they are looking forward to in the group. After several rounds, the leader can ask group members to come up with additional categories. Another icebreaker activity involves having group members each tell the group three statements about themselves: two statements should be true and one should be a lie. Then, teens guess which statement is not true of that person. Another option is to have group members interview each other and introduce their partner to the rest of the group. We have typically used the first activity because it provokes the least anxiety, but the leader can use his or her discretion with a particular group to choose the most appropriate activity.

Collaboratively establish group rules. Before establishing group rules, the leader reminds teens that the purpose of the group is to work on communication and interpersonal problem-solving to help improve relationships and decrease or prevent depression symptoms. To help group members feel comfortable talking to each other about these topics, it is helpful to establish guidelines that will make group a safe place. When encouraging teens to set group rules, the leader guides the group members to generate rules themselves. In this way, teens' independent behavior is encouraged, and group members own the rules of their group, rather than having rules imposed on them by an adult. It also ensures that teens' actual concerns about the group will be addressed. The leader should write down rules as they are generated so that they can be printed and distributed at group session 2. The rules can be kept in the teens' binders as a reminder of what has been agreed on.

Although rules are collaboratively set, it is important that several areas of common concern are addressed: confidentiality, how group members will interact outside group, mutual respect for others, giving feedback to others in a constructive manner, time commitment to group, and policies regarding lateness or cancelling. When teens bring up other topics of concern, these should be discussed as well to help teens feel heard.

Perhaps the most important area to address is confidentiality. This includes keeping others' personal information private and agreeing to use fake names when talking about people who other group members might know. It is important for teens to agree that they will not share other group members' personal information outside the group. However, a strict policy of "what is said in the group stays in the group" might not be appropriate because it is suitable (and even encouraged) for a teen to talk to a parent about what he or she is working on in the group, without mentioning another group member by name. On the other hand, it would not be appropriate to tell a friend what another teen said in group. The leader helps to make this distinction for group members. In addition, it is best to remind group members of the limits of confidentiality as they pertain to the leader sharing information with parents (concerns about suicidality or risk of harm to self or others) or reporting to authorities (concerns about suspected abuse). Hearing group members discuss friends or acquaintances is likely to increase the temptation to break confidentiality. For this reason, it is helpful for teens to agree not to identify others by name if people in the group are likely to know them.

Another important topic to discuss is group members' interactions outside the group. This will vary depending on the setting and the adolescents' level of comfort. Some teens will feel comfortable referring to group in the hallway at school, while others will want more privacy. For groups of teens who do not know each other already, discuss what kind of contact outside the group feels comfortable (e.g., social media, texting, seeing each other outside the group). Leaders working in various settings may feel differently about this and can set expectations accordingly. It is important that all group members are on the same page regarding contact outside the group, whatever decision is made about how much contact, if any, is appropriate. It is typically not realistic for a group leader to limit teens' contact outside the group, particularly in settings where teens live in the same community or go to the same school. However, talking about topics discussed in the group or about other group members should be discouraged, especially on public forums. When necessary, the leader can explain the rationale for this rule, given that discussion of these topics may break confidentiality, make other members of the group uncomfortable, or make others feel left out.

Two related topics that are necessary to discuss are maintaining mutual respect for group members and giving feedback to others in a constructive manner. This includes listening attentively to others when they speak and taking turns appropriately. It also means not putting down other group members' ideas or contributions to discussions. The idea that people can disagree while remaining respectful should be discussed. Adolescents can be oriented to the fact that they will be asked to give each other feedback regarding communication, and at times they may not agree with each other's ideas or advice. While constructive feedback is encouraged, group members should agree to provide this feedback respectfully.

Last, the leader raises the topic of time commitment to group as well as policies regarding lateness or cancelling. Depending on the setting, rules regarding missing group meetings and procedures to follow in the case that someone will be late or has to cancel may differ. Given the time-limited nature of the group, the leader should encourage regular attendance, both for each member's benefit and for the benefit of the rest of the group. The leader can predict that the teens' motivation to attend group sessions may fluctuate, while emphasizing that it is important for teens to participate in the group in its entirety to get the maximum benefit and to respect the other group members. It can be beneficial for the group leader to remind teens that they will help each other by providing ideas and feedback, so their absence will mean that others will miss out on their contributions.

Example: Establishing group rules

LEADER: As we discussed in your individual meetings before group started, this is a depression prevention group. We are going to work together on communication and problem-solving so that we can help you improve your relationships. You all set goals to work on in this group. Over the next 8 weeks, we are going to spend some time learning new skills and helping each other practice different ways of communicating to help you work toward those goals. For you all to get the most out of this group, I want to talk about guidelines to make sure that this is a fun and safe place for you to talk about those things. What are some rules or guidelines that you think are important for this group?

MARY: We shouldn't talk about what happens in group with anyone else. What happens in the group stays in the group.

LEADER: *That's a great point. It is important to keep what people share in here private. That's called confidentiality. So, Mary, if you shared something about yourself with the group, you wouldn't want anyone else here to tell people outside of group about it. What kinds of things are okay to talk about outside of group? What if there is a topic, let's say it is bullying, and after group you feel upset or worried about what we talked about in the group? Who could you talk to about that?*

RYAN: *We could talk to you about it.*

LEADER: *Yes, that's right; you can always talk to me about that. Do people think it's okay to talk to a parent if something comes up in group that bothers you, as long as you don't say anything about a specific person from group?*

FARRAH: *Yeah, I think that's okay.*

LEADER: *Great. So far, we have a rule that group members should keep what others share in the group private. What if someone shares something related to someone else you know? Would that make it hard to keep that a secret?*

JESSICA: *I think we should try not to talk about other people in group. If I heard about one of my friends in here, I would want to tell them.*

MICHAEL: *Maybe we could just not use names.*

LEADER: *What do other people think? I know some of you have goals related to friends, so it might be hard to avoid talking about those people at all. Would it be okay either to not use names or to use code names when we have to talk about other people?*

JESSICA: *That sounds good to me.*

LEADER: *So, besides privacy and keeping other people's names out of the group, what else should we do in here to make this a safe place to talk?*

Discuss purpose of group, role of group members, and role of the group leader. Although the leader provided some information about the group in the pre-group sessions, it is helpful in this first group session to remind group members about the structure and purpose of the group so that everyone is on the same page. This may also include a discussion of why the teens have been put together in this group. This explanation will vary depending on the type of group as well as the setting. For a selective prevention group in a school, the leader might say: "You are all participating in this group because you have recently transferred to this school, and we know that can be a hard transition for some teenagers." For an indicated prevention group, the leader might say: "You are all in this group because you are experiencing some minor symptoms of depression." Next, the leader should highlight how the group members can use the group meeting times most effectively. This includes learning new ways to communicate and behave in significant relationships. The leader also emphasizes the commonality of group members' symptoms (for indicated prevention groups) and problems they may be having in their relationships (for all levels of prevention). As a result of these commonalities, group members can be helpful coaches to each other. The leader's role is described as that of an expert assistant to facilitate teens' participation, in contrast to a teacher who imparts all of the information to a class without much participation. Another way to describe the leader's role is to compare the leader to a coach who will encourage group members to work toward goals and to help each other learn new ways to communicate.

Example: Introduction to the purpose of the group

LEADER: You are all in this group in the hope that it will prevent you from developing depression. As you know from your pre-group sessions, we are going to spend a lot of time in group learning new ways to communicate with important people in our lives. We are going to do this because I believe that improving your relationships and learning new skills will help you to handle problems better as they come up and prevent you from feeling worse in the future. As group progresses, you'll see that a lot of you are dealing with similar issues with family or friends. We are going to use the group to address these problems. You all have a lot in common, which means that you can really help each other a lot. As the group leader, my job is to introduce new strategies that can help you to improve your relationships. All of you are going to help each other practice these new skills.

Discuss signs and symptoms of depression using depression vignettes. Given that IPT-AST is a preventive intervention for depression, it is important for the adolescents to learn about the symptoms of depression and to begin to distinguish between normal sadness and more significant mood disturbances. It may be helpful for the leader to first introduce the concept of symptoms with an analogy that teens can relate to (e.g., symptoms of the flu). The leader can then provide a rationale for why it is important for them to learn about depression to help them understand the disorder that the group aims to prevent and to help them recognize symptoms if they occur.

Example: Discussion about symptoms of depression

LEADER: The purpose of this group is to prevent depression, so first I want everyone to have an understanding of the signs and symptoms of depression. Does anyone know what I mean by "symptoms"?
MARY: Yeah, they are like things that let you know someone is sick.
LEADER: Exactly. So, for example, if I had the flu, what symptoms would I have?
MICHAEL: A fever.
JESSICA: A headache, and you'd feel nauseous.
LEADER: That's right. So, now we are going to talk about symptoms of depression so you can become more familiar with what depression looks like.

Next, the leader introduces the activity that follows, where group members are asked to identify symptoms within made-up examples of teenagers experiencing varying levels of difficulty. The depression vignettes listed next are also provided in a printable form in the Appendix. It is best to have teens read the examples aloud to increase engagement in the group, but the leader can read each example aloud instead if group members are reticent. After the vignette is read aloud, group members identify the depressive symptoms for each adolescent, using a blank copy of the depression checklist to help them if needed.

Example: Introduction to depression exercise

LEADER: *We are going to listen to a few made-up examples of teenagers who might have some symptoms of depression. Please listen closely, and when the example has been read, you are going to tell me which symptoms you heard. You can use a blank depression checklist from your binder to help you because those are all symptoms of depression right there. Ryan, can you get us started by reading the first example out loud?*

This exercise is meant to provide an engaging way for teens to familiarize themselves with depression symptoms and to begin to appreciate the variety of ways that depression can look to an outside observer. It also serves as a springboard for the leader to discuss differences between normal low mood, which everyone experiences; subthreshold symptoms of depression that might mean someone is at risk for developing depression; and an actual depressive episode. The first two examples are adolescents who meet criteria for a depressive episode. The third example is the type of adolescent who might be in a selective or indicated prevention group, with some symptoms of depression but not enough symptoms to meet criteria for a depressive episode. The last example is an adolescent who is experiencing normal sadness who might be included in a universal prevention group.

Depression vignettes

- Anna is a 15-year-old girl. For the past month, she has been feeling sad. She's not sure why, but thinks maybe it has to do with starting a new school and not knowing a lot of people. She has been having trouble falling asleep. Sometimes, she lies in bed for 2 hours before she finally falls asleep. During the day, she feels really tired, and, although she is going to school, she finds that her mind wanders in her classes. As a result, she failed her last three quizzes. Anna feels really guilty about this and worries that her mom will be disappointed. Anna used to love going out with friends, but lately she doesn't feel like it. Instead, she goes home and sits in front of the television by herself.

Symptoms: depressed mood, insomnia, feeling tired, poor concentration, feeling guilty, loss of interest

- Jose is a 13-year-old boy. He has been getting in a lot of arguments with his mom and brother since the school year started. It seems that whatever Jose's brother does, it bothers Jose. In addition, Jose has been having a lot of headaches, and he has lost his appetite. He went to the doctor, but the doctor said that nothing was wrong. Lately, Jose has been thinking about his dad, who died when he was younger. Sometimes when he thinks about this, he feels like life is not worth living anymore. All Jose wants to do is sleep. If he could, he would sleep all day. In addition, he has been having a hard time making decisions, such as what to do after school or what to wear in the morning.

Symptoms: irritability, somatic complaints (not a symptom for diagnosis of depression but a common associated feature), loss of appetite, thoughts of death, hypersomnia, indecision

- George is a 16-year-old boy who feels sad almost every day. He's not sure what happened, but in the past few months, he just hasn't felt like himself. He has been spending time alone a lot and can't pay attention in class. When he does hang out with friends, he has a good time and feels better.

Symptoms: sadness, withdrawal, poor concentration

- Carla is a 12-year-old girl who feels sad a couple of times a week. The sadness lasts for about an hour or two and then goes away when Carla finds something to do. Some of the sadness is related to the fact that Carla hasn't been getting along with her best friend, Marie. Ever since they started seventh grade, Marie has been hanging out with a new group of girls, and Carla feels left out. On Sundays, Carla has a hard time falling asleep because she thinks about the upcoming week at school and wonders whether Marie will include her.

Symptoms: sadness a few times a week that doesn't last long, some difficulty sleeping

The leader should encourage the adolescents to discuss the symptoms noted. This includes pointing out that different people can experience different symptoms and still have depression (e.g., some people eat more, while others eat less). The leader also highlights differences between normal sadness and depression, noting differences between the examples in terms of number of symptoms, severity, duration, and effect of symptoms on functioning. The purpose of this discussion is to get group members to think about how they would know when they are experiencing more than just a passing bad mood. The leader emphasizes duration (lasting for at least 2 weeks); number of symptoms (sadness, irritability, or loss of interest in activities, plus three or four other symptoms); and effect on functioning. It is not necessary to teach diagnostic criteria for depression, but teens should get the sense that everyone has bad days and that it is normal to feel sad sometimes. However, if one experiences a cluster of symptoms that lasts for a week or two, help from an adult might be needed. If issues of self-harm or suicidal thoughts are raised by group members, the leader should emphasize that immediate help from an adult is required in those situations.

Example: Discussion about depression versus normal low mood

LEADER: What did you all notice about these examples?

RYAN: I think the second one, Jose, was the most depressed because he was even thinking about suicide.

LEADER: That's a great point. Thoughts of death or suicide are definitely a sign that someone needs help. What are some other reasons that you think Jose is more depressed than some of the other teenagers?

JESSICA: Well, he had more symptoms than George or Carla did. I think he had about five.

LEADER: That's right. So, both the number of symptoms and the severity of those symptoms let you know that Jose is probably depressed. What about Anna?

MARY: I think she was depressed, too; she had five or six symptoms.

LEADER: Right. Her symptoms were a little different, but she would also be considered depressed. For both Anna and Jose, you also heard that they have been feeling down for a while; for Anna, it was the past 3 weeks, and for Jose, it was since the beginning of the school year. You might have noticed that Anna had trouble sleeping, while Jose actually slept a lot more than usual. One thing that's interesting about depression is that it can affect people in both of those ways. Depression can also affect your appetite in different ways. Some people might not feel like eating, and other people might eat even more than usual. Does that make sense?

JESSICA: *Yeah.*

LEADER: *What about George and Carla?*

RYAN: *George had a few symptoms for a while, but he wasn't as bad as Anna and Jose. I don't think he was depressed.*

LEADER: *That's right. What do other people think? Would he be someone who could be in a prevention group like this one? [for a selective or indicated prevention group]*

MARY: *Yeah, because he isn't depressed but he still has some symptoms.*

LEADER: *Right. So, you all picked up on the fact that George had fewer symptoms. You also might have noticed that he was still able to have fun sometimes when he spent time with friends. What about Carla?*

MICHAEL: *She was sad sometimes, too.*

LEADER: *She was. Did she have a lot of symptoms?*

JESSICA: *No, she was sad sometimes but just about her friend. I don't think she was depressed.*

LEADER: *Right, she is an example of someone who feels down sometimes, but wouldn't be considered depressed. It is normal for everyone to feel sad from time to time or to be in a bad mood.*

Discuss issues and problems that teenagers face. The last task of the first group session is to have group members talk about some of the problems they experience as teenagers (i.e., fighting with friends, not knowing how to talk to parents about romantic relationships, having trouble adjusting to a new school). The leader can emphasize that while he or she has expertise about depression and helping teens with relationships, group members are experts on what it is like to be a teenager right now. This should be an open-ended discussion about adolescence and is a good opportunity to get the adolescents talking. It is helpful to frame the discussion as a general conversation about issues that come up for teenagers, rather than asking teens to disclose their own particular problems. While often teens do volunteer issues or problems that are personal to them, it is important not to pressure them to do so, particularly given that they have been told that they will not be obligated to share personal information right away in the group. Most adolescents will be much more comfortable participating if this is framed as a discussion about issues that many teenagers experience, including their friends or people at school. For a group that is reticent to begin the discussion, the leader can list a few problems to get the adolescents started (e.g., "When I was a teenager, there were problems at my school with people spreading rumors. Does that happen in your school?"). The leader should facilitate the discussion, keeping group members focused on one area at a time (e.g., focus on expanding a discussion about parents before moving on to talk about peer issues) to deepen discussion of a given topic.

Example: Discussion of problems in adolescence

LEADER: *I want to take some time now to hear from you all about what types of issues teenagers face these days. I know a lot about depression and how to help kids, but I don't know as much about what it is like to be a teenager right now. What are some problems that teenagers have these days? You can talk about things you have experienced or things that you have heard about from friends or seen in school.*

JESSICA: *I've noticed that people spread a lot of rumors at my school. Everyone knows everyone else's business.*

LEADER: *That is definitely a problem for lots of teenagers. Has anyone else noticed that, too?*

FARRAH: *Yeah, it's so annoying, but I try to stay out of all that.*

This discussion can take more or less time depending on how talkative the group is and how much time there is left in the session. When wrapping up the conversation, the leader should put these problems in the context of the interpersonal psychotherapy (IPT) problem areas (grief, interpersonal role transitions, interpersonal role disputes, and interpersonal deficits), using language the adolescents can understand. Group members often spontaneously discuss issues related to role transitions or recent life changes (e.g., switching schools, moving) and role disputes (e.g., fighting with peers or family members). It is less common for teens to spontaneously bring up the interpersonal problem area of interpersonal deficits, which refers to difficulty forming close relationships with others. If they do not, the leader can encourage discussion about difficulties making friends or trusting people as this will be related to the goals of many group members. If the group does not spontaneously bring up issues related to the death of significant others, we do not recommend initiating a discussion of grief, as IPT-AST does not explicitly address this area. However, if group members do bring up grief, it is important to acknowledge that this is a significant interpersonal event that group members may have experienced.

Example: Summary of problems of adolescence

LEADER: *You have mentioned a number of issues that teenagers deal with. These issues fall into a few different categories. The first is changes in our lives. One of you mentioned switching from middle school to high school. Another mentioned your mom had a new baby. These are good examples of life changes. The second is conflict with people who are important to us, things like fighting with family members and arguments with peers. Some of you mentioned having difficulty meeting or staying close to people. That can be hard sometimes for people your age. Another issue that comes up for some people is having lots of friends but finding it hard to talk to them about how you are feeling. The strategies we are going to talk about later in the group can help people handle issues like these. We'll learn things like how to talk to people about our feelings and how to understand other people's points of view.*

Closing tasks: encourage consistent attendance. Before ending the session, the leader should remind group members that there are seven more groups, encourage consistent attendance at sessions, and let them know he or she is looking forward to seeing them next week.

It is not unusual, particularly with a quieter group, to have some time left over at the end of group session 1. If there is time left, there are several options to make use of any remaining time. One option is to briefly review depression symptoms. For example, the group leader can ask everyone to close their binders and think of as many symptoms of depression as they can in 30 seconds. This helps teens to solidify what they learned in the session. Another option is to provide group members with an opportunity to think of any additional group rules that they may have thought of during the second half of group. These new rules can then be incorporated into the written rules to be distributed at the second group meeting. If a significant amount of time is left and the group could benefit from more time getting to know each other, the leader can also conduct an additional icebreaker activity or continue the icebreaker activity from the beginning of the session (e.g., candy activity, two truths and a lie).

Group Session 2

Group Session 2 Checklist:

- ☐ Distribute binders and have adolescents complete the depression checklist and mood rating
- ☐ Distribute a printed list of rules
- ☐ Discuss the relationship between mood and interactions with significant others
- ☐ Use a hypothetical situation to illustrate how interactions affect mood and relationships
- ☐ Conduct activity to illustrate impact of teens' communication on others
- ☐ Conduct activity to illustrate impact of teens' communication on interpersonal interactions
- ☐ Introduce communication analysis
- ☐ Closing tasks: encourage adolescents to think about the link between their relationships and mood

Materials Needed:

- ☐ Binders and pens
- ☐ Printed group rules
- ☐ Communication notecards (see Appendix)
- ☐ Interpersonal scenario notecards (see Appendix)

Session goals and tasks. Group session 2 provides continued opportunities for group members to build rapport with each other as they learn about the relationship between mood and interactions with others, as well as the importance of communication in influencing others' perceptions and the course of an interaction. Activities are used to illustrate these points and to help teens become comfortable with role plays. Teens also learn the technique of communication analysis, which will be used throughout the rest of the group program to help teens analyze interactions they have with others. This session is intended to provide a fun introduction to these concepts and techniques; in fact, many teens have shared that this session is the most enjoyable for them.

Distribute binders and have adolescents complete the depression checklist and mood rating. Adolescents should complete the depression checklist and give a mood rating for the past week on a scale of 1–10. As the weeks progress, the group leader monitors depressive symptoms and mood ratings. The leader should pay particular attention to items 14 and 15 and meet after group with any adolescents who endorse these items to get a better sense of the situation.

Distribute a printed list of rules. It is helpful to distribute a printed list of group rules generated in group session 1 and to ask teens if they have any questions or would like to add anything to the list. This is a good opportunity to review the rules and to emphasize any rules that were particularly salient for group members.

If one or more group members missed the first group session, it is also useful to review the purpose and structure of group and to briefly review symptoms of depression. Engage the rest of the group as much as possible in this discussion, for example, by asking group members to recall and share what happened in group last week and to name some symptoms of depression. If all group members were present for group session 1, this review is typically not necessary.

Discuss the relationship between mood and interactions with significant others. As discussed in Chapter 2, IPT-AST, like IPT for depression, is based on the premise that depression occurs in an interpersonal context. Thus, it is important for teens in the group to understand the connection between interpersonal relationships and mood and other symptoms, as this provides a rationale for the focus of the program. In this discussion, the leader should emphasize that everyone (including the leader) has difficulty with communication sometimes, and that this can affect how people feel about the relationship, which can affect one's mood. The leader should not share significant personal information, but admitting occasional difficulties with communication in relationships normalizes this for the group members and makes the leader appear less intimidating. An illustration of how a leader might provide a personal anecdote is included in the example that follows. Through the anecdote, the leader illustrates the sequence of how communication or lack of communication can affect relationships, relationships can affect feelings, these feelings can affect the next communication, and so on. For this personal anecdote, it is best to use a situation in which the leader did not communicate as effectively as possible. This imparts the sense that all people have some difficulties with communicating their thoughts and feelings. It also serves to illustrate the point that communication mistakes can have an adverse effect on mood; therefore, changing small aspects of the way we communicate might help to improve mood.

Example: Personal example of mistakes in communication

LEADER: Today, we are going to focus on how communication affects your relationships and how you feel and in turn how your mood can affect the way that you communicate. These are issues that everyone has to be aware of. We have all made mistakes in communicating with other people at times. There have been times when I wished I had said something in a different way or when I did not say anything and wished that I had. I want to give you an example from my own life to help you understand what I mean. This past Sunday, my friend and I were supposed to go see a movie. She called me at 3:00 that day to say she wasn't going to be able to make it because her boyfriend needed her to do something. I was really mad, but

I didn't say anything. I just said it was fine and got off the phone quickly. For the next couple of days, I was in a bad mood, and whenever she would call, I would let it go to voice mail. On Wednesday, I ran into her, and she asked me why I hadn't called her back. I told her that I couldn't believe she cancelled on me to spend time with her boyfriend, and that I was really mad that she waited until the last minute to cancel. After talking about it for a couple of minutes, she apologized and explained that her boyfriend's car had broken down, and he was stranded an hour away. I felt better knowing that, but wished I had said something to her sooner. If I had used some of the communication skills we will be learning and had spoken to her, I probably wouldn't have been upset for 3 days.

Use a hypothetical situation to illustrate how interactions affect mood and relationships. To illustrate how each interaction in a relationship can affect people's feelings, the leader provides a brief description of a hypothetical situation (one example is provided next) and then asks group members at each point to identify different possible feelings and outcomes. This should be an interactive exercise, but the leader guides the conversation so that the chain of poor communication → negative emotions → additional poor communication → negative emotions and poor outcome is illustrated. In summarizing this exercise, the leader emphasizes the connections between the person's feelings, manner of communication, and outcomes in terms of both the relationship and the feelings generated by the conversation.

Example: Illustrating link between mood and interpersonal events

LEADER: Let me give you another example of what I am talking about. Let's say someone named Janet gets in a fight with her mom. During the fight, her mom tells Janet that she can't go out with her friends. How does Janet feel?

JESSICA: Angry.

LEADER: So, what does Janet do next? [Solicit thoughts from the group and then pick one of these options]

LEADER: Let's go with what Mary said. Janet tells her mom that she wishes she could live with her dad. How does Janet feel after the fight?

RYAN: Mad and I think sad, too; she probably feels bad for saying that to her mom.

LEADER: That's right. She feels mad and sad. She goes to her room and spends the rest of the evening by herself. Because she doesn't talk to her mom, nothing gets resolved, right?

RYAN: I guess not.

LEADER: What happens next? Does Janet get to hang out with her friends?

FARRAH: No, definitely not now.

LEADER: So, it ends up that she feels mad at her mom, but also sad and guilty that she said something mean to her mom, and she doesn't get what she wants either. The idea behind this group is that by working on communication and problem-solving skills, relationships with others should improve. This will help you feel better and may prevent you from developing depression later on. Even if your relationships don't change, I hope we can change the way you handle difficult situations so that when bad things happen, like a fight with your mom, it won't make you feel as upset as it used to.

Conduct activity to illustrate impact of teens' communication on others. The next two activities are designed to illustrate the importance of communication and how what you say and the way in which you say it has an impact on the interaction and ultimately the relationship. The first activity focuses on the way in which teens' words, tone, and body language influence how others interpret what was said. Each group member is given a notecard with a statement on it, and each teen is asked to say the statement in a particular way (these communication notecards can be found in the Appendix). For example, a card might state: Say the following in a whiny and complaining voice. "Mom, it's not fair. All of my friends get to hang out at the mall and I am stuck babysitting my sister." After someone reads the statement out loud, the leader asks the other group members how they think the teen was feeling and how the adolescent's words, tone of voice, and body language led to that conclusion.

Example: Introduction to the communication exercise

LEADER: *We are going to spend a lot of time in group paying attention to how we talk to people and what we convey to people through our words and how we say them. We are going to start by doing an activity that will show you what I mean. I am going to hand you each a notecard. It is going to tell you something to say and ask you to say it in a certain way. For instance, a card might ask you to say in an angry voice, "You're not my friend. I can't believe I thought you were my friend." We are going to go around the room. The rest of the group members get to guess how the person is feeling, and we are going to talk about what the person said or did that conveyed the feeling. There is no right or wrong answer because it is realistic for people to interpret what you say differently sometimes. I will go first, and then all of you will get a chance.*

This communication exercise helps teens to appreciate that both what you say and how you say it has an impact on how the other person interprets your message. The leader should be the first person to read a statement out loud to reduce any discomfort. If possible, the leader chooses the statements that will be most appropriate for different group members, based on the issues they discussed in the pre-group sessions as well as the leader's sense of teens' comfort with speaking in front of the group. For example, if one group member is particularly shy, it would be a good idea to avoid having that member read a statement that calls for a loud or angry voice, as this may be more difficult and anxiety provoking for the teen. After each statement is read aloud, group members discuss how the person might have been feeling and what in the verbal or nonverbal communication was important in helping them discern how the person was feeling. The leader emphasizes that there are no right or wrong answers in terms of how teens interpret each statement because part of the point of this exercise is to show that different people might interpret an ambiguous statement differently. In some cases, there are examples of the same words stated in different ways. This is meant to illustrate for adolescents that how you say something can influence how the same statement is heard by another person. Other statements are intentionally less ambiguous to demonstrate that communicating feelings clearly leads to fewer misunderstandings about how a person is feeling. At the end of the exercise, it is helpful for the leader to reiterate that the activity illustrates that what you say and how you say it influence how others interpret the meaning.

Example: Summarizing the communication exercise

LEADER: Great acting everyone! So, you get the general idea that what you say and how you say it conveys a lot to the people around you. You saw that you can let others know how you feel both by the words that you use and by things like your tone of voice and your body language. Next, we are going to do another activity to show how the way you communicate also affects how the other person responds. If you are angry and start yelling, the other person is more likely to start yelling back. If you stay calm, the other person might react differently.

Conduct activity to illustrate impact of teens' communication on interpersonal interactions. The second exercise extends the previous activity by asking teens to role play scenarios rather than reading stand-alone statements. The leader should prepare notecards with different interpersonal scenarios written on them. It is helpful to utilize situations that are likely to resonate with the group members. In the Appendix, we provide 20 common interpersonal scenarios. These situations include interactions with parents, siblings, peers, and teachers. The leader can print out the notecards with these interpersonal scenarios and create additional scenarios if they would be helpful. These interpersonal scenario notecards will be used again in session 3. They can also be utilized in the middle phase of IPT-AST as a backup if there are no pressing interpersonal situations that group members bring up in session.

There are several goals for this role-play activity. First, it should be a fun exercise that gets group members engaged in the session. The leader encourages group members to say whatever comes to mind and gives them permission to be silly. Often, group members have told us that this is the most fun they had in group (even though later sessions may have felt more helpful to them personally).

Second, it should get group members comfortable with the process of participating in role plays and introduce them to communication analysis, given that these will be two key techniques used throughout the rest of the group sessions. Communication analysis involves dissecting communication into discrete components, analyzing the impact of the communication, and discussing how changing the communication might alter the impact of the interaction. Communication analysis differs from how people typically describe an interaction because much greater detail is elicited about what exactly was said, how it was said, and what emotions went with each interchange. It can be described to teens as a way to provide a play-by-play of the interaction. The goals of communication analysis are to help group members understand the impact of their words on others, the feelings they convey through verbal and nonverbal communication, and the feelings that generated the verbal/nonverbal exchange. This will be a large part of what is done in middle phase sessions.

Third, this activity illustrates the point that what you say and how you say it influences not only how the other person interprets what you say but also how the person will respond to you, which in turn influences your reaction and ultimately influences both the outcome of the conversation and the feelings associated with the interaction.

If there are two group leaders, they should act out the first scenario in a role play to illustrate what is expected and reduce any discomfort. In this role play, the leaders should model how negative communication can escalate the problem. When leaders are engaged and demonstrate that the activity is fun, it helps group members to become engaged as well. If there is only one group leader, a more outgoing group member can be asked if he or she is willing to volunteer to be part of the first role play.

Example: Introduction to the role-play activity

LEADER: *This next activity is going to show you how what you say and how you say it also affects how the person responds to you and influences the outcome of the conversation. We are going to act out situations together instead of reading single statements. These conversations don't have to go well, and I want you to have fun with this and be silly. We will worry about improving the way we communicate later, but for now we just want to see what happens. After we act out a scenario, we are going to talk together about what happened in the conversation. I want you to try to remember who said what and to pick out how each thing a person said influenced the direction of the conversation. So, everyone who is not acting is going to listen really closely to help us remember what happened.*

After the leader and another group member have demonstrated the activity with the first interpersonal situation, there are several options for how to engage the teens in role plays. The first option is to have two group members act out each scenario. If group members are hesitant to participate in this way, all teens can participate in the role play, while the leader stays consistent in the role of the other person. This way, group members take turns responding; therefore, each person only says one or two things during the role play. Another option is to engage more than two group members in a role play so that each teen feels less on the spot. Some scenarios are well suited to this, particularly if they specify that multiple friends or both parents are involved, but other family member or peer roles can be created as needed for many of the interpersonal situations provided in the Appendix.

Each role play should be long enough that a conversation occurs between the role players (i.e., at least five exchanges back and forth). There should be time in this session to act out three or four of the interpersonal scenarios. The leader chooses the scenarios that will be most appropriate for a particular group. Scenarios that involve conflict tend to engage the group more. Choosing conflict-oriented scenarios for this session allows the leader to save some of the more nuanced scenarios for later in the group after the interpersonal strategies have been introduced.

Introduce communication analysis. After each interpersonal scenario is role played, the group answers the questions that follow to illustrate communication analysis. It is helpful to use the people involved in the role play to reflect on their own feelings and reactions to the other person, in addition to engaging other group members to share their observations about the interaction. Questions in communication analysis include the following:

- What did you say?
- What did he [she] say?
- Then what happened?
- How did you feel?
- Could you tell him [her] how you felt?
- Was that the message you wanted to convey?
- How do you think it made _____ feel?

The leader can also initiate a discussion about ways in which the interaction could have gone differently and how this might have affected the person's feelings. This aspect of the communication analysis should receive less attention at this point because group members have not yet learned communication skills that would help them consider more effective ways of communicating. Questions to facilitate this process include these:

- How do you think it could have gone differently?
- What could have been said differently by either person?
- How would it have changed the way they felt and the interaction itself?

Example: Communication analysis

LEADER: *Great job acting, Mary and Ryan! Who can remember how the conversation started?*

JESSICA: *Well, Mary started by telling her dad she absolutely has to go to this party on Saturday.*

LEADER: *That's right; good memory, Jessica. She said, "Dad, I absolutely have to go to this party on Saturday!" Mary, what were you feeling when you said that? Do you remember what your tone was like?*

MARY: *I was already pretty annoyed because I thought it was so unfair that my dad didn't want me to go. I think I sounded annoyed, too.*

LEADER: *Ryan, how did you feel when you heard Mary say that?*

RYAN: *Well, I don't know, but I figured if I was her dad I would be pretty mad. It seemed like she was telling me instead of asking me. I felt disrespected.*

LEADER: *What did you say back?*

RYAN: *I said, "You absolutely do not have to go! I already told you once."*

LEADER: *Who can remember what Mary said back to him?*

FARRAH: *She said that she didn't care what he said, that it was her best friend's birthday and she was going to go to the party no matter what.*

LEADER: *Right; thanks, Farrah. Mary, how were you feeling at that point?*

MARY: *Really angry because I felt like he wasn't even listening to me.*

LEADER: *What about you, Ryan?*

RYAN: *Well, after she said that, I was really mad, too. I decided to ground her instead of just not letting her go to the party on Saturday.*

LEADER: *That's right. So, how did you end the conversation, Mary?*

MARY: *I just stormed off. I was so mad I couldn't think what to say next.*

LEADER: *So, did anything get resolved there?*

FARRAH: *No, I think she made it worse for herself because now she's grounded, and she and her dad are really mad at each other.*

LEADER: *That's right. So, not only did she not get the outcome she wanted, but also she feels pretty upset. What do you guys think Mary could have done differently in that conversation?*

MICHAEL: *Maybe the way she started. She could have asked nicely to start and maybe told her dad that her friend's parents will be there. That sometimes works with my parents.*

FARRAH: *Her dad might have listened more if she weren't yelling.*

LEADER: *Those are both great ideas. Do you think that even if her dad would not change his mind, Mary might have avoided getting grounded?*

MICHAEL: *Yeah, if she had stayed calm, maybe her dad wouldn't have gotten so mad.*

Closing tasks: encourage adolescents to think about the link between their relationships and mood. At the end of group, the leader should encourage group members to begin thinking about the link between their relationships and their emotions. The leader asks teens to pay attention to any difficult interpersonal situations that occur during the week: how it started, the sequence of events, how it ended, and their feelings about the situation. It is also useful to forecast for the group members what will happen in the next group, letting them know that they will be learning new communication skills and that in later sessions (group session 4 and beyond) they will be working to apply these new ways of communicating to situations in their own lives.

Example: Closing tasks

LEADER: *You all did a great job today. You could see from that exercise that what you said and how you said it really influenced how the other person felt and how they responded, and then their response influenced how you felt and what you said next. We are going to do more role-play activities next week. I am also going to teach you some new communication strategies that will help make these conversations go better. Over the next week, your job is to pay attention to any difficult conversations that you may have. You probably noticed today that it's pretty hard to remember what happens, even when we try to remember a conversation right after it happened in here! So, I want you to practice paying close attention to how your conversation started, the sequence of events, how it ended, and how you felt about the situation. That way, later on, starting in our fourth group, you will be ready to talk about those things in here.*

Group Session 3

Session goals and tasks. In group session 3, teens learn the communication strategies that they will use throughout the group to improve their relationships. The session begins with two additional role plays that the leader can refer to when teaching the strategies and that can serve as a starting place for teens to practice applying skills toward the end of the session. Because the leader teaches the six communication strategies in this session, it can feel more didactic. It is important for the leader to work to keep group members engaged and to make the process as interactive as possible.

Group Session 3 Checklist:

☐ Distribute binders and have adolescents complete the depression checklist and mood rating

☐ Role play additional interpersonal scenarios and conduct communication analysis

☐ Interactively teach six communication strategies

☐ Practice applying new communication strategies

☐ Closing tasks: highlight transition to middle phase sessions and discuss mid-group sessions

Materials Needed:

☐ Binders and pens

☐ Interpersonal scenario notecards (see Appendix)

☐ Communication strategy cue cards (see Appendix)

Distribute binders and have adolescents complete the depression checklist and mood rating. Group members complete the depression checklist and mood rating. The leader should review symptoms and mood ratings.

Role play additional interpersonal scenarios and conduct communication analysis. At the start of group session 3, pick two new interpersonal scenarios from the Appendix to conduct two additional role plays with the group members before the new communication strategies are taught. One reason to do additional role plays at the start of this session is so that these scenarios will be fresh in group members' minds to use as models as they learn to apply the new skills. The leader can reference these different scenarios when teaching each new skill to help the teens think about how the strategy might apply to that situation. After the leader teaches the new communication skills, group members will be asked to redo one or both of the scenarios using the new strategies.

Unlike the role plays in group session 2, this role-play activity is intended to include all group members. This both increases engagement and ensures that there will be variety in types of responses. The varied responses allow group members to see changes in the direction of the conversation based on individual differences in tone, word choice, and other aspects of communication. For example, one group member may consistently turn the conversation in a more argumentative direction, while another may be more conciliatory. If a group approaches this activity by being too nice, the leader should insert realistic pitfalls, such as whining, yelling, or refusing to compromise to have some communication mistakes to reflect and improve on.

There are two options for how to conduct these role plays. The first option is to divide the group into two halves, so that half the group will play Person A and the other half will play Person B. Have a group member start the conversation by being Person A, have the next group member (in the B half) respond as Person B, have the next person (in the A half) respond as Person A, the next as Person B, and so on. Thus, while going sequentially to each group member, they are alternating between responding as Person A or Person B. Another option is to have the group leader play a consistent role (e.g., the parent, sibling, friend, or teacher in a scenario) in the role play. The group members then take turns playing the role of the teen in the scenario and interacting with the group leader in the role play. Have a group member start by being the teen (Person A), then the leader responds as the other person (Person B), the next group member responds as the teen (Person A), then the leader again responds as Person B, then the next group member responds as Person A, and so on. The role play should continue for several minutes so that there are multiple exchanges between Persons A and B to examine in the ensuing communication analysis.

After the role play, the leader guides the group through a brief communication analysis. This should be less detailed than the communication analyses that were conducted in group session 2 to ensure that there is enough time to introduce the communication strategies and practice utilizing the strategies during this session. The leader can ask people who were Person A how they felt. How do they think Person B felt? Ask people who were Person B how they felt and how they think Person A felt after particular statements were made in the role play. It is useful to discuss any discrepancies between group members' perceptions of the conversation and to identify moments when the conversation took on a different tone, becoming either more or less negative. What did the person say to change the tone? How did the other person respond after this change of tone? This illustrates that a small change by one person can lead to a big change in the conversation and the associated feelings. This is an important message to convey in order to help adolescents understand that making small changes in their communication can lead to significant changes in their interactions with others. Because there will be an opportunity to redo the role play later utilizing the communication strategies, it is not necessary to discuss how saying things differently might have led to a different outcome, as is typically done in a communication analysis. This will be highlighted later in the session, when group members role play the same scenario utilizing the new strategies.

Interactively teach six communication strategies. One of the goals of the group is to help teens find better ways of communicating with important people in their lives. In the group members' binders, there should be cue cards (see Appendix) of different strategies to keep in mind when talking to someone. The leader should ask adolescents to open their binders and go through each of the cards, discussing what each one means and giving examples. To engage the group members in this activity, the leader can ask the adolescents what they think each of the sayings mean. The leader should also elicit examples of each of the communication strategies, both from adolescents' experiences and by referencing scenarios that teens role played either at the start of this session or in group session 2. This allows teens to participate throughout the discussion of the strategies and gives the leader an opportunity to correct any misunderstandings about the strategies right away. The leader should acknowledge that while these strategies are helpful in many situations, they will not apply to every situation, and there may be some situations when some of these strategies are not appropriate or helpful. In later group sessions, teens will be encouraged to engage in interpersonal problem-solving (also known as decision analysis) to identify additional actions or ways of communicating or behaving that may be helpful in a given situation.

Example: Introduction of communication strategies

LEADER: We have talked a lot about communication and we have acted out several situations where conversations ended with both people feeling upset and not getting what they wanted. Now, I am going to teach you some strategies that will help these types of conversations go more smoothly. You all have six cue cards in your notebooks. Can you all open up to the first one? It says **Strike while the iron is cold.** *I'm going to explain that, but first, does anyone have any idea what it might mean?*

The following are descriptions of each of the six communication strategies taught in this session, along with important points for the leader to convey to teens during this discussion:

Strike while the iron is cold. The purpose of this strategy is to encourage teens to pick the right time to have a conversation. Picking the right time involves considering both the teen's and the other person's moods; how distracted the teen or the other person may be by other tasks or concerns; as well as logistical concerns, such as having enough time and having a private space to talk if this is desired. Having a conversation when one or both parties are angry often leads teens (and others) to say things that they later regret. The purpose of this strategy is to help teens recognize that they can have a much more constructive conversation if they choose to talk once they (and the other person) have calmed down.

Some teens have particular difficulty with this strategy once a conversation has escalated and they are feeling angry. If this is a concern, the leader can help teens identify appropriate ways to pause or end a conversation to allow themselves time to cool off. A common pitfall is for teens to end a conversation by simply walking away; this may feel helpful in the moment but often leaves the other person feeling confused or angry and sometimes is counterproductive. It is often more helpful for teens to explain to the other person why they need to take a break from a particular conversation and come back to it later (e.g., "I am getting really upset right now, and I would like some time to calm down and collect my thoughts before we continue. Can we talk about this another time?").

Strike while the iron is cold also means finding a time when the other person is not busy or distracted by something else and can spend time focusing on the conversation. Thus, part of this strategy is *asking* the other person if they have time to talk or *scheduling* a time to talk about something in advance. The leader can help teens to find ways of asking to talk that feel comfortable and natural and that set the stage for a productive conversation. For instance, a teen might say, "Mom, I would like to talk with you about something. Do you have time now or is there a better time for us to talk later?"

I statements. *I statements* are used to tell another person about how you are feeling. The purpose of this strategy is to encourage teens to express feelings to others in an appropriate way while avoiding statements that blame or alienate the other person. Often, when people argue, they say things like, "You are so rude." This blames the person, is not very clear, and often causes the other person not to listen to the rest of the communication. It is more effective to begin with a feeling statement, such as, "I feel angry when you interrupt me when I am talking to you because it seems like you don't care about what I am saying."

The leader should explain to teens that *I statements* can give them the upper hand in a discussion because the other person cannot argue with how they are feeling. While teens might believe they give up power by exposing their feelings, it is likely to help them gain power, particularly when the other person (e.g., a parent, close friend) cares about how they feel. The leader should encourage teens to name a feeling (e.g., sad, disappointed, angry) in each *I statement* and should warn teens that starting a sentence with "I feel" does not automatically make it an *I statement* (e.g., "I feel like you're being rude" is not using this strategy correctly). The emotion word following the "I feel" is a key component of the communication that can lead to a different response and should come first in the conversation.

Some teens may feel uncomfortable with expressing feelings, either generally or to particular people in their lives. If teens express discomfort with expressing feelings, it can be useful to explore these concerns and to help teens identify how to use this skill in a way that is more acceptable to them (e.g., saying "upset" instead of "sad"). The leader can also acknowledge that this technique is not appropriate for every situation (e.g., If a peer at school teases them, telling that person "I feel sad when you tease me" is probably not a helpful response). An example of how to introduce and discuss concerns about *I statements* is provided next. If group members are open to using this strategy, it is not recommended that the leader discuss concerns or modifications to *I statements* at this time. The leader can refer to this example for language to address concerns if they come up at a later date.

Example: Explaining *I statements*

LEADER: *Some of you may have heard of an* **I statement** *before. What does that mean to you guys?*

RYAN: *That's like, "I feel <blank> when you <blank>." We learned about that back in elementary school.*

LEADER: *Yeah; that is the basic idea of it. The point of an* **I statement** *is to tell the other person what you're feeling and to avoid blaming the other person. So instead of saying "You are so rude, I can't believe you keep interrupting me," you could say, "I feel angry when you interrupt me while I'm talking. It makes me think you don't care about what I'm saying." What are some advantages to using an* **I statement**?

JESSICA: *The other person might not get as mad at you. I would be mad if someone called me rude.*

LEADER: *Right; it might avoid the other person getting defensive or mad. Are there any other advantages?*

FARRAH: *Well, the way you said it first, I think it would lead to an argument.*

LEADER: *That's true; it might. The other person might say, "No, I'm not rude!" but they can't argue with how you are feeling. So, using an* **I statement** *can help you make a stronger point without arguing. Does anyone have concerns about using* **I statements**?

MICHAEL: *I just wouldn't really say that; it sounds kind of cheesy to me, telling someone how I feel like that.*

LEADER: *Okay. So, what's another way to get the same message across without sounding cheesy? Even though this skill is meant to help you express feelings, it doesn't mean you have to say "I feel angry." What's another way to say it?*

RYAN: *What about "I don't like it when you interrupt me"?*

LEADER: *That is definitely better than saying, "You're so rude," but let's try to use a feeling word. Could you say, "I get angry when you interrupt me," instead of, "I feel angry when you interrupt me"?*

MICHAEL: *Yeah; I think that would be okay.*

LEADER: *Let's go back to our role play from the beginning of this group. What is an example of an* I statement *that someone could have used in that conversation?*

Be specific. This strategy encourages teens to *Be specific* and avoid overgeneralizing by saying things like "you always" or "you never." It is unlikely that someone always or never does something. It makes the other person feel bad and makes that person less likely to listen to the teen's message. The leader can emphasize that this will often lead to an argument, while naming a specific time that a problem happened is less likely to elicit objections. Also, in general, teens should try to focus on the present, rather than bring up things that happened a long time ago. It can be helpful for the leader to ask teens if they have ever been in an argument when someone brought up something that happened a while ago. How did they feel? This helps group members recognize why this technique is worthwhile.

While the concept *Be specific* is useful in conversations, teens can bring up a pattern if one exists. Teens might object to using this skill if someone in their life does seem to do something that upsets them on a regular basis. For example, it is possible that a sibling frequently borrows the teen's clothes without asking first or that a parent often yells at a teen before asking for the teen's side of the story. In these types of situations, the leader can encourage teens to avoid using the word *always*, while still getting the point across. For instance, teens could say, "I feel upset when you borrow my clothes without asking." It can also be helpful to be prepared with specific examples when these things happened. Teens could say something like, "This has happened several times in the past week, for example, on Monday when . . ."

As with the other strategies, it is useful for the leader to ask the group members how *Be specific* might have helped in the role plays that were conducted at the beginning of the session. The leader can ask for actual statements that an adolescent might say. This ensures that all group members understand the skills and makes the process of learning these skills more engaging for the group members. In addition, this discussion highlights that these skills can be used in combination, for instance, combining *Be specific* with an *I statement* such as in the example, "I feel upset when you borrow my clothes without asking, like this past Monday."

Put yourself in their shoes. This strategy helps teens to appreciate that understanding another person's perspective, while also expressing one's own feelings, makes it easier to come to a compromise. The leader emphasizes that understanding another person's perspective is not equivalent to agreeing with that perspective. However, it is helpful to start a conversation by acknowledging the other person's feelings or needs. In this way, this interpersonal strategy can be used as a negotiation tool. *Put yourself in their shoes* involves two steps: (a) thinking about how the other person feels and (b) communicating that to them as a way to diffuse the argument. This technique can often be paired with an *I statement* so that the teen also has an opportunity to express his or her point of view. If the adolescent wants to use this strategy but is unsure about how the other person feels, the teen can be encouraged to ask the other person.

Some adolescents may have difficulty seeing issues from someone else's perspective and should be encouraged to practice this skill. This may be particularly challenging for younger teens. Other teens may object to this idea because they worry that it means accepting the other person's side of the argument. Still others may be skilled at considering another person's point of view but may have difficulty understanding the need to explicitly say this to the other person. Many teens consider attempts to alter their own behavior in light of their knowledge of other people's points of view to be equivalent to putting themselves in others' shoes. For example, a teen may be aware that her mother is stressed and tired when she gets home from work. As a result, she is quiet and cooperative around that time to avoid arguments with her mom. While that is an adaptive and sensitive response to her mother's perceived mood, it is not a communication strategy. To be useful as a communication strategy, this teen would have to communicate to her mother that she knows that her mother must feel stressed and tired after a long day. An example is provided next of how *Put yourself in their shoes* can be illustrated for the group. The leader is encouraged to use this example when teaching this skill and to ask teens questions that will help them learn this strategy.

Example: Explaining *Put yourself in their shoes*

LEADER: *Let me give you an example of this. Imagine Carlos, who is 14 years old. He has an argument with his mom because his mom thinks that the reason he isn't doing well in school is because he is not doing his homework. How do you think Carlos feels?*

JESSICA: *He's mad at his mom because she doesn't trust him.*

LEADER: *Right; he thinks his mom doesn't trust that he's doing his homework, and that makes him feel angry. How do you think his mother feels about the fact that Carlos is doing badly in school?*

MICHAEL: *She's probably worried. My mom worries about that.*

LEADER: *Right. She might be worried because she wants Carlos to do well in school so he can do something with his life. Great job! So, in this situation, if Carlos put himself in his mom's shoes, he might say, "Mom, I know you are worried about me not doing my homework, but I feel frustrated when you ask to see my work." This is a better way to start a conversation than, "Mom, you're so annoying. Leave me alone!"*

LEADER: *Can people think of an example of* **Put yourself in their shoes** *for the role play we did earlier? The one where your mom calls you every 5 minutes?*

FARRAH: *I know you're worried that something bad will happen to me.*

LEADER: *Great. Can anyone add an* **I statement** *to that?*

RYAN: *But I feel like a child when you call every 5 minutes.*

LEADER: *What about a feeling? How did people feel in the role play?*

RYAN: *But I feel embarrassed when you keep calling me.*

LEADER: *Good. So, combining the two would be, "Mom, I know you are worried that something bad will happen to me when I am out with friends, but I feel embarrassed when you keep calling me."*

Have a few solutions in mind and remember to compromise. This strategy encourages teens both to prepare in advance with some ideas of how they might wish to resolve the conflict and to be flexible in the moment to compromise with the other person. It is helpful for teens to brainstorm in advance, coming up with three or four possible solutions to resolve the conflict. For instance, if a parent calls every 5 minutes when the teen is out with friends, possible solutions could include the teen calling every hour, calling when leaving a friend's place to go to the movie, calling if plans change, or texting instead of calling. The leader should emphasize that having solutions of your own in mind is useful, but it is also important to be willing to negotiate and compromise if the other person has ideas as well. Group members can be encouraged to ask the other person about his or her ideas as part of a conversation and to be open to trying one of these solutions.

It is helpful to discuss how the compromise may not feel as good as the ideal outcome but may be better than what is happening currently. For instance, the teen may want the parent to not call to check in when the teen is out, but this is not realistic for the parent. The group can help the teen think through which solutions will feel best for the teen and will also appease the parent's concerns. For instance, the teen might be uncomfortable if his or her mom calls every hour (so this would not be a good solution to suggest to his or her mother), but the teen would feel comfortable texting his or her mom every hour as this would be less disruptive.

The success of this technique lies not only in thinking about possible solutions and coming to a compromise, but also in ensuring that both parties follow through with what was decided. Adolescents often agree to a solution with a parent but then do not follow through with their end of the bargain. It is important for the leader to help the teens recognize that this might work in the short term, but may decrease the likelihood of successful negotiations in the future. For instance, if the teen repeatedly does not follow through on texting the parent as agreed, the parent will be more likely to say no to a future request and might resort to calling frequently when the teen is out.

Don't give up. The leader should point out that changing the way one communicates and behaves in relationships is not easy. However, teens can expect to see a difference over time if they are persistent and keep working to change their interactions. This strategy refers both to not giving up on learning new ways to communicate and to not giving up on solving an interpersonal problem that is important. A distinction should be made between relentlessly nagging someone and being appropriately persistent. This skill does not mean continuing a conversation when it is counterproductive. Rather, it is important to recognize when a strategy is not working, end the conversation appropriately, and find another strategy to address the issue. In some situations, it will not be possible to "get your way"; instead, it might be necessary to change expectations. However, the strategies may be helpful in another situation so teens should be encouraged to continue to apply them to improve their interactions.

Practice applying new communication strategies. After learning and discussing the communication strategies, the group should redo one of the interpersonal scenarios that the group already role played (either in session 2 or earlier in session 3) to highlight differences when using these communication skills. Given that this is the first time that teens apply the new communication strategies to a scenario systematically, it is helpful to break this process down into smaller steps. In later group sessions, this process will become more streamlined as group members become more comfortable with planning and practicing conversations using these skills.

First, the group discusses how the various communication strategies may apply to this situation, with the teens offering examples of how they might use each of the strategies. The focus of this exercise is on changing how the teen responds, not the other person in the scenario (given that the teen cannot change another person's behavior in real life). Thus, the discussion should focus on how the teen in the scenario can use the strategies (rather than the friend, parent, or sibling) to create new statements to express in the conversation. Once the leader has helped teens to identify how each strategy may apply, the group should put these statements in order, based on what group members think is the best approach to achieve the goals of the conversation. This process should lead to a clear script for several back-and-forth interactions.

Once this script has been developed collaboratively within the group, group members should act out the conversation in a role play. It can be tempting for group members (and the leader) to talk through the interaction, rather than act it out. But, it is most helpful for the adolescents to gain experience practicing the new strategies in the context of a role play. This role play can be done with two group members who volunteer or can involve the entire group. The group leader should act as a coach, reminding the group member doing the role play of which strategy to use by holding up the appropriate cue card as the role play is going on. When there are two coleaders, it is helpful to have one leader act as the coach while the other leader plays the role of the parent, friend, or other person in the role play. The group members can then take turns being the teen, allowing all group members to have practice applying the communication skills as planned.

In either case, the leader should explain the coaching role to the group because this is the first time it is being used. The leader also lets group members know that this time he or she will act as coach, but later group members will be asked to coach each other in role plays. By this point, group members should be comfortable with the role-play format but may become nervous now that they are being asked to apply particular strategies and remember the plan that the group came up with together. While coaching is helpful during the role play, it is important to stay in the role play as much as possible without breaking out of the roles to discuss why a strategy is being recommended. This is why the coach is asked to quietly hold up the appropriate cue card rather than talk through what can be said.

After the role play, the group discusses the difference between the two role plays (before and after skills were learned). How was the outcome different? Did the people feel differently? The leader helps group members identify what went well in the conversation and any parts that were difficult or did not feel comfortable. It is important to emphasize strengths to encourage teens to continue to practice these strategies. However, this is also an opportunity for the leader to gently correct any mistakes or misunderstandings about any of the skills.

Example: Applying the skills to rescript a role play

LEADER: Let's go back to the role play from the beginning of the group. We acted out a situation where your mom calls every 5 minutes when you are out with your friends. Let's think of how we could use the strategies we just talked about in that situation, and then we will act it out again to see if we can make the conversation go differently. Let's start with **Strike while the iron is cold.** *How would you use that skill in that situation?*

MARY: You could talk to your mom before you go out instead of waiting for her to call you while you're out.

LEADER: That is a great idea! That way, you and your mom will be much calmer. So, assuming you're at home before you go out, how could you start the conversation to let your mom know that you want to talk about something?

MARY: I'd probably just say, "Hi, Mom, would this be a good time for us to talk about something?"

LEADER: Okay; good idea. So, once you get your mom to talk to you, let's think of how some of these other skills would apply. What is an **I statement** *someone could use?*

FARRAH: I don't like that you always call me.

LEADER: Let's try to use a feeling here.

JESSICA: She could say, "I feel mad when you call me every 5 minutes."

LEADER: That's a better **I statement**. *How do you all think a mom might respond to that?*

RYAN: I think my mom would be mad; she would think I'm telling her what to do.

LEADER: Okay. So, that wouldn't work so well for your mom. Can you add anything to that to help her mom understand why it makes her mad?

RYAN: What about saying, "I feel upset when you call me every 5 minutes because it's like you don't trust me."

LEADER: Great; you added another level by telling your mom that it seems like she doesn't trust you when she calls that often. You also changed it to upset instead of mad. That may also make her mom less angry. What about using **Be specific?** *Let's think of ways to use that strategy here.*

FARRAH: She probably shouldn't say, "You always call me." Maybe she can think of a specific time it happened.

LEADER: Exactly, So, let's make up some details here. What could she say instead of "You always call me"?

FARRAH: How about, "Last week when I was out with my friends, you called me eight times, and I was embarrassed."

LEADER: That was a great example! I noticed you ended that with an **I statement**, *too, letting your mom know that you felt embarrassed. What about* **Put yourself in their shoes?** *How could that apply to this situation? First, let's think about how someone's mom might be feeling in this situation.*

MARY: I think her mom worries a lot; she probably wants to make sure her daughter is safe.

RYAN: Maybe her mom doesn't like her friends. She might think she is doing something bad.

LEADER: Those are two possibilities. Let's say that we think her mom is worried. What could the daughter say?

MICHAEL: *She could say, "I know you want to make sure I'm safe."*

LEADER: *Can you add to that to express your thoughts about the situation once you have conveyed your understanding?*

MICHAEL: *I know you want to make sure I'm safe, but I want to figure out another way for you to do that so I can have fun with my friends, too.*

LEADER: *That sounds good. You really acknowledged how your mom sees the situation. What skill does it seem like we need to use next?*

MARY: *We should use* **Have solutions in mind,** *so that we can find another way for her mom to check in on her.*

LEADER: *So, what are some ideas?*

MARY: *Maybe she can call her mom to let her know where she is.*

RYAN: *Or, maybe she and her mom can text.*

LEADER: *Those are two good ideas. Any others?*

FARRAH: *What about if she agrees to call her mom every time she goes somewhere different, like if she leaves her friend's house to go to the mall, she would give her mom a call.*

LEADER: *Great. We have some good ideas here. Let's put it all together in a role play now. Farrah, can you play the teenager? Mary, you can be her mom. I will act as a coach this time, so I will hold up a cue card with the communication skill I think you should use in case you get stuck. Next time, someone else in the group will be the coach, but I'll demonstrate what that means this first time. Farrah and Mary, let's get started.*

FARRAH: *How do I start again?*

LEADER: *[Holds up* **Strike while the iron is cold** *cue card] Remember, we decided you would ask your mom if you can talk to her about something.*

FARRAH: *Mom, can I talk to you about something?*

MARY: *Sure.*

FARRAH: *I feel upset when you call me every 5 minutes because it's like you don't trust me.*

MARY: *Well, I just want to make sure you're safe. I'm your mom; I worry about you.*

FARRAH: *[Hesitates and looks at the group leader]*

LEADER: *[Holds up* **Put yourself in their shoes** *cue card, pointing to it]*

FARRAH: *I know that you worry, but it's embarrassing when you call me when I'm with my friends. Can we find another way for me to check in with you?*

MARY: *Maybe. But what do you have in mind?*

FARRAH: *What if I call you as soon as I get someplace with my friends, and then if we leave and go anywhere else, I will call you again. Then, when I need to get picked up, I will call you and let you know.*

MARY: *That sounds okay, but you have to promise not to forget to call. And, if I don't hear from you at least once per hour, I'm going to call.*

FARRAH: *Okay, that sounds fair. How about if I stay put, I can text you after an hour just to tell you I'm still there. Texting is a little easier to do when I'm with my friends than calling.*

MARY: *Okay, let's try it this way next time you go out, and we will see how I feel after that.*

FARRAH: *Okay. [Looks at group leader]*

LEADER: *How do you want to end the conversation?*

FARRAH: *Thanks, Mom.*

LEADER: *That was great. Thanks so much for giving that a try, Farrah and Mary! You both did an excellent job. Let's talk about how we think that went. What was different this time compared to the first time we acted it out?*

Alternative: Practice applying communication strategies using a real interpersonal situation. Sometimes, a group member has an interpersonal situation he or she would like to discuss in the group session. This is rare in group session 3 but can happen on occasion. An adolescent might bring something up when role playing the hypothetical situations or at the beginning of the group session. If one of the group members comes into session 3 with something to discuss, the leader can use this issue to practice the communication strategies instead of redoing a hypothetical situation from one of the role plays. It is important to be clear that there will not be enough time to resolve the issue, but that it will give everyone a chance to talk about how these strategies apply to a real-life situation. Because these strategies are still new, it is important not to expect the adolescent whose problem it is to come up with examples of each of the communication skills. Instead, the leader should encourage all of the group members to think about how the strategies apply to the situation. The leader can plan to return to this interpersonal issue in the beginning of the next session. At that point, more focused work can continue.

Example: Applying the strategies to a real-life problem

LEADER: *Jennifer, you mentioned during one of the role plays that you could relate to the scenario because your mom yells at you when you and your brother fight. We have a little time left to practice the strategies today. I am wondering how you would feel if we used your situation to talk about these skills.*

JENNIFER: *That would be okay, I guess.*

LEADER: *Because we are just learning these skills, we won't have time to discuss this in depth, but it will give us an opportunity to think about how to put these strategies together to solve a real-life problem. Let's pretend that Jennifer was going to have a conversation with her mom about her brother. Can anyone think of when might be a good time to have the conversation—when could she* **Strike while the iron is cold?**

TIM: *Well, she wouldn't want to do it when she was mad.*

DENISE: *Or when her brother was around.*

LEADER: *So, finding a time when it was just the two of them and they were both calm would be important. What about an* **I statement?** *Jennifer, how do you feel when your mom yells at you?*

JENNIFER: *Mad, like it's not fair.*

LEADER 2: *Can anyone turn that into an* **I statement?**

JUAN: *Mom, I don't like it when you yell at me about us fighting. It's not fair that I am always the one getting blamed.*

LEADER: *Let's remember that* **I statements** *usually start with "I feel . . . ."*

DENISE: *I guess she could say, "I feel mad when you yell at me for fighting with my brother."*

Closing tasks: Highlight transition to middle phase sessions and discuss mid-group sessions. There are two important tasks at the end of session 3. First, the group leader highlights the transition to the middle phase sessions, starting in the next group session. The focus of the group to date has been on hypothetical situations. In the next session, the focus will switch to working on interpersonal problems that different group members may be experiencing. Group members should be encouraged to bring in interpersonal events pertaining to their own lives to discuss in the next group, particularly those related to the goals that they set before the start of group. Teens are asked to pay attention to any difficult interpersonal situations and what they would have done if they had the chance to do an instant replay of the event (i.e., what strategies they might have used). The leader encourages the adolescents to bring in these interpersonal situations to discuss in the next group session, emphasizing that the group will be more helpful if focused on their own issues. In particular, teens should think about situations that come up that are related to the interpersonal goals they set in the pre-group session before group began, as these will be the most helpful to discuss as a group to bring teens closer to their goals.

Second, this is a good time to remind adolescents that the mid-group session will take place after group session 4 or 5. This is particularly important if parents will be invited to the mid-group session, as the leader will need to begin scheduling these sessions before group session 4. The mid-group session is an opportunity to review how the group is progressing, talk about gains made, and practice the interpersonal skills the teens have been working on. If parents are not able to attend, the teen and group leader will meet alone. If parents will attend, it is helpful to remind teens of this and to discuss any concerns about this meeting, such as confidentiality of information already discussed in group. Many teens will be anxious about having their parent or another caretaker participate in the session. The roots of their anxiety often include being afraid their parent will embarrass them or will be negative about their behavior. To alleviate some of the anxiety, it is helpful for the leader to describe in detail the structure and goals of the mid-group session.

Example: Discussing mid-group sessions

LEADER: *Sometime in the next 2 weeks I will be meeting with you for an individual meeting. I am going to invite your parents to join the session. The purpose of the meeting is to discuss how things are going in group, review your goals for the group, and give you a chance to practice some of the new communication strategies we just learned. If your parents can attend the session, I will invite them in for part of the time.*

SHEILA: *Are you going to tell my mom what we talk about in here?*

LEADER: *I can understand that you might be concerned about what I will share with your parents. At the beginning of the session, I will meet with you alone to make sure that I don't share anything that you are uncomfortable with. During that time, we will make a plan of what will be discussed. Does that sound okay?*

Summary of the Initial Phase

By the end of the initial phase, group members should be familiar with symptoms of depression, the concept of prevention, the connection between mood and relationships, how to break down an interaction using communication analysis, how to use role plays to plan conversations and refine communication, and the six communication strategies taught in group session 3. Group members should also feel more comfortable with each other and with the group leader by this time. This sets the foundation for the interpersonal work that group members will do in the middle phase, described in the next chapter.

6

IPT-AST Middle Phase

In the middle phase of Interpersonal Psychotherapy – Adolescent Skills Training (IPT-AST), the focus of the group shifts from learning communication strategies to implementing these skills in specific situations that are important to the group members. It is important to connect the situations of each adolescent to those of others in the group and to point out when particular strategies may be applicable across different situations and different interpersonal goals. Ideally, group members will spend these sessions working on their interpersonal goals by planning and practicing conversations using the skills they learned in group session 3, along with other strategies that might be helpful. The format for helping group members plan and practice a conversation follows this basic structure:

1. Identify an interpersonal situation to work on
2. Conduct a communication analysis to learn more about relevant prior interactions
3. Use decision analysis (if needed) to consider how best to resolve the interpersonal situation
4. Help teen clarify the goals for a future conversation, as well as the main message the teen wants to convey
5. Discuss how the communication strategies can be used to increase the likelihood of a successful interaction
6. Script the conversation in detail
7. Role play the conversation and debrief about how it went
8. Assign the teen work at home to have the conversation

The communication strategies are a useful starting place for the middle phase sessions and apply to many different interpersonal problems. However, these strategies may not be sufficient or applicable for a given situation. In these situations, group members can be encouraged to think about other ways of communicating effectively or come up with other solutions to a given problem. While the logical next step to solving an interpersonal problem is sometimes obvious (e.g., talking to a parent to resolve an ongoing dispute about chores), at other times the solution is not immediately clear. In those cases, the leader can facilitate a decision analysis to help the teen identify and evaluate a number of possible approaches before settling on the first solution to try. Other times, it may be that a relationship cannot be improved. In these instances, the group can discuss how the adolescent can modify his or her expectations so that problems in the relationship do not affect the teen's mood as significantly or, in the case of a problematic peer relationship, determine whether it may be time to end the relationship.

One of the challenges of the middle phase is that the content of sessions will differ based on the particular issues and interpersonal situations that group members bring in. The leader must make decisions during group sessions about which issues to prioritize and how to guide the discussion in the most effective way possible. When setting an informal agenda for each session, consider relevance to interpersonal goals set by group members in the pre-group sessions, urgency of addressing a particular issue, and group members' eagerness to share and work on an issue. It will also be important to manage time so that all group members who are interested have a chance to discuss issues of importance to them at some point during the middle phase.

Sometimes, adolescents do not readily bring up a particular interpersonal issue to discuss. In this situation, the leader can bring up an interpersonal topic that is common to several group members, such as difficulty talking about feelings or frequent arguments with parents. This can be done using one of the interpersonal scenarios in the Appendix or in a more open-ended discussion. Often, this will prompt a teen to give an example from his or her life that can then be worked on in greater detail. If this happens, the group can discuss how this situation may be similar to those experienced by other group members and how the same techniques may apply. Another option is to encourage teens who have scheduled mid-group sessions with a parent to use group time to plan a conversation they would like to have during that session. If the leader anticipates that teens might be hesitant to share interpersonal situations, the leader can also call the adolescents in between group sessions or check in with them before the session starts to identify issues they might want to discuss and encourage participation. The leader can then explore any resistance to sharing with the group on an individual basis without breaking confidentiality.

The structure of group sessions 4 through 6 is similar, and the same techniques (communication analysis, decision analysis, application of the communication strategies, scripting, and role playing) are used across all of the middle phase sessions. The section on session 4 provides detailed examples of each of these techniques and how they are applied to different interpersonal problems. The section on sessions 5 and 6 provides additional details about discussing the mid-group sessions and following up on interpersonal work at home because these are important tasks of the later middle phase sessions. The leader is encouraged to read through the entire chapter before beginning the middle phase sessions and to return to the section on session 4 when more detailed examples would be helpful.

The individual mid-group session, described in Chapter 7, takes place between group 4 and group 6. It is helpful to schedule this session in advance so that parents can be invited to attend. We encourage the leader to invite the parent for the mid-group session, rather than relying on the teenager. In groups where there are coleaders, the same leader who met with an adolescent for the pre-group sessions should meet with the adolescent (and the teen's parent) for the mid-group session.

Group Session 4

Group Session 4 Checklist:
- ☐ Distribute binders and have adolescents complete depression checklist and mood rating
- ☐ Remind group members of the transition to middle phase group sessions
- ☐ Complete mood ratings aloud
- ☐ Review communication strategies (if needed)
- ☐ Collaboratively set an informal agenda for the session
- ☐ Discuss group members' interpersonal situations
- ☐ Script a conversation using communication strategies
- ☐ Role play the conversation and debrief after the role play is complete
- ☐ Use decision analysis (if needed)
- ☐ Assign and prepare for interpersonal work at home
- ☐ Closing tasks: remind group members about upcoming mid-group sessions and mark the midpoint of the group

Materials Needed:
- ☐ Notebooks and pens
- ☐ Communication strategy cue cards (see Appendix)

Session goals and tasks. Group session 4 is the first middle phase session; teens begin to bring in their own interpersonal situations to work on with the help of the group. This session can be the most anxiety provoking for group members, as teens do not yet know what to expect. This session requires the leader to provide more direction to the group members than the leader likely will need to provide in later sessions. The objective of the session is for one or two adolescents to have the opportunity to work on something relevant to their interpersonal goals and for the other group members to participate in the discussion, helping the adolescents apply the strategies learned in session 4 to real-life situations. It is also important for teens to understand the rationale for interpersonal work at home. Work at home provides an important opportunity for teens to apply the strategies to improve their relationships and meet their interpersonal goals for group.

Distribute binders and have adolescents complete depression checklist and mood rating. Group members complete the depression checklist and mood rating. The leader should review symptoms and mood ratings.

Remind group members of the transition to middle phase group sessions. The leader explains to teens that, as mentioned in the past group session, they will be asked to begin working on their own interpersonal issues in this session.

Example: Transition to middle phase

LEADER: As we talked about last time, we are going to be doing things a little bit differently from now on. We have been doing some role playing in the past couple of sessions, and we have acted out some made-up situations to help you learn new ways of communicating. In the rest of group, we are going to be doing a lot of role plays as a way of practicing the new communication strategies we talked about, and we are going to be applying those strategies to real situations that you bring in. If one of you brings in a problem, say you want to talk to a friend who said something behind your back, we are going to talk about how you can best handle the situation, and then we can role play the conversation. It is going to feel funny at first, but it really helps you think about what you want to say and the best way to say it.

Complete mood ratings aloud. As the group shifts to the middle phase, teens are asked to share their weekly mood ratings aloud. It is helpful for the leader to provide a rationale for this practice. The mood rating aloud serves several purposes. Sharing a mood rating and a personal situation from the week helps all group members to feel heard during middle phase sessions, when the bulk of the sessions may be focused on only one or two teens. This process also helps the leader stay attuned to how each member of the group is doing. Most important, this activity provides the basis for the group to decide which interpersonal situations to prioritize for more in-depth discussion.

The leader asks group members to share a general mood rating (better, worse, or the same as last week) rather than a 1–10 number rating to maintain privacy for adolescents who might be embarrassed about consistently low mood ratings. Teens are also asked to share one interpersonal event in the past week that has affected their mood in a positive or negative way to continue to facilitate group members' understanding of the link between mood and relationships. In particular, teens are encouraged to focus on relationships that are linked to their goals for group. It is best for the leader to model this first to demonstrate what is expected and to reduce any discomfort teens might have. Extensive self-disclosure is not encouraged, but modeling can be helpful to highlight for teens the types of interpersonal issues they might attend to (e.g., arguments with important people in their lives; not spending enough time with friends or family; conversely, spending more quality time with someone or resolving a disagreement successfully). Teens may initially have difficulty identifying interpersonal events that are linked to their mood ratings but will become more able to make this link as the group progresses. To help with this process, the leader can acknowledge noninterpersonal events that an adolescent brings up, such as feeling better this week because he or she did well on a test, but can ask additional questions to help the adolescent identify any interpersonal events that may also be linked to mood. For instance, doing well on a test may mean that the teen had less conflict with a parent around academics. As each group member shares a mood rating and an interpersonal event, the leader highlights and explores any significant changes from the previous week.

Example: Mood ratings aloud

LEADER: *We are going to start our group meetings a bit differently by sharing whether our moods are better, worse, or the same as last week. You don't need to share the exact number. But, I would like you to share one thing that happened in your relationships this week that affected your mood, in either a good or a bad way. Try to focus on relationships that are related to the goals you set before group started. This check-in will give me a sense of how everyone is doing and will help me figure out what we should talk about during the group. I will go first. My mood was a little bit worse this week because I had an argument with a good friend of mine. Michael, can you go next?*

MICHAEL: *I guess my mood was a little better. I played basketball with my friends this week.*

LEADER: *Great; thank you for sharing that, Michael. How about you, Farrah?*

FARRAH: *I didn't have a great week. I failed my math test.*

LEADER: *I'm sorry to hear that. Was there anything that happened in your relationships that affected your mood as well, especially relationships connected to your goals for group?*

FARRAH: *Well, because I failed my math test, my mom was upset with me. We had a big fight, and then she didn't let me hang out with my friends this weekend, so that made my mood worse.*

LEADER: *Thanks for sharing that, Farrah.*

MARY: *My mood was the same this week. Nothing really happened.*

LEADER: *Mary, can you think of anything related to your relationships that affected your mood at all?*

MARY: *Well, I went to a friend's house this weekend. That was fun. I guess that made my mood a little better.*

JESSICA: *I don't know; I guess my mood was a little worse. I found out that a friend of mine was talking about me, and I haven't talked to her since.*

LEADER: *That sounds like a difficult week, Jessica. Ryan, what about you?*

RYAN: *My mood was awful this week. My girlfriend dumped me.*

Review communication strategies (if needed). Before proceeding to discuss a particular interpersonal issue, it is important that all group members have at least basic knowledge of the strategies that were introduced in the previous group session so that the discussion can be productive. If anyone was absent from group session 3, spend 5–10 minutes reviewing the communication strategies. Group members who were present can be asked to name as many skills as they can remember and can take the lead on explaining the strategies. This allows the leader to find out if there are any misconceptions and, if so, to correct them. This also ensures that any adolescents who missed group session 3 have some idea of the strategies that will be used to address whatever interpersonal problems will be discussed in the rest of the session.

Collaboratively set an informal agenda for the session. The mood check-in helps the leader to identify and prioritize topics to be discussed during group. Unlike in other manualized interventions, setting an agenda in IPT-AST is done informally to provide a guide for what will be discussed in the session. The leader does not write down the agenda and may not even explicitly share it aloud. This agenda can be modified if needed during the course of a group session to best meet the needs of group members. An example of how the agenda is shared with group members is provided next. In setting an informal agenda, the leader should consider which group members have the most pressing issues to discuss, which group members are most interested in sharing and working on issues, and which group members have raised issues related to their interpersonal goals. Although the leader does not disclose what adolescents' goals are to protect confidentiality, knowledge of the teens' goals can help guide the leader in deciding which issues to focus on during the rest of the session. In later group sessions, providing relatively equal attention for all group members across the sessions will become an important consideration as well.

Example: Setting an informal agenda

LEADER: Ryan, Jessica, and Farrah all had some issues come up this week. We should have time today to focus on one or two issues. Who do you all think we should start with?

RYAN: I'm not sure if I really want to talk about it right now. I'm not talking to my ex-girlfriend anymore anyway.

FARRAH: I wouldn't mind talking about what happened with my mom. That happens all the time with her.

JESSICA: Farrah can go first; I can wait.

LEADER: Okay, let's start with Farrah. We may also have time to talk with Jessica or Ryan if you feel up to it and we have time today. If not, we will make sure we get to both of you next time. Does that sound okay?

If teens do not initially bring up a topic to discuss, the leader can draw on hypothetical situations to start a conversation. One source of hypothetical situations is the set of scenarios in the Appendix, used in group sessions 2 and 3. The leader should attempt to select a situation that is likely to resonate with group members, based on the leader's knowledge of teens' interpersonal goals. The leader may also create novel hypothetical situations that are more closely related to group members' particular concerns if needed. If a topic is chosen carefully, one of the group members may bring up a related issue early in the discussion, and the leader can quickly direct the conversation to focus on that person. An example of this type of discussion is provided next. If no one volunteers a specific interpersonal issue, the group can discuss how the communication strategies would apply in the hypothetical situation and then script and role play a conversation. This provides useful practice for all group members.

Example: Transition from hypothetical to specific interpersonal issue

LEADER: Since no one mentioned anything pressing they want to talk about today, let's start with a hypothetical situation. One issue that comes up a lot for teenagers is people talking behind other people's backs. So, let's say you heard that someone in your class was spreading rumors about you. What are some things you could do?

FARRAH: You could talk to that person, tell them to stop.

MARY: Something like that happened to me, except I actually overheard them talking about me. I was really mad.

LEADER: *That sounds like a tough situation. Would you mind sharing what happened with the group?*

MARY: *I don't mind. Yeah, it was actually someone people might know, so I'll use a code name. . . . I'll call her "Barbie." So, I heard Barbie telling someone that I cheated on my boyfriend.*

LEADER: *Can you tell us what happened next?*

Discuss group member's interpersonal situation. First, the leader should ask the teen to give a brief description of the situation. The leader and other group members can ask questions for clarification, gathering information about how long the problem has been going on, what the teen's primary concern is, and what strategies the teen has already tried to address the situation. This is followed by a discussion of the feelings associated with the experience, which helps the teen link his or her mood to interpersonal events. When appropriate, the leader might conduct a communication analysis of what happened. Communication analysis is helpful if the teen's interpersonal problem involves conflict with an individual. It is also used when the adolescent tells the group that he or she has attempted to resolve an issue with someone, but the conversation went poorly or the outcome was not what the teen wanted. In these situations, communication analysis can help the group to better understand any communication problems the teen might have. This will then inform next steps in approaching the problem. A communication analysis should include a play-by-play of what was said and done in the conversation as well as exploration of feelings associated with each statement and any important nonverbal behavior that might have occurred. Communication analysis (described in detail in the section in Chapter 5 on group session 2) should involve addressing the following questions:

- What did you say?
- What did he [she] say?
- Then what happened?
- How did you feel?
- Could you tell him [her] how you felt?
- Was that the message you wanted to convey?
- How do you think it made _____ feel?
- How do you think the conversation could have gone differently?
- What could you have said differently?
- How would it have changed the way you felt or the interaction itself?

It is important to get enough information in the communication analysis to inform next steps, while leaving enough time to plan and role play a follow-up conversation. This can be challenging, especially when a teen talks about a conflict that took place over several interactions. It can be helpful for the leader to ask for a brief overview of the situation so the leader can decide which piece of the interaction is most important to focus on in a communication analysis.

When the problem does not involve a previous interaction, such as wanting to ask a restrictive parent to go to a party or figuring out how to handle a situation when a friend is speaking about the teen behind the teen's back, a communication analysis will not be necessary. Before moving on, the leader can ask other group members if they have had similar experiences, and if so, if they have tried anything that worked. This can be a good way to involve members of the group and to lead into a discussion about what the group member can do next.

Example: Discuss group member's interpersonal situation

LEADER: Farrah, first tell us more about what happened with your mom.

FARRAH: We had a big fight last Friday. I wanted to go to the movies with my friends, and she wouldn't let me. She never lets me go out!

LEADER: Farrah, this argument sounds very upsetting for you, but this is just the sort of thing I want you to bring in to work on in group. Can you tell the group more about what happened? How did the fight start? Who said what first?

FARRAH: I don't really remember. I think I said, "Mom, Maya asked me to go to the movies with her. I can go, right?"

LEADER: What did she say?

FARRAH: No, you can't go. I looked up your grades and saw that you failed your math test. That's just not okay. What's wrong with you?

LEADER: How did you feel when she said that?

FARRAH: I was pissed off. I started yelling at her and told her I hated her.

LEADER: How do you think your mom felt?

FARRAH: Upset.

LEADER: The rest of you, how do you think Farrah's mom must have felt when she found out that Farrah failed her test?

MICHAEL: She was mad. My mom gets mad if I don't do well; she thinks I'm not trying.

FARRAH: Yeah, my mom only cares about grades. She doesn't care about what I want to do.

LEADER: How else could Farrah's mom have been feeling?

JESSICA: She could have been worried.

FARRAH: I know she worries, but she never bothers to ask what's going on with me; she always just yells.

LEADER: What about when Farrah got upset and told her mom she hated her? How do you think her mom felt then?

FARRAH: She was definitely mad then; she yelled back at me.

LEADER: What did she say next?

FARRAH: She said if I kept this up, she would ground me for a whole week.

LEADER: How did you feel then?

FARRAH: I was mad, but I didn't want to get grounded, so I just walked away after that and went into my room.

LEADER: Okay; I think we have a pretty good idea what happened. Does anyone have any questions for Farrah to make sure we understand the situation before we move on to thinking about what she can do next?

MARY: Do you usually have fights with your mom like that?

FARRAH: Yeah, it happens all the time, but this time was a little worse.

LEADER: Good question. Have other people been in a situation like this?

MARY: Well, it's for different reasons, but I get into fights with my mom all the time, too. It really puts me in a bad mood.

MICHAEL: My dad gets really upset with me about school stuff. He's always on my case if I don't get my homework done.

LEADER: So, it sounds like this is a situation that a number of you can relate to. Let's spend some time thinking about what Farrah can do next. Does anyone have any ideas that have worked for them?

Script a conversation using communication strategies. Once the group has a good understanding of the situation, the leader should help the teen identify what he or she would like to do to change the situation. When deciding how to address a particular interpersonal problem, it is most helpful for the teen to plan a conversation that can happen proactively, rather than practice how a conversation in the past could have gone differently. If the teen learns strategies to improve on a past conversation, this will only be helpful if the teen has the same kind of argument with the same person in the next week. On the other hand, planning a proactive conversation allows the teen to take steps to improve a situation without waiting for another problem to come up. This idea is sometimes difficult for teens to grasp, as they are often used to a reactive approach to relationships, responding when something comes up rather than planning ahead to resolve an issue. Some teens worry that they will "rock the boat" by bringing up an issue before an argument occurs. In those cases, the leader should provide a rationale for addressing an issue outside the context of an argument (i.e., teens will have more control over the conversation, and both parties are more likely to have a calm, productive discussion).

If it is not feasible to plan a new conversation or if the teen is unwilling to do so, the teen, with the help of the group, can generate alternative communications that could have been used in an exchange that already happened. This can be helpful if this type of argument happens frequently. In these cases, the leader facilitates the same type of scripting that would be used to plan a proactive conversation and engages the teen in a role play to practice different ways of responding to a similar argument. This helps prepare the teen for future interactions with the person in question.

Before scripting a conversation, it is helpful to ask the teen what his or her goals are for the interaction. What would the teen like to achieve? This step is important for the teen and the rest of the group to keep the discussion focused on helping the teen reach these goals. It is important to choose a goal that is achievable in a conversation. If the teen wants to address multiple problems in one conversation, the leader, with the assistance of the group, helps the teen focus on one or two areas that are most relevant. Often, teens are emotional when discussing important interpersonal situations, and it is easy to become sidetracked by bringing up issues that are tangentially related to the topic at hand. Having a clear goal from the beginning can help keep scripting on track and make sure that the teen plans a conversation that addresses the teen's goal. If a teen continuously returns to a different topic when planning what to say in an interaction, it is an indication that the goal for the conversation may need to be clarified.

Once the goal of the conversation is clear, the group should help the teen plan at least four or five exchanges, drawing on communication strategies learned in session 3 as needed. While it is not possible to script an entire conversation exactly as it will occur, it is useful for the adolescent to think about how to start and end the conversation and the main points the teen would like to convey. Because it is often difficult for teens to engage in a proactive conversation about a problem, it is important for the group to discuss the best way to introduce the topic, utilizing the strategies of *Strike while the iron is cold* and *Be specific* about what the teen wants to discuss. It is also important for the group to help the teen plan how to end an interaction, either thanking the other person if the conversation went well or thinking about how to end a conversation gracefully before it escalates. During the scripting, the leader asks the teen how the particular person he or she plans to talk to might respond, rather than assuming typical or generic responses to what the teen plans to say. While it will not be possible to anticipate every possible direction the conversation might take, it is useful for the teen to consider the most likely responses from the other person. If the most likely response is not clear, the group should help teens prepare for a more difficult (or worst case) scenario because this will present the biggest challenge for the teen. The following is an example of how to facilitate scripting a conversation:

Example: Scripting a conversation

LEADER: *Farrah, it sounds like this argument was really upsetting for you. Not only were you not able to go out, but also you ended up in a really big fight, which made you feel even worse. Do you think it might be helpful to talk with your mom when you're calmer about what's been going on?*

FARRAH: *Nothing's going to change.*

LEADER: *I can understand why you feel that way. But, I am hopeful that you can make some small changes. I am not sure she'll let you go out as much as you'd like, but I do think we can find a way for you to talk with her so that you both don't end up so angry. If you were to have a conversation with your mom, what would you like to happen?*

FARRAH: *I know I should study more so I do better in math, but it's hard for me, and when I don't get to see my friends, it doesn't make my grades get better. It just makes me feel worse, and then I really don't feel like studying. I wish she would understand that and loosen up.*

LEADER: *That sounds like a good reason to have this conversation. So, you want to tell your mom that you have trouble doing schoolwork when your mood is low, and one thing that brings your mood up is spending time with friends. You are hoping that when she understands that, she will let you spend time with friends. Is that right? Anything else you hope to achieve in this conversation?*

FARRAH: *No, I think that's it. I think I should be able to see friends at least once a week.*

LEADER: *I think that is a reasonable goal, but I wonder if your mother might be more willing to listen to what you have to say if you also acknowledge your part in this, which is that you got an F on your math test. Do people think that it might be helpful for Farrah to acknowledge that part?*

MARY: *Yeah. Her mom probably wants her to say it won't happen again.*

FARRAH: *I do feel badly that I failed, but I worry that if I bring it up, she'll get mad about it all over again.*

LEADER: *I can understand being nervous about it, but we can try to think of a way for you to acknowledge your part in this in a way that might make your mother less angry, rather than angrier.*

FARRAH: *Okay, that might be all right.*

LEADER: *So, you are going to add the part about taking responsibility for your grade. Do you specifically want to get permission to see friends at least once per week as well?*

FARRAH: *That would be great, but I'd be okay if my mom at least said she would think about it.*

LEADER: *Great; it is a good idea to be clear before going into a conversation on what you expect to achieve, and it sounds like you are realistic about what one conversation can accomplish. Does anyone have ideas for how Farrah could start the conversation?*

JESSICA: *Mom, is this a good time to talk to you about what happened on Friday?*

LEADER: *Great start. That is a good way to make sure that now is an okay time to talk and to* **Be specific** *about what the conversation will be about. Farrah, what would she say to that?*

FARRAH: *Okay.*

LEADER: *What could Farrah say next? Maybe she could use an* **I statement** *or acknowledge her mom's perspective?*

RYAN: *Mom, I know you were mad that I got that F in math and you think I need to focus on school, but I was really upset that I couldn't see my friends.*

LEADER: *That is a great way to use* **Put yourself in their shoes** *and an* **I statement**, *Ryan. Farrah, what do you think?*

FARRAH: *I am not sure how she will respond. I don't think she will care that I want to see my friends.*

LEADER: *What about adding what you said before, that it actually makes it harder to concentrate because your mood is worse if you don't see your friends?*

FARRAH: *Okay, so I could say, "Mom, I know you were mad that I got that F in math and you think I need to focus on school, but I was really upset that I couldn't see my friends, and when I don't get to see them, it puts me in such a bad mood that it's actually harder to study."*

LEADER: *That was great! What do you think your mom would say to that?*

FARRAH: *I don't know; she might understand better, but she will still want me to just focus on school.*

LEADER: *Okay, who can help Farrah out? What else might she be able to say to her mom?*

MARY: *What about letting your mom know you can spend time with friends and still make time to study?*

LEADER: *That's a good idea, Mary. That sounds like* **Have a few solutions in mind**. *What are some suggestions for how to make time for both?*

JESSICA: *She could see friends Friday night but agree to do homework on Saturday or Sunday.*

MICHAEL: *My mom likes it better if I finish my homework first. Maybe she could do her homework Friday and Saturday, and if she's done she'd get to go out Saturday night?*

LEADER: *How do those options sound to you, Farrah? What would you be willing to offer to your mom as a compromise?*

FARRAH: *Well, on a weeknight I am okay doing homework first, but I don't think I should have to do all my homework on Friday night.*

LEADER: *It sounds like the first option that Jessica suggested feels more comfortable for you. Would your mom want to hear that you are going to make sure you study more for your next math test?*

FARRAH: *Yeah, I think she would. But, I don't know if that will help. Math is just hard this year.*

LEADER: *Okay, what about other solutions besides studying more?*

RYAN: *You could ask your mom if she could help you.*

FARRAH: *Oh, she wouldn't be any help. She doesn't know how to do this stuff either.*

JESSICA: *What about telling your mom you will ask your teacher for help?*

FARRAH: *That could work. She would probably like that idea.*

LEADER: *Great! So, it sounds like we have a few possible solutions: One is to offer that if your mom lets you see friends on Friday night, you will promise to do your homework on Saturday, and another idea is to let your mom know that you plan to ask your teacher for extra help with math. Farrah, how would you put those together in your own words?*

FARRAH: *I could say, "I want to do better in math, so I am going to ask my teacher for extra help."*

LEADER: *Great. Do you think your mom would want you to also agree to get homework done, or is getting extra help from your teacher enough?*

FARRAH: *I think I can start with getting help from a teacher because she already expects me to get my work done on the weekend anyway.*

LEADER: *Okay, great. So, Farrah, your goal was to help your mom understand that seeing friends makes you feel better and that helps you to focus on schoolwork, too. You want to acknowledge that you are upset about your poor grade in math and let her know that you plan to get extra help before you ask her for permission to see your friends once per week. Is there anything else you anticipate coming up that we should plan out before we practice?*

FARRAH: *No, I think that's it.*

LEADER: *If Farrah's mom listens and agrees to let her see friends more, how can Farrah end the conversation?*

FARRAH: *I could just say, "Thank you."*

LEADER: *That sounds great. Now, what if the conversation doesn't go as well as you hope, and it starts leading to an argument? How could you end the conversation so that things don't get worse?*

FARRAH: *Usually, I just walk away at that point.*

LEADER: *Ending the conversation is good, but what could you say before you walk away so that your mom doesn't think you're blowing her off? Does anyone have any ideas?*

JESSICA: *Maybe she could just say she needs some time to cool off.*

LEADER: *That's a great idea. How about, "Mom, I think we are both pretty upset, and I need some time to cool off. Can we talk about this again later when we're both calm?"*

FARRAH: *My mom would be really surprised if I said something like that.*

LEADER: *Do you think she might feel better than if you just walk away?*

FARRAH: *Yeah; she'd think I was being pretty mature if I said it like that.*

Role play the conversation. Once alternative strategies have been identified and the conversation has been scripted, the teen and another group member role play the interaction using these strategies. Prior to the role play, it is helpful for the leader to reiterate the main points of the conversation and to remind the teen how he or she planned to use the different strategies. The goal of the role play is to get group members comfortable with a new way of communicating. The goal is not for them to be perfect. It is important for the group member to have a chance to practice this conversation realistically, so if another teen will play the role of the other person in the conversation, that teen should be instructed to respond in character. For that reason, it is helpful for the teen to describe how his or her parent or friend is likely to react. The group leader can play the role of the other person in the role play if group members do not volunteer or if the leader anticipates that the adolescents will not be able to respond accurately enough to be helpful.

For each role play, identify one group member who can be the coach. The coach helps the teen remember which strategies he or she planned to use during the role play by holding up cue cards as a reminder of each skill. Before the role play, the coach can put the cards in order according to the plan that the group developed. However, if the role play takes a different turn, the coach can also suggest using a particular strategy even if it was not planned in advance. It is best to have only one coach during a role play. Having more than one coach in a role play is more confusing than helpful, particularly if the two coaches recommend different skills at the same time. Nonparticipating group members can watch to see how the situation resembles situations of their own, listen for strategies they should or should not try, try to think of helpful suggestions for the teen, and learn new ways to look at a problem and to find a solution.

The group leader assists the group during the role play in several ways. First, the leader might participate in the role play if needed. Second, the leader can prompt the coach or other group members to offer a brief suggestion if the group members are struggling and can then encourage the teens in the role play to continue. Although it is often best to allow the role play to keep going so the teens can practice the entire interaction, in some instances, it is best to briefly stop the conversation if it seems like either party needs more significant assistance. In these cases, the leader asks the other group members to suggest another problem-solving or communication strategy before returning to the role play. These time outs should be minimized both to improve the realism of the experience and to boost teens' confidence that after preparing for a conversation, they can carry it out largely on their own.

Typically, the leader encourages the teen whose situation is being discussed to play him- or herself in the role play to maximize the amount of practice the teen gets using the communication strategies in preparation for the upcoming conversation. An example of this type of role play is provided next. There are some situations when the leader or another group member might take the role of the teen instead. If the group member whose situation is being discussed has substantial difficulty or is not willing to give the conversation a try, the group leader or another teen may choose to model the strategies by acting in the role of the teenager and having the group member play the teen's family member or peer. This strategy can also be used when a teen insists that a parent is particularly difficult because it gives the teen a chance to demonstrate this to the group. After the leader or another group member models the role of the teen, roles should be reversed so the teen has the opportunity to practice the new communication strategies.

Example: Role play

LEADER: Now that Farrah has some good ideas for what she can say, let's help her practice it. Who can be Farrah's mother for the role play?

JESSICA: I'll do it.

LEADER: Great; who can help by coaching Farrah? If you remember from last time, that means holding up a cue card if she gets stuck to remind her which skill she can use.

RYAN: I can do that.

LEADER: Wonderful. Now, let's quickly review what she wanted to say: First, she was going to use **Strike while the iron is cold** by asking her mom if this is a good time to talk for a few minutes. Next, she was going to put herself in her mom's shoes by saying that she understands that her mom wants her to do better in math. Here would be a good place to also acknowledge that she shouldn't have gotten an F on her math test and that she will try harder next time. She was going to add an **I statement** to that, letting her mom know that she was really upset that she couldn't hang out with her friends, and it made it even harder to concentrate because she was in a bad mood. Then, she was going to suggest some solutions, such as getting extra help from her math teacher so that she can bring her math grade up. At the end, she was going to ask permission to see her friends at least once per week, provided she works hard to bring her math grade up like she said she would. Does anyone remember how she was going to end the conversation?

RYAN: Either thanking her mom if she listened and agreed to at least think about it or asking her mom for some time to cool down if the conversation started getting too heated.

LEADER: That's right. Let's get started.

FARRAH: Wait, what do I do first?

LEADER: [Looking at Ryan] Coach, which skill should Farrah use first?

RYAN: [Holding up **Strike while the iron is cold** cue card] This one?

LEADER: That's right.

FARRAH: Mom, is this an okay time to talk for a minute?

JESSICA: Sure.

FARRAH: I wanted to talk about what happened last Friday.

JESSICA: Okay, go ahead.

RYAN: [Holding up **Put yourself in their shoes** card]

FARRAH: Well, I know you want me to do well in math, and you think that keeping me from seeing my friends is going to help, but it just isn't going to help.

JESSICA: I'm your mom, and I am not going to let you run around town with your friends when you are failing your math class!

FARRAH: I understand, but when I don't get to see my friends, I feel really down, and when I'm in a bad mood like that it makes it harder to concentrate.

JESSICA: I know you like to see your friends, but school has to come first.

FARRAH: [looks at group leader] She would probably say that, what can I say next?

LEADER: This could be a good time to acknowledge your part in this: You got an F on your math test, and you want to do better next time.

FARRAH: I know school comes first, and I messed up when I got that F on my math test. I was thinking I could go ask my teacher for extra help tomorrow to see what I can do to get my math grade up. But, I want to get to see my friends, too.

JESSICA: *I don't know, I still think you have to show me an improvement in your math grades before you get to go out with your friends again.*

FARRAH: *Okay. Will you think about it at least?*

JESSICA: *Talk to your teacher tomorrow and let me know what she says. Then, we can talk about it again after your next grades are posted.*

LEADER: *That seems like a good place to stop. Farrah, how can you end the conversation?*

FARRAH: *Thanks for listening, Mom.*

LEADER: *Great job everyone!*

Debrief after the role play is complete. After the role play, facilitate a discussion about what went well and what could still be improved. In this discussion, the leader should point out strengths as well as areas to improve to avoid discouraging teens from trying out strategies. The leader can ask both parties involved in the role play as well as other group members to notice what the teen did well and to make suggestions for improvement, highlighting which communications skills the teen used and those that could be added or improved. Open-ended questions will help facilitate a discussion among the group members, including asking other teens how they would feel in the chosen situation, discussing teens' feelings, and working to generalize the role play to the other group members' situations. It is helpful to consider whether the conversation achieved the goals the adolescent set for the interaction and to help the teen anticipate how having this conversation in real life might address the interpersonal problem and improve his or her mood.

Example: Debrief after the role play

LEADER: *So, Farrah, what do you think went well in that conversation?*

FARRAH: *Well, I was a lot calmer than I usually am. I didn't yell or raise my voice.*

LEADER: *That's a great observation! The tone you use in a conversation is really important, so staying calm is one thing you noticed. What did you notice, Jessica, in playing the part of Farrah's mother?*

JESSICA: *She did a good job ending the conversation; it was nice that she said thank you. She also had some solutions; I thought that was good.*

LEADER: *That is good feedback, Jessica. Farrah, one thing I noticed is that you made it clear how you felt when you didn't get to see your friends, and I thought it helped when you linked that to how it affects your schoolwork. I also liked it that you put yourself in your mom's shoes. Is there anything you wish you had done differently?*

FARRAH: *I noticed that when I started out, I had a little bit of an attitude when I said that it didn't work for my mom to stop me from seeing my friends. I think my mom would get mad if I said that.*

JESSICA: *Yes, I did feel a little angry when you said that.*

LEADER: *Okay. So, what could you say differently early on? What about taking a moment to acknowledge that you should have done something to avoid getting an F? Would that help your mom want to listen to what you have to say?*

FARRAH: *Yeah, but that feels kind of weird. Like, what would I say?*

LEADER: *Does anyone have any ideas for Farrah?*

MARY: *What about, "Mom, I understand that you were upset that I got that F, and I know I should have done more to get ready for that test." I think if I said that to my mom, she would feel like I was listening to her for once.*

FARRAH: *Yeah, that would be okay, I guess. I could also let her know up front that I want to find ways to bring up my math grade. Maybe then she'd be more interested in at least thinking about letting me see my friends.*

Following this discussion, it is helpful to give the teen another chance to role play the conversation, incorporating any of the changes discussed. If the first role play was unrealistically successful (for instance, a parent agreed immediately for the teen to go out with her friends regardless of her grades), it is important to practice the conversation again with a more challenging partner so the teen practices a more difficult situation. Otherwise, the teen will be ill prepared for her work at home, have a negative interaction, and will question the utility of these strategies.

Use decision analysis (if needed). While the format described so far is appropriate to address many interpersonal situations, group members sometimes bring up issues that require additional problem-solving. For example, a teen might be unsure about whether to continue a difficult friendship; someone might have an issue with a peer and need help from an adult to handle it; or another group member might need to consider modifying behavior rather than having an explicit conversation about something. In these situations, the leader can use another interpersonal psychotherapy (IPT) technique called decision analysis, or interpersonal problem-solving, to help teens think about how they might approach the interpersonal problem. Decision analysis involves identifying possible solutions to an interpersonal problem, assessing the pros and cons of each solution, deciding which solution to try, and then determining what needs to be said or done to implement the solution. Group members should be encouraged to generate ideas before the leader provides possible solutions to help teens learn to engage in the process. Decision analysis helps to decrease adolescents' tendency toward black-and-white thinking that there is only one solution to a problem. Thus, the leader wants to encourage the group members to generate several solutions to practice being flexible in thinking about alternative options.

For instance, in the case of someone spreading rumors about a teen, the group would explore the situation and help the teen think through pros and cons of different solutions. Options might include talking to the person who spread the rumor; involving another adult or peer in the situation (e.g., talking to parents, friends, or a school counselor); deciding not to be friends with the teen; or ignoring the situation if it is likely to pass. If a decision is made to talk to someone, the leader can encourage the teen to think through what to say in the conversation. The leader can then facilitate scripting and role playing this conversation. While it is important to emphasize interpersonal solutions to problems, a direct conversation may not always be the best solution. Group members are encouraged to implement whatever solution is considered best after weighing the pros and cons of each option. In subsequent sessions, the group can discuss whether this solution was successful. If not, an alternative strategy may need to be identified and implemented. The following is an example of a decision analysis:

Example: Decision analysis

LEADER: *Jessica, you've done a great job of telling us what happened this week at school. It sounds like it was pretty upsetting when you saw Amy, your best friend, sitting with people who she knows you don't like. You recognized that it wasn't the right time to talk to her, so you just walked away and sat with someone else, but it's still upsetting you. The rest of you think Jessica should tell Amy what is upsetting her. Jessica, what would you like to do next?*

JESSICA: *I don't know; I could say something to her, but it isn't the first time something like this has happened. I'm just not sure if it's worth it.*

LEADER: *Let's talk through this so you can decide what you want to do. What are your options?*

JESSICA: *I could ignore Amy and see if she says anything.*

LEADER: *Okay, what else?*

MARY: *It seems like this has happened a lot with Amy. If I were you, I wouldn't really want to be friends with her anymore if she ignores you when other people are around.*

FARRAH: *Yeah; she's not being a good friend to you.*

LEADER: *So far, the options are telling Amy that you are upset; ignoring her to see if she says something to you; or ending the friendship. What are some other ideas?*

JESSICA: *I think you guys are right that she hasn't been a good friend, but it's hard to just stop being friends with someone who you've known for a long time.*

LEADER: *It seems like you're not ready to give up on this friendship. Let's think of all the options of what you might do next.*

MARY: *What about talking to someone else about it, someone who knows you and also knows Amy?*

JESSICA: *Well, my mom has known Amy for a long time, and I know she has noticed that Amy hasn't been around as much lately. Maybe I could talk to her about it.*

LEADER: *That's another great idea. So, of all the ideas we have so far, which one might you want to start with?*

JESSICA: *I think I might want to start by talking to my mom. That seems like a good idea to me. I don't think talking to Amy is going to help right now.*

LEADER: *Okay. Let's think about pros and cons of talking to your mom. What are some of the possible downsides?*

JESSICA: *I don't think there is much of a downside. I guess maybe my mom won't have good ideas for me. I don't think she will be annoyed with me talking to her about it, and usually she is pretty helpful.*

LEADER: *Have you talked to your mom about Amy before?*

JESSICA: *Yeah, but not for a long time. Lately, my mom and I haven't talked as much as we used to.*

LEADER: *In the past, was your mom helpful when you talked to her about Amy?*

JESSICA: *Yeah, most of the time. She gives pretty good advice about that sort of thing. I think she would listen and try to help.*

LEADER: It sounds like there is a chance she would help and would have good advice, and you don't think it would be difficult or there would be much of a downside. So, let's think through how you can approach your mom about this.

If the solution does not involve talking to someone, continue to use decision analysis for as long as it is useful. Examples of possible solutions include deciding to wait and see what happens with a relationship, deciding to change one's own behavior to see how that affects the other person (e.g., doing chores before a parent comes home to avoid arguments), or deciding to spend more time with other people instead. In the example provided, Jessica might decide to avoid Amy for the next week, spending time with other friends. Alternatively, Jessica might decide to try spending time with Amy and her new friends to see if she can get along with them better. The leader encourages the group member to try the chosen solution and to report back on how it goes at the next group session. At that point, the group can discuss whether additional action is needed.

Discuss another interpersonal situation. If there is time, a second group member can talk about an interpersonal event and begin the process of planning and role playing a conversation or conducting a decision analysis if this would be helpful. The remaining time can also be used to link the situation that was discussed to something one or more group members brought up. For instance, if the situation related to conflict with parents, another group member might be able to briefly discuss how strategies already discussed might apply to conflicts with his or her parents as well. If there is not time to finish the discussion of another interpersonal situation, the group can continue the conversation next session. Another option would be to continue this discussion in the individual mid-group session.

Assign and prepare for interpersonal work at home. It is important to emphasize the need for teens to work on their interpersonal goals in between sessions so they can problem-solve any difficulties in the remaining group sessions. Because this is the first time that teens will be assigned interpersonal work at home, the leader should emphasize that these assignments provide an opportunity to apply the communication strategies to real-life situations. This out-of-group practice will help the teens feel more comfortable with the skills, improve their communication with other people, and address their interpersonal goals for the group.

Interpersonal work at home is assigned to group members who worked on an interpersonal problem during the session. At the end of the discussion of each interpersonal issue or at the end of the session, the leader assigns these adolescents interpersonal work at home. Depending on what was discussed in the session, this work at home might involve having a planned conversation, thinking further about the interpersonal issues, or modifying their behavior to address the problem. For instance, if the teen planned and role played a conversation, the teen should be asked to try to have this conversation at home and to report on it next session. In preparation for this, the group can help the teen identify the best time to have the conversation, as well as anticipate possible obstacles to having the planned conversation, including having difficulty finding a good time and worrying that the conversation will go poorly. It is helpful to emphasize that, even if a conversation does not go as planned, it is worthwhile for the teen to try new ways of communicating. Further problem-solving may be needed in future sessions to continue to work on the relationship.

If the teen does not seem prepared to have a planned conversation by the end of the group session, he or she should not be asked to have the conversation. While the leader should not wait for a perfect role play to assign work at home, it is important that the teen is adequately prepared. This helps to avoid setting the adolescent up either for an unsuccessful conversation or failure to attempt the conversation at all. In this case, the teen can be encouraged to continue to think about ways to approach the situation, to consult with another friend or family member about the problem, or to work on addressing identified obstacles to having the conversation (e.g., finding a good time). Finally, if a decision analysis occurred and the teen chose a specific solution, the work at home might involve the teen implementing this solution. The teen would be asked to report in the following session on how the solution worked. For instance, if a teen decided to do chores before his or her mom gets home from work, the teen should be asked to try this out and report back on whether this plan was implemented and if this had an impact on the frequency and intensity of their arguments.

Example: Assigning interpersonal work at home

LEADER: Farrah and Jessica, we spent time today discussing both of your relationships. Farrah, as we talked about earlier, I think it would be helpful for you to have a conversation with your mom about your grade in math and your desire to spend time with friends. Is that something you can do this week?

FARRAH: Yes.

LEADER: Is there a particular time you have in mind to have the conversation?

FARRAH: Well, I am hoping she will let me see my friends on Friday, so I should have the conversation as soon as possible. Maybe I can do it on Tuesday because I don't have to stay late for swim practice.

LEADER: That sounds like a good idea. It is really important for you all to have an opportunity to try these strategies out in your relationships so you can see how it feels to use them. This is also the best way for you to see improvements in the relationships you identified as part of your interpersonal goals for group. Farrah, if you communicate with your mom in the way we practiced, I hope she will let you spend more time with friends. Even if that doesn't happen, I think if you can stay calm and use the strategies, it is less likely to escalate into an argument like it did this week. What do you think?

FARRAH: I hope so.

LEADER: Are there any things that might get in your way of having the conversation like we planned?

FARRAH: Well, if she is in a bad mood on Tuesday, I should probably wait for another time. I would try to do it on Wednesday then.

LEADER: That sounds good. We are looking forward to hearing about it next week. Jessica, we didn't get to finish talking yet about the situation with Amy. You were leaning toward talking to your mom about it. Can you think about this over the course of the week? If you still think that is the best solution, we can discuss what you might want to say in this conversation next time.

Closing tasks: remind group members about upcoming mid-group sessions and mark the midpoint of the group. At the end of this session, the leader takes time to praise adolescents' participation in the group, including self-disclosing, role playing, and generating strategies to use in the interpersonal situations. Before the end of the session, the leader reminds group members that between group sessions 4 and 6, teens will be meeting with the group leader and their parent(s). The leader should provide additional information about the content and structure of these sessions as needed, particularly if teens are nervous about them. If there is time at the end of the session, the leader can use this time to mark the mid-point of the group. Teens are often surprised at how quickly time has passed. Reminding teens that there are only four sessions left helps motivate the adolescents to discuss interpersonal situations in group. This is also an opportunity to discuss teens' experience of being in a group. This discussion can include thoughts and feelings about (a) getting enough attention for their own problems, (b) learning by hearing about others' experiences, (c) learning to role play different ways of interacting and communicating, and (d) sharing personal feelings or experiences with other peers. The leader can also ask if there is anything teens would like to do differently during the remainder of the group.

Group Sessions 5 and 6

Group Sessions 5 and 6 Checklist:
☐ Distribute binders and have adolescents complete depression checklist and mood rating
☐ Complete mood ratings aloud
☐ Discuss mid-group sessions
☐ Review interpersonal work at home assigned in the previous session
☐ Collaboratively set an informal agenda for the session
☐ Discuss group members' interpersonal situations
☐ Closing tasks: assign interpersonal work at home

Materials Needed:
☐ Notebooks and pens
☐ Communication strategy cue cards (see Appendix)

Session goals and tasks. In sessions 5 and 6, the leader can set the agenda flexibly to fit the needs of group members. There should be time for teens to share their mood ratings and interpersonal events from the week, discuss mid-group sessions, review interpersonal work at home that was assigned previously, and discuss one or two new interpersonal situations. The order of these tasks may vary based on the priorities of a particular group, although we recommend that the group begin with teens sharing their mood ratings to make sure that anyone with a pressing issue has a chance to share and discuss it.

The leader should be mindful of managing time in the group so that each group member can address issues related to his or her interpersonal goals. Teens who have not yet worked on an interpersonal issue should be prioritized over those who have already worked on something. If a teen has already had a chance to discuss an interpersonal problem in depth, try to limit the time spent discussing that teen's issue (e.g., reviewing work at home, discussing why the teen did not have a conversation, planning a follow-up conversation), unless this discussion would be beneficial for other group members or there are no other interpersonal issues to discuss. If a planned conversation took place, this might mean doing an abbreviated communication analysis and briefly discussing how the teen might follow up to either maintain gains or make further progress. If a planned conversation did not happen, the leader might take a few minutes to remind the teen of what the teen already planned to say and briefly discuss how to overcome obstacles to initiating a conversation, particularly if this can be generalized to other group members. Similarly, the leader should avoid allowing one or two group members to dominate discussions and may have to tactfully limit the amount of time spent discussing a topic brought up by a group member.

Some adolescents may be reluctant to share personal issues with the group or may have difficulty acknowledging interpersonal problems. It is helpful to get these adolescents involved in group sessions in other ways, such as encouraging them to act as coaches during role plays, calling on them to generate ideas when planning conversations, or asking them to provide fellow group members with feedback. By the end of group session 6, the goal is for all group members to have the opportunity to work on at least one interpersonal situation related to their goals, although some teens may choose not to discuss their interpersonal relationships in depth.

Distribute binders and have group members complete depression checklist and mood rating. Group members complete the depression checklist and mood rating. The leader should briefly review symptoms and mood ratings.

Complete mood ratings aloud. Each session begins by having the group members briefly comment on any changes in their mood ratings and how these changes relate to interpersonal events that happened over the past week. The leader also reports on changes in his or her mood and links these changes to interpersonal situations as a model for the teens. In addition, the leader prompts teens to identify links between their mood and their relationships during this check-in.

Discuss mid-group sessions. If any group members had individual mid-group sessions since the previous group meeting, the leader asks them to share something with the group about the session. The leader asks open-ended questions to facilitate this discussion, including how each teen felt about the session, any positive or negative aspects of the session, and any information they are willing to share about the content of the conversation. Particularly for mid-group sessions with parents, it is helpful for group members to hear that some teens had difficult mid-group sessions and others had sessions that were easier. Teens are able to observe other group members' progress and understand that relationships can change as the result of effective communication. If issues that are raised in the mid-group session warrant further discussion, this can be added to the informal agenda for the group to discuss, and if necessary a follow-up conversation can be planned and role played. This is beneficial for the target group member as it results in additional problem-solving about an interpersonal problem and awareness that, if you do not initially have success, you can continue to work toward the desired outcome. It also helps all teens to recognize how the mid-group sessions complement the work done in group.

Example: Discussing mid-group sessions

LEADER: *Does anyone want to talk about the mid-group sessions? Mary?*

MARY: *It was okay. My mom was pretty cool in the meeting. We talked about my chores at home, and she agreed to let me go out on Saturday if I got everything done beforehand. It was weird. She doesn't talk to me like that at home. Part of me felt like she was being nice, just because you [the leader] were there. But, I got everything done and she let me go out, so I guess it worked.*

LEADER: *That's great to hear! I know that sometimes it feels like things go better because your parents are on their best behavior in the session. But, I think there were a lot of things you did in the conversation that were really positive. What did you do to help it go more smoothly than usual?*

MARY: *Well, I put myself in her shoes. I think she appreciated that I mentioned that I get how it must be frustrating for her when I don't help out. That probably was part of why she listened more, too.*

LEADER: *I agree; I think that was really important for her to hear, and you did a great job staying calm in that conversation, too. How about you, Michael?*

MICHAEL: *It wasn't as bad as I thought it would be. My dad came, and I told him I wanted to spend more time with him on the weekends. He was okay about it, but so far nothing has changed, so I'm not sure if it was worth it.*

LEADER: *Okay, so you were able to talk to him about this for the first time, which is good, but you didn't get the result you wanted right away. That happens sometimes, because it often takes more than one conversation to really make a change. So, even if you said things just the way you wanted to the first time, you might have to talk to someone a few more times before things really get to be the way you want them. What do other people think?*

RYAN: *I think that's right; I had to ask my mom a bunch of times before she let me sign up for the baseball team.*

LEADER: *That's a good example. Michael, if we have time today, would you be willing to talk more about what happened with your dad so we can think together about whether or not you want to talk to him again?*

MICHAEL: *Yeah, that would be okay I guess.*

LEADER: *That sounds good. Ryan, what about your mid-group session?*

Review interpersonal work at home assigned in the previous session. If a teen was assigned interpersonal work at home, it is important to ask how the conversation went during the next group meeting. This conveys to teens that the leader believes that interpersonal work at home is important. While it is always critical to check in about previous work at home, the leader can decide when this fits best into the session agenda. The leader can review the work at home before moving on to new interpersonal work or can wait until the end of the session. This decision will depend on how many group members have pressing interpersonal situations to discuss, how much time was spent focusing on the teen with work at home in the previous session, and any knowledge the leader has about whether the teen completed the work at home and how this went. Because this knowledge is important in setting the informal agenda for the group, it is useful to ask the teen informally about the interaction before the start of group when the teens are settling in and completing their depression checklists.

The leader should ask any teen with a work-at-home assignment if he or she was able to have the conversation and how it went. If the conversation went well, it may be helpful to do an abbreviated communication analysis to highlight the use of the various communication strategies. If it went poorly, the leader should use communication analysis to determine exactly what was said and discuss what the teen could have said differently. If the group member is willing and if time permits, the group can role play the conversation again, incorporating any suggestions for change. This is particularly useful if the teen wants to attempt the same conversation again. If a teen has not completed assigned interpersonal work, the group should briefly discuss the barriers the teen encountered, which may include difficulty finding a good time to have a conversation, worries about the other person's reaction, or difficulties expressing feelings. The leader can provide encouragement and a rationale for practice of communication strategies even if the teen has doubts about whether the other person will listen. It is often helpful for the leader to engage other group members in this discussion if possible. If other teens have been able to do interpersonal work between sessions, they may be able to provide encouragement for a group member who has been more reluctant to do so. The teen may also benefit from a brief review of the strategies he or she had planned to use and a discussion of any necessary revisions to the conversation. If time permits, rehearsal of a revised conversation can be helpful.

Example: Reviewing work at home

LEADER: Farrah, were you able to have the conversation with your mom that we planned last week?

FARRAH: Yeah, I talked to her. It went okay, I guess, but she didn't let me hang out with my friends on Friday.

LEADER: Okay, let's briefly talk through what happened, and we can figure out what worked and what didn't work.

FARRAH: That would be okay I guess.

LEADER: How did you start the conversation?

FARRAH: It was Thursday. I think she was in the kitchen, and I just asked her if I could see my friends the next day because it was a Friday and they were all going to see a movie I wanted to see.

LEADER: What did she say next?

FARRAH: My mom said, "Farrah, you know that you can't go out with your friends until you bring your math grade up. We talked about this last week." She sounded a little frustrated with me then, and that made me remember that I had wanted to use the **Put yourself in their shoes** *strategy.*

LEADER: That's great that you remembered that. So, what did you say next?

FARRAH: Well, then I said, "Mom, I know you are worried about my math grade, but it is really important to me to spend time with my friends. When I don't spend time with them, I feel really down, and then it is hard to concentrate on my schoolwork."

LEADER: That is just how we practiced it. What did your mom say?

FARRAH: *Well, she was understanding and all, but she said that even though she gets why I want to see my friends, I have to put my schoolwork first. I got pretty discouraged then, and I just said okay and went to my room.*

LEADER: *It sounds like you had a really good start to the conversation, but you were upset when she didn't agree to let you see your friends, and it was hard for you to continue the conversation at that point.*

FARRAH: *Yeah; the whole thing went okay I guess, and we didn't fight or yell like we sometimes do, but I still didn't get to hang out with my friends.*

LEADER: *I'm glad to hear that the conversation did not lead to a big argument like it sometimes does. I have a few ideas about what to do next, but first let's see if other people in the group have ideas. What do you all think?*

Collaboratively set an informal agenda for the session. One of the most challenging tasks in sessions 5 and 6 is selecting which interpersonal issues to focus on during the remainder of the session. Often, the leader will have a sense of who to focus on based on what group members mentioned in either the mood check-in or the discussion about the mid-group sessions. If it is not clear, the leader can ask the group if anyone has a pressing issue to discuss in group today. If one or more teens volunteers to talk about a relevant issue, help the group prioritize the most pressing or relevant topic and proceed to discuss the situation and plan and role play a conversation with that person. It is helpful to prioritize those teens who have more pressing interpersonal issues, those who bring in situations closely related to their interpersonal goals, or those who have not had a chance to discuss an interpersonal situation in depth in previous group sessions. As discussed in the section on session 4, the leader can use hypothetical situations to get a conversation started if group members do not identify any of their own interpersonal situations to discuss.

Discuss group members' interpersonal situations. Once the group agrees on an issue to discuss first, ask the group member to tell everyone about the issue or event, as described in the section on session 4. If an argument occurred, a communication analysis may be helpful to understand what happened before deciding what to do next. If the person brings up a different type of interpersonal issue that is not conflict based, such as wanting to talk to a friend about feeling distant and wanting to spend more time together, the group might conduct a decision analysis to help the teen decide on a course of action before proceeding. When the teen decides that a follow-up conversation is the best next step, the leader can ask the group member what the goal is for the conversation. It is helpful for the teen to focus first on what he or she would like to say and then apply the communication strategies to say it in the best possible way. Then, the group can proceed to help the group member plan and practice the conversation as described in the section on session 4.

During sessions 5 and 6, as teens report on conversations they have tried, it is helpful to use the momentum that some teens have built to encourage other group members to try new ways of communicating. Some group members may try to communicate with someone but find that the other person is either not receptive or cannot change something (e.g., a parent is too busy to take the teen to an activity or a friend continues to spend time with another friend instead). It is helpful for the leader to acknowledge this and help teens to recognize when they should keep trying (using the ***Don't give up*** strategy) and when they might need to modify expectations about a relationship. One conversation is rarely enough to make an important change in a relationship, and it is useful for everyone to keep this in mind. Time can be spent in group sessions planning follow-up conversations to bring about or maintain a desired change.

Example: Follow-up conversations

LEADER: Michael, you were telling us that you talked to your dad in your mid-group session about wanting to spend more time with him, but you weren't sure if it made a difference. Can you fill in the group on what you discussed?

*MICHAEL: Well, I used an **I statement** to tell him that I have fun when we do stuff together and I want to try to do that more often. He said he would like that, too, and that maybe we could go fishing this weekend. But then this weekend came and went and he didn't say anything about it again.*

LEADER: So, after he said you could go fishing this weekend, did you set a plan or a date for that?

MICHAEL: No, it was more like, we'll figure it out this weekend.

LEADER: Do other people have questions for Michael so far?

FARRAH: Did you remind him at all? Sometimes, my mom totally forgets what we talk about. Is your dad like that also?

MICHAEL: No, I didn't remind him. I figured if he really wanted to go fishing with me, he would remember.

JESSICA: I thought that too with my parents, but I notice that when I do remind them about something we planned to do, they are more likely to follow through, and we have a good time.

LEADER: That's a good point, Jessica. Michael, it sounds like it would feel much better to you if your dad remembered that you had plans to go fishing. But, Jessica is suggesting that if you remind him, you would be more likely to go fishing, and that would feel better than not going at all.

MICHAEL: Yeah, I guess that's true.

RYAN: Is your dad really busy on the weekends?

MICHAEL: Yeah, he has a lot to do because he works a lot during the week.

RYAN: Maybe going fishing takes up too much time? When I went fishing with my dad, we were gone the whole day.

MICHAEL: I guess it does take a while, and there is all the fishing gear to pack up. Maybe I could ask him to do something else, like go to the park to play basketball? That would take up less time.

LEADER: So, people have a couple of good ideas for you, Michael. One was picking a different activity that might be easier, and it seems like you're okay with that. The other is actually reminding your dad about plans. I wonder if it might also help if you set a day and time to do something; that way, he knows how to plan around it. What do you think?

MICHAEL: Yeah, that could be okay. I still wish he would remember himself, but I guess I can remind him.

LEADER: *So, now that you have some good ideas, let's plan a follow-up conversation you can have with him.*

Closing tasks: assign interpersonal work at home. At the end of each role play or at the end of the session, encourage adolescents who did interpersonal work during the session to try these strategies at home. This may flow directly from the role play, for instance, asking a group member to have a conversation that was planned and role played during the session. At other times, it may be appropriate to assign interpersonal work at home that is targeted at addressing a particular depression symptom that continues to be problematic. For instance, if an adolescent continues to report social withdrawal, work at home might involve calling a friend and making plans. If by group session 6 some adolescents have not implemented the communication strategies at home despite the practice in group, it might be helpful to ask each group member to use one or two of the strategies in the next week with someone in their lives. The leader should convey to group members how important it is to do these exercises during the week so they become more comfortable with these new strategies. The leader can emphasize the time-limited nature of the group and encourage group members to try these strategies while they have the benefit of talking these conversations over with the group. It is helpful to let the teens know that the leader is excited to hear about these interactions during the next session.

Summary of the Middle Phase

By the end of the middle phase, all teens should have had at least one opportunity to work on an interpersonal situation related to one of their goals for group. This may have occurred in the context of a middle phase group session or during an individual mid-group session. Ideally, teens will also have started trying out new communication strategies outside the group setting, either at home or with a parent during the mid-group session. The teens are encouraged to continue this work during the remainder of the group, although the focus of the group shifts somewhat in the termination phase, as described in Chapter 8.

7

IPT-AST Mid-Group Session

The mid-group session is scheduled with each teen individually and takes place sometime between group sessions 4 and 6. The purpose of the mid-group session is to review how the teen is doing, discuss areas that still need to be addressed, and allow the teen to practice new communication strategies, either with the parent or with the group leader. When parents are included in the mid-group session, it is useful to obtain parents' perspectives on whether there have been noticeable changes in the teens and to identify continued problematic areas. For teens whose identified goals involve parents, this session is a particularly useful opportunity to practice new communication strategies with parents in a safe environment. When a parent cannot attend the mid-group session, the session serves as an important opportunity to help the teen do targeted work toward interpersonal goals in a one-on-one session. A 45-minute session is recommended to accomplish the tasks of the session. This session can be slightly shorter or longer, depending on what is feasible in the setting where Interpersonal Psychotherapy – Adolescent Skills Training (IPT-AST) groups are offered.

Mid-Group Session

Session goals and tasks. The goals for the mid-group session are to review progress made so far, discuss any group issues that need to be addressed, and to apply the new communication and problem-solving strategies to an interpersonal issue related to the teen's goals for the group. The basic structure and goals of the mid-group session are similar whether or not parents are available to attend. In particular, the opening and closing tasks of the session are the same regardless of whether a parent attends the session. There are two primary differences. First, the middle tasks of the session differ depending on whether parents attend the session. As such, there are separate sections that follow in this chapter that describe the middle tasks of the session with parents and without. Second, the allotment of time is different. When a parent can attend the session, the leader should meet with the teen alone for 15 minutes, then together with the teen's parent(s) for 20 minutes, and then wrap up alone again with the teen for 10 minutes. This gives the leader and teen time alone in the beginning to discuss the teen's experience of being in the group and to plan what will be

Mid-Group Session Checklist:

Opening tasks
☐ Discuss and address any concerns about the group
☐ Review communication strategies (if needed)
☐ Review progress toward interpersonal goals

Middle tasks
If parent attends:
☐ Collaboratively decide what the teen will discuss with the parent (with teen alone)
☐ Discuss what will be shared with parent (with teen alone)
☐ Review the teen's progress in the group and elicit parent feedback and concerns
☐ Facilitate communication between the teen and parent
☐ Debrief regarding conversation with parent (with teen alone)

If parent does not attend:
☐ Identify an issue related to the teen's interpersonal goals to work on in session
☐ Discuss the teen's interpersonal issue
☐ Assign interpersonal work at home (if appropriate)

Closing tasks
☐ Discuss what the teen will share with the group

Materials Needed:
☐ Communication strategy cue cards (see Appendix)

discussed with the parent, while reserving sufficient time for the teen and parent to engage in a conversation about the chosen topic. It is helpful to leave time at the end to meet with the adolescent alone to discuss how he or she felt the interaction went and to decide what the teen will share with the group. If the parent is not able to attend the session, the leader meets with the teen alone for the entire session.

Opening Tasks for All Mid-Group Sessions

Discuss and address any concerns about the group. The group leader should begin the individual portion of the session by asking how the teen feels about the group so far. Have the teen's needs been adequately addressed? Does the teen feel comfortable talking in the group? The leader and teen can discuss any concerns the teen may have about the group. This is also a good opportunity for the leader to gently voice any concerns about the teen's group participation, including issues regarding group attendance, engagement, or behavior. It is important to raise these concerns and address them in the individual session before return-ing the teen to the group. This might involve strategizing about how the teen can attend the remaining sessions or identifying specific ways that the teen can participate more in group discussion.

Example: Discussing group so far

LEADER: *Joyce, I would like to talk a little about how you've been feeling in the group so far.*

JOYCE: *I like the group a lot, but I am nervous about talking about my family. I don't want them to know that my dad cheated on my mom. I don't want them to judge me or my dad.*

LEADER: *I can understand why it might be hard for you to bring that up in group. Even if you don't want the other group members to know that your dad cheated on your mom, what would you feel comfortable sharing about how you have felt about your parents' separation?*

JOYCE: *Well, I guess it would be okay for them to know my parents are separating. I am just worried that they will ask questions about why.*

LEADER: *I think it would be helpful to talk about your parents' separation to some degree because one of your goals is related to talking to your parents about this, and I think group members could really help you think of some ways for you to talk to your mom or dad so that the separation is not as hard for you.*

JOYCE: *I am really nervous about talking to my parents.*

LEADER: *Would you be willing to bring this issue to the group to get some help with it? So far in group, some people have opened up about some tough things in their lives, so I bet that even if other people haven't experienced exactly what you're going through, they will try to understand. And, we can think together about ways to talk about it so that they won't find out about what happened with your dad.*

JOYCE: *Okay, I guess that would be all right. As long as I can avoid talking about my dad's cheating, I think it will be okay.*

LEADER: *Let's think about some things you can say if anyone in group asks why your parents are separating.*

Review communication strategies (if needed). If the teen was absent from group session 3, the mid-group session is an opportunity to review the skills before moving to targeted work on one of the teen's interpersonal goals. A review is also appropriate if the teen seems to have trouble understanding the strategies. More or less time should be spent on skill review depending on the teen's level of understanding and whether a parent is waiting. If a parent is participating in the session, the leader and teen will need to review the communication strategies quickly so there is adequate time to prepare for the conjoint part of the session. If a parent is not attending, there is more flexibility, and the leader can determine whether a more intensive review would be helpful. Please refer to the section on group session 3 in Chapter 5 for more details on how to introduce the communication strategies.

Review progress toward interpersonal goals. Next, the leader reminds the teen of his or her interpersonal goals, set during the individual pre-group sessions, and reviews any prog-ress made on these goals. Many teens do not remember their goals, so the leader should be sure to review them before the start of the session. If the mid-group session is held between groups 4 and 5, the teen is likely to report little change because the middle phase has just begun. If the session is held between groups 5 and 6 and the teen reports little or no change in interpersonal relationships, engage the teen in a discussion about difficulties the teen may be having in generalizing from the group discussions. The leader and the teen can then make a specific plan about how the teen can best work toward progress both in and outside the group. This might involve identifying specific skills the teen might want to address in the group and at home. In some cases, the teen might report that a particular goal is no longer relevant, either because it has been resolved or because it no longer seems as important. Together, the leader and teen can identify another interpersonal issue that might be more relevant at this point so that the teen can focus on that goal for the remainder of group.

Middle Tasks for Mid-Group Sessions When Parents Are Present

Collaboratively decide what the teen will discuss with the parent (with teen alone). The leader works with the teen to decide what the teen will discuss with his or her parent in the session. If the teen has a specific goal related to the parent, the teen is encouraged to discuss a topic related to this goal. It is important to choose an issue with a greater likelihood of a successful outcome. This means picking a topic that is more specific or circumscribed, rather than a large or complicated issue. For instance, a teen's interpersonal goal for group might be to fight less with his or her mom. For the purposes of the mid-group session, the leader should help the teen focus this goal more. For example, the teen and parent might discuss arguing less about chores in particular. Ideally, the leader and teen will also pick a lower intensity topic. For example, the parent and teen might discuss the teen's desire to go to a friend's house after school, rather than having a conversation about being allowed to date when this is clearly forbidden by the parent. However, it is not always possible or preferable to pick a low-intensity conflict, and this should be balanced with maximizing the opportunity of having teen and parent in a joint session. We have worked with many teens who decided to bring up high-intensity topics in mid-group sessions, often with positive results.

Regardless of the topic chosen, it is helpful to emphasize that, given the limited time available, it is unlikely that the parent and teen will completely resolve the issue. The expectation is that the parent and teen can begin to work on the problem, and this is primarily an opportunity to practice a new way of communicating. The leader can help decrease the teen's anxiety by helping to identify a good way to begin the conversation and by discussing which communication strategies may be particularly applicable. Although there is often not enough time to plan a detailed script, it may be helpful, if time permits, to briefly plan and role play the first few interactions. The leader should assure the teen that the leader is there to help everything go as smoothly as possible and will meet with the teen at the end of the session to debrief.

If there is no need to practice communication with the parent or the teen refuses to do so, there are several options for how to maximize the time. One option is to have the teen teach the parent the communication skills learned in group. It is best for the teen to take the lead, with the leader providing support as needed. Another option is to ask the parent if there is an issue he or she would like to discuss. In this case, the leader and teen should spend time in the individual portion of the session anticipating the issues the parent might bring up and discussing the communication strategies that the teen might use in the conversation. The leader can actively coach the teen during the conversation as well. If the teen has been difficult to engage in the group, the leader can also take this opportunity to discuss obstacles to attendance with the teen and parent together, particularly if the parent might be able to help address those obstacles (e.g., if the teen is expected to care for younger siblings after school, the leader can ask the parent if alternate child care is available on group days).

Discuss with the teen what will be shared with the parent (with teen alone). Before inviting the parent into the session, the leader discusses with the teen what will be shared with the parent. The leader informs the teen that he or she will first provide the parent with a summary of the group so far, but will not share any specific information with the parent without the teen's permission. It is important to allow the teen an opportunity to express concerns over sharing any of the information and then address the concerns before the parent joins the session. Following this, the leader will facilitate a conversation between the teen and the parent.

Example: Discussing what will be shared with the parent

LEADER: *So, now that you and I have thought through what you want to talk to your mom about, I'm going to invite your mom in. I'd like to first fill her in on what we've done in group so far, generally, and give her a brief summary of how you've been doing in group. Does that sound okay to you?*

JOYCE: *Well, what are you going to tell her? I don't want her to know I've been talking to you about my dad cheating on her. That would be really awkward.*

LEADER: *I'm glad you asked about that. I won't share your goals with your mom if you don't want me to. I was planning to tell her that you have done a great job picking up on the skills in group, but you are not so comfortable sharing with other group members yet, and that is something that we have talked about and that we are working on together. Would that feel all right to share with your mom today?*

JOYCE: *Oh, that sounds fine then.*

LEADER: *Great. Then, after that, I will ask your mom if she has anything she'd like to talk about briefly, and then I will give you a chance to talk to her about how you are feeling about your parents' separation.*

JOYCE: *Okay.*

Review the teen's progress in the group and elicit parent feedback and concerns. Once the parent joins the session, the leader begins by explaining the purpose and structure of the session. It is helpful for parents to know the structure of the session so they know what to expect, making them less likely to dominate the discussion with their own concerns or feedback. If the teen has identified an issue to discuss with the parent, emphasize that the primary purpose of the session is to give the teen a chance to practice new communication strategies. The leader can inform the parent that to this end, the teen has chosen a topic to discuss with the parent in session, and the leader will be there to facilitate the conversation.

The parent is told that the leader will review what the teen has been learning in group, and there will also be time to discuss any concerns or feedback that the parent wants to share with the teen and leader.

Next, the leader can briefly review the teen's progress in the group and any areas identified that need further work. In particular, it is important to address issues related to group attendance and engagement with the parent to identify a plan to overcome any obstacles. The leader then asks the parent to discuss his or her observation of the teen's progress since beginning the group program, noting that significant change is not expected given that the active working phase of the group has only recently begun. It is important to maintain a positive outlook on the teen's experience by highlighting the teen's progress, hard work in group, and steady attendance. This will make the adolescent more comfortable in the joint session and will set a positive and hopeful tone for the remainder of the session.

If there is time, the leader can ask the parent if there are any parental areas of concern, listening and acknowledging the parent's perspective. If the parent has a particular issue to discuss, this can lead to a conversation with the teen and parent to clarify each person's perception of the problem and to identify how best to approach these continued areas of concern. More time can be spent on this conversation if the adolescent has not identified a specific topic that the teen would like to discuss with the parent. However, if the teen has identified an issue to discuss with the parent, care should be taken to leave adequate time for this conversation. Thus, the leader needs to balance being attentive to the parent's perspective and concerns with ensuring that the majority of the session is available for the teen to practice communicating with the parent.

Example: Summarizing group and eliciting parent feedback

LEADER: *Mrs. Smith, I am really glad that you could make it today.*

MRS. SMITH: *Me, too.*

LEADER: *First, Joyce and I wanted to fill you in on what we have done in group and how she has felt about it so far. Then, I'd like to hear your feedback. I also want to make sure that Joyce has a chance to practice some new communication skills she has learned with you.*

MRS. SMITH: *Okay. That sounds good.*

LEADER: *So far in group, we have talked primarily about how what you say and how you say it influences the other person and the direction of the conversation. We went over six communication strategies to help everyone in the group improve the way they communicate with people in their lives. Joyce has been a pleasure to have in the group. She has really picked up on the skills, and she has been great at coming up with examples to help other people in the group. She hasn't been so comfortable sharing with the group, which is something she and I have talked about and are trying to work on together.*

MRS. SMITH: *I can understand that. It is hard to open up to new people, but I'm glad she is working on communication. That's something that we definitely think is important at home.*

LEADER: *I want to make sure that Joyce has time to practice those communication skills with you, but first I wanted to ask what you have noticed at home since group started. Have you seen any changes?*

MRS. SMITH: *I can't say I have noticed major changes, but Joyce has been a little more patient with me; in the past week she hasn't been snapping at me when I ask how her day was, so that is something.*

LEADER: *That is good to hear. Are there any concerns you have that you wanted to talk about in here?*

MRS. SMITH: *Well, I have been worried about her since her father and I separated. I have noticed she has been nicer to me this week, but in general since her dad moved out, maybe a little before that even, she hasn't been her old self.*

Facilitate communication between the teen and parent. Before the teen starts talking to his or her parent about the topic the teen has chosen, it is important to emphasize that the focus is on practicing the communication skills that the adolescent has been working on in the group, rather than on solving the problem that the adolescent has raised. The goal is for the teen and parent to communicate with each other more effectively, so they should be encouraged to talk to each other directly rather than addressing the leader. The leader can inform parent and teen that he or she is there to help guide the discussion and will focus on how both of them are communicating rather than on finding a solution.

If the teen has identified a particular issue to discuss with the parent, the leader should prompt the teen to initiate the conversation. During the conversation, the leader actively coaches the teen as needed. It may be necessary to help structure the conversation by asking the parent or teen to respond to something the other person said or to encourage both parties to speak to each other rather than to the leader. If the teen has difficulty remembering what she wants to say, the leader reminds the teen of the communication strategies in the moment, either verbally or using the cue cards. The leader can also call a brief time out if needed to speak with the teen for a couple of minutes to regroup if the conversation has gone in an unexpected or undesired direction. In the unlikely event that the conversation becomes too heated or counterproductive, the leader should end the conversation, modeling an appropriate way to do so.

Example: Facilitating communication between teen and parent

LEADER: *Mrs. Smith, before Joyce gets started, I want to let you both know that the primary purpose of today's meeting is to give Joyce a chance to practice using the new communication skills she has been learning in the group. She is going to bring up an issue that is important to her, and I don't expect that we will have time today to fully resolve the issue. It might require another conversation later, but this is a chance for her to get started and especially to practice these skills. My role here is to help Joyce communicate, so I might interrupt to remind Joyce of a particular strategy, or I might slow the conversation down and ask each of you to respond to something. I want both of you to make sure you are talking to each other and not to me, because that will be more useful for Joyce.*

MRS. SMITH: *Okay, that sounds fine.*

LEADER: *Joyce, why don't you start?*

JOYCE: *Mom, I wanted to talk to you about how your ... uhh ... about you and dad separating ... and how that is affecting me. I know how hard it must have been for you, but I want you to know it was hard for me, too.*

MRS. SMITH: *I know it must have been.*

JOYCE: *I am starting to feel better now. But, there are still some things that are bothering me. I know you need to work full-time and that you are working to make sure that you can pay the bills. But, I always have to take care of Bobby and I have no time to hang out with my friends . . . uhh . . .*

LEADER: *Joyce, you are doing such a great job. Remember our strategy* **Be specific***, so try not to use the word always. Can you let your mom know how you feel?*

JOYCE: *Okay . . . when I have to take care of Bobby, I feel frustrated because I can't hang out with my friends.*

LEADER: *That was great. Your mom is really listening to you. Do you want to respond, Mrs. Smith?*

MRS. SMITH: *Well, I need someone to take care of Bobby, but I do know it's frustrating not to be able to see your friends. I have made a lot of sacrifices lately, too, and I'm sorry that you have to do that right now.*

LEADER: *Now might be a good time for you to put yourself in your mom's shoes, Joyce.*

JOYCE: *I know that you have had to make a lot of sacrifices with dad not being around, and I don't mind helping out with Bobby sometimes, but I wanted to see if we could figure out a way for me to get to see my friends a little more, like maybe once a week or so.*

LEADER: *Joyce that was a good possible solution. Maybe you and your mom can talk about whether there is a way to make that happen?*

Once the teen and parent have finished talking about the issue that the teen raised, the leader should help the parent and teen reflect on how the conversation went. This includes talking about the outcome of the conversation and, more importantly, the way that both parties communicated with each other, highlighting the strategies used and how it made the other person feel in the conversation. It is helpful to ask teen and parent whether this interaction was typical of conversations they have at home. If the conversation went significantly better than usual, the leader can help teen and parent think about ways to communicate like this in the future. If the teen or parent note any particular issues in communication that came up during the conversation, this can be something that the teen and parent continue to work on at home. This also informs how the leader guides the teen in subsequent group sessions as the teen continues to work on improving interpersonal relationships.

Debrief regarding conversation with parent(s) (with teen alone). It is helpful to spend time with the teen alone to assess the teen's feelings surrounding the joint session. First, the leader asks the teen to reflect on how the conversation went, asking about what went well as well as any areas that could have gone differently. Next, the leader highlights the teen's accomplishments and efforts and provides feedback on the teen's use of the new communication strategies. The leader can ask the teen whether this conversation went differently than conversations the teen and parent typically have and how these changes can be applied to future conversations.

If the conversation with the parent was not finished, the leader encourages the adolescent to continue the conversation at home, utilizing the strategies that were successful. During this discussion, the leader provides the teen with an opportunity to ask questions and address any concerns. This is particularly important if the conversation with the parent became heated or if the teen believes that the parent only responded in a supportive manner because the leader was present. The leader should validate these concerns and discuss how the leader and the group will continue to help the teen navigate this relationship.

Middle Tasks for Mid-Group Sessions When Parents Are Not Present

Identify an issue related to the teen's interpersonal goals to work on in session. When parents are not present, the bulk of the mid-group session can be spent working on an interpersonal issue that is related to the teen's goals for group. Given that this is a one-on-one session, this is an excellent opportunity to work on any goals that the teen may be reluctant to discuss in a group setting, such as maintaining contact with an incarcerated parent or dealing with a family member's substance abuse. In most cases, however, teens are willing to work on both of their interpersonal goals in the group setting, so there is more flexibility about which interpersonal situation to work on. Thus, the leader helps the teen identify the most relevant or pressing interpersonal situation to discuss, making sure that the situation is clearly related to the teen's interpersonal goals for group. For instance, the teen might discuss a recent argument that is related to his or her goal of fighting less with a peer.

Discuss the teen's interpersonal issue. The leader guides the teen through a brief discussion of the interpersonal problem. If there was a previous interaction or argument, the leader can conduct a communication analysis to better understand what was said and the resulting feelings. Next, the leader and teen can talk about next steps to resolve the disagreement. This might involve a decision analysis to decide how best to resolve this problem. Ideally, the bulk of the session should be spent scripting and practicing a conversation that the adolescent can have to try to resolve the interpersonal problem, applying the communication strategies to increase the likelihood of a successful interaction. In the case of a teen who is fighting a lot with a friend, this might involve scripting and practicing how to talk to a friend to let the friend know how the teen has been feeling about these disagreements. The leader can help the teen identify which communication strategies are applicable to the situation and then to script the interaction utilizing these strategies. This discussion should follow the same framework used in the middle phase group sessions (see session 4 for a thorough description).

Example: Identifying and working on an interpersonal situation

LEADER: *Because it's just the two of us today, it would be great to spend some time working on one of your interpersonal goals. As we discussed, the goals we identified before group are to decrease arguments with your friend, Robin, and to stay connected to your older sister who started college this year. Is there anything related to these goals that you think would be helpful to talk about today?*

MARY: *Yeah. I had a big argument with Robin this week because she said we were going to hang out on Saturday night, and then she cancelled at the last minute. I was really angry.*

LEADER: *I'd like to hear more about what happened [conduct a communication analysis and a decision analysis if needed].*

LEADER: *Thanks. I have a good sense of the argument and how you want to try to address this problem. Let's think about what we've been talking about in group and how this might help you talk with Robin about what is going on. Without worrying about the right way to say it, what would you like to convey?*

MARY: *I want Robin to know that I was pissed off that she cancelled our plans at the last minute. I feel like she has been doing that more since she started dating John. I want things to be like they were before, with us spending more time together. I also wish we would stop fighting all the time.*

LEADER: *It sounds like you have a good sense of what you want to say.*

MARY: *Yeah, I tried to tell her how I was feeling before but it just turned into an argument. I am worried the same thing will happen if I try again. I am also not sure that Robin will care how I feel.*

LEADER: *You know what you want to say, but you aren't sure how Robin will respond, and you are worried that it will turn into another argument. Let's think about the skills and how they might be helpful. I hope we can find a way to communicate with Robin about how you have been feeling so she will respond more positively.*

MARY: *Okay.*

LEADER: *So, what skills would be most helpful here? [Discuss communication strategies, script conversation using strategies, role play conversation]*

LEADER: *Great job, Mary. I think you have a good plan in place for talking to Robin. I know you are worried about how she will respond. But, when I was acting and responding as Robin in the role play, I could see how much you cared about our friendship and that made me want to work things out. I hope she will respond in a positive way, but if she doesn't, we can talk more in group about other possible solutions. I imagine the other group members will have some good ideas.*

Assign interpersonal work at home (if appropriate). If the leader and teen have been able to script and role play a conversation, the teen should be given a work-at-home assignment to have the conversation before the next group session so the teen can report back to the group about how it went. If the leader and teen made some progress on scripting a conversation but did not finish or were unsure about the best way to proceed, the leader discusses with the teen the benefits of sharing this situation in the next group session. In addition, if the teen has been quiet in group thus far, the teen should be encouraged to bring up interpersonal events in the remaining group sessions, particularly situations related to the teen's goals for group.

Closing Task for All Mid-Group Sessions

Discuss what the teen will share with the group. At the end of the session, it is important to discuss what the teen feels comfortable sharing with the group about the mid-group session. There are several reasons we encourage group members to briefly discuss what happened in the mid-group sessions during the following group meeting. First, it provides teens with an opportunity to obtain additional help from the group (e.g., the group can help generate ideas for a follow-up conversation). Second, it can be helpful for other group members to hear how these sessions went. Hearing about a difficult session can help others feel better if they also had a difficult discussion with a parent. If the teen had a productive discussion with a parent, this can motivate other group members to try out new ways of communicating with important people in their lives. Third, it opens the dialogue between group members about what they are all working on, making it easier for the group and the leader to prioritize the interpersonal work in the remaining sessions.

The leader should let the teen know that he or she can share with the group as little or as much about the mid-group session as the teen feels comfortable sharing. For instance, in one of the previous scenarios, Joyce described feeling reluctant to discuss her parents' separation with the group, in particular her father's infidelity. In this case, the leader would first ask Joyce if she is willing to share with the group that her parents have separated. If Joyce is not comfortable with this, the leader can discuss whether Joyce can report that she was able to speak with her mom about spending more time with friends. Specifically, Joyce would be encouraged to share that she was able to negotiate with her mom so she can have 1 day a week when she does not need to watch her brother and can be with friends instead. Frequently, teens end up disclosing more with the group than they originally planned. Nonetheless, it is important to have this discussion during the mid-group session to decrease any anxiety that teens may have about sharing information with the other group members.

Example: Discussion of what to share with the group

LEADER: *In the next group meeting, we are going to ask everyone to report back on how their mid-group session went. What would you feel comfortable sharing about what we talked about today?*

JOYCE: *I still don't want to tell them about the reason for my parents' separation, but I can say that I talked to my mom about how I've been feeling lately.*

LEADER: *That is fine if you don't want to share anything about your parents' separation. One thing you did really well today was that you asked your mom if someone else can watch your brother after school so you could spend time with friends. Is that something you could share with the group?*

JOYCE: *Yeah, I could tell them that.*

LEADER: *Great, I think it would be helpful for the group to hear about that conversation, and I will be eager to hear if you and your mom were able to follow through with that plan so you can have a little more time with friends.*

Summary of the Mid-Group Session

The mid-group session is intended to give all teens a chance to work on an issue related to one of their interpersonal goals in depth with the group leader. Ideally, the teen has the opportunity to practice using new communication strategies with a parent while being coached in real time by the leader. This allows the leader to give valuable feedback, facilitating more rapid acquisition of skills. When a parent cannot attend, the leader works with the teen individually on an interpersonal issue, again facilitating both skill acquisition and work toward goals in a targeted manner. This session can also serve as a springboard for further work on a teen's interpersonal goals. For this reason, it is important for the leader to encourage the teen to bring issues raised in the mid-group session back to the group for further discussion.

8

IPT-AST Termination Phase

The main goals of the termination phase of Interpersonal Psychotherapy – Adolescent Skills Training (IPT-AST) are to establish group members' sense of competence and to solidify gains made during the middle phase of the intervention. To this end, termination-phase tasks include discussing which communication strategies have been helpful and challenging for each teen and reflecting on the changes teens have made in important relationships. The termination phase is also a time to help group members identify warning signs that would let them know they might be experiencing symptoms of depression as well as strategies to improve their mood if they notice these warning signs. In addition, this is a good time for the leader to consider whether any of the group members need additional services.

Session 7 is a transition session between the middle phase and the termination phase, including both middle phase work and some termination tasks. The leader should emphasize how the communication and interpersonal problem-solving strategies being discussed generalize to other situations so it is relevant for all group members and for future work outside the group. The tasks of the termination phase can all be accomplished during group session 8 if needed, but it is recommended that at least part of group session 7 is devoted to discussing termination issues. The tasks of the termination phase are described in the recommended order, but the leader can modify this if needed to keep the conversation flowing.

In session 8, there is time for the group to reflect on what it was like to participate in a group and to process the end of the group. There is also time to discuss what qualities to look for in other people who teens might confide in or seek support from now that the leader and other group members cannot be a weekly source of support. It would not be unusual for there to be flare-ups in interpersonal stressors as teens anticipate the end of group and become anxious about their ability to solve their difficulties on their own. If this occurs, it is helpful to emphasize that group members have gained many skills they can now use on their own to address interpersonal difficulties. Teens can also talk about how to maintain and build on what they have learned in group, whether on their own or by enlisting the help of others in their lives.

Group Session 7

Group Session 7 Checklist:

☐ Distribute binders and have adolescents complete depression checklist and mood rating

☐ Complete mood ratings aloud

☐ Mark the transition from the middle phase to the termination phase of the group

☐ Review interpersonal work at home assigned in the previous session

☐ Collaboratively set an informal agenda for the session and discuss any pressing interpersonal situations

☐ Discuss communication strategies that were most helpful/challenging for group members

☐ Address barriers to using interpersonal strategies

☐ Closing tasks: emphasize importance of attending the last session, plan last group activities, and assign interpersonal work at home

Materials Needed:

☐ Binders and pens

☐ Communication strategy cue cards (see Appendix)

Session goals and tasks. This session marks the transition from the middle to the termination phase of the group. Often, group members will benefit from devoting part of this session to continued interpersonal work as described in Chapter 6. When significant issues remain, some group time can be devoted to reviewing previous interpersonal work at home as well as discussing pressing issues that there was not time to discuss in session 6. Even when a significant portion of this session is devoted to middle phase work, approximately 30 minutes should be reserved toward the end of the session to begin termination tasks. Specifically, the group discusses which communication strategies were most helpful and challenging for each of the group members and barriers to utilizing these strategies outside the group.

Distribute binders and have group members complete depression checklist and mood ratings. Teens complete the depression checklist and mood rating. The leader should review symptoms and mood ratings.

Complete mood ratings aloud. As in the middle phase sessions, teens and the group leader briefly comment on any changes in their mood ratings and how these changes relate to interpersonal events that happened over the past week.

Mark the transition from the middle phase to the termination phase of the group. The leader should inform teens that this session marks the transition from the middle phase to the termination phase of the group and discuss the changes in the group tasks from this session forward. While there will still be time for new interpersonal work, the remaining groups will focus on reviewing main themes of the previous sessions. This will include highlighting the progress that each teen has made, discussing the effective strategies that have been practiced in the group and implemented at home, and preparing group members for continued work on their interpersonal issues after the group has ended.

Example: Transition to termination phase

LEADER: *We only have today and one more group meeting left before we stop meeting as a group. That means that this week we are going to start talking about some different things to wrap up. We will still talk about situations that are ongoing for all of you, and we may have time to work on a new issue today, too. But, we are going to leave time later today to start looking back at what you have all learned and accomplished since we started meeting, especially in terms of your relationships. As we talk about relationship issues today, I am also going to rely on all of you to take the lead more, now that I know you have gotten the hang of the communication strategies.*

Review interpersonal work at home assigned in the previous session. If teens were assigned work at home in the previous session, the leader should ask about these interactions. If a teen initiated a planned conversation, the leader can conduct a brief communication analysis to highlight the strategies that were used and to briefly discuss any difficulties the teen encountered. If a group member has not done assigned interpersonal work, the group can briefly discuss barriers and help the teen to address those barriers. This may include reminding the teen of the strategies he or she had planned to use. The leader should encourage teens to have any planned conversations before group session 8, as this will be the last opportunity for them to report back to the group and receive feedback.

Collaboratively set an informal agenda for the session and discuss any pressing interpersonal situations. If any of the teens brought up a significant interpersonal event during the mood check in, or if there is lingering work left over from session 6, the leader should briefly discuss the situation as described in Chapter 6. Although it is appropriate to spend an entire session in the middle phase working on one or two interpersonal situations, discussion of interpersonal situations in session 7 should be briefer so there is time to begin termination tasks. Specifically, the group can have a brief discussion of what skills may be helpful and how these skills can be applied to address the interpersonal problem but may not always conduct a role play of the conversation due to time constraints. This can be a good opportunity for the group members to draw on their prior experiences utilizing the communication strategies in similar interpersonal situations. The adolescents can be encouraged to take the lead in identifying what strategies would be helpful for the teen to use, given that they should be more familiar with the strategies and the process of planning a conversation by this point. This helps the teens recognize their own competencies at handling challenging interpersonal situations and aids in the generalization of skills to different types of relationship difficulties.

Example: Helping teens address interpersonal situations

LEADER: *Jessica, you brought up that you want to talk to your friend because you think she might be interested in the same guy that you're interested in. How can you approach this conversation?*

JESSICA: *I don't know. If I bring it up, it might end up starting a fight.*

LEADER: *How might the skills apply? A few people have talked about issues with friends, and you all came up with some great ideas. I want to give you more of a chance to take the lead this week because group will be ending soon. It's important for you all to have practice doing this on your own so you can see that you have the ability to handle these types of situations.*

JESSICA: *I guess I could tell her how I feel about it, but I can also let her know I get that she may also like him and that I can't tell her who to like.*

LEADER: *That sounds like a great message. You are already thinking about using an* **I statement** *and* **Put yourself in their shoes**. *Before we talk a bit more about it, what do you hope to walk away with from this conversation?*

JESSICA: *Well, I would really like it if she said she would back off so that we aren't going after the same guy, but I know that might not be fair. I would be okay with it if we could just both be honest about it and agree not to fight over him. I don't want this to get in the way of our friendship.*

LEADER: *It seems like you are being realistic about this, which is great. Let's quickly get some ideas from the group about what other strategies you could use to help get your message across without it turning into a fight.*

Discuss communication strategies that were most helpful/challenging for group members. Once the group has addressed any pressing issues that group members brought in, discuss how the teens have increased their knowledge of the different communication and problem-solving skills. It is helpful to ask teens to identify which strategies have been most helpful to them and to link the use of those strategies to changes in relationships or mood. This solidifies the adolescents' mastery of skills and helps them generalize use of the strategies to other situations. Teens also benefit from hearing about which skills other teens found most useful, given that others may have applied the strategies in diverse ways and in different types of situations. While all of the skills can be helpful, it is not unusual for teens to identify two or three that are particularly relevant for them or comfortable to use.

Teens also can discuss communication strategies that were particularly challenging for them. This is helpful so that teens become aware of skills they may want to continue working on in the future. Some teens may express discomfort with implementing certain strategies, while others may have tried to use a skill but had difficulty applying it effectively. For example, some teens feel uncomfortable with the use of *I statements* to express feelings, thinking that this can make them vulnerable or that others will not understand them. Other teens may want to use *Put yourself in their shoes*, but may struggle to identify the other person's perspective or forget to communicate this to the other person during a conversation. The leader and other group members can help teens address these challenges, while acknowledging that not every teen will feel comfortable with every skill. This may include, for example, helping teens think of other ways to express feelings that may feel more comfortable or helping group members problem-solve about how to remember to use the skills in the moment when things are more heated.

Example: Discussion of challenging communication strategies

LEADER: You have all identified at least one new communication strategy that you found help-ful. Which skills were more difficult to learn or to use?

MARY: I really didn't use **Put yourself in their shoes** *much. It was just really hard to remember to do, even if I meant to do it beforehand.*

LEADER: Thanks for sharing that, Mary. That was something we talked about a little bit in here. I remember that even when we planned a conversation, it was hard for you to use that technique, especially with your dad because you really didn't agree with him. Did anyone else find that strategy more difficult?

MICHAEL: That was hard for me, too.

LEADER: Sometimes, we focus so much on trying to get our point across, it can be hard to remember to take the other person's perspective. Farrah, I remember you saying that once you tried this strategy it was really helpful with your mom. How did you use **Put yourself in their shoes** *even when you did not totally agree with her?*

FARRAH: Well, it was hard at first, because I didn't want to acknowledge her side of things when she wouldn't let me go out after I failed my math test. But, once I told her that I understood why she was upset that I failed my math test, she was more willing to listen to me.

LEADER: Thanks, Farrah. Mary and Michael, does that make sense for you?

MARY: Yeah, that does make sense. Sometimes I just don't even know what my dad is thinking, so that makes it hard too.

LEADER: What can Mary do if she wants to use the skill **Put yourself in their shoes,** *but doesn't know what the other person thinks or feels about something?*

JESSICA: She could ask, right?

LEADER: Exactly. Mary, could you ask your dad what he is feeling?

MARY: I don't know; I guess so.

LEADER: It seems like this is something you're willing to try, but maybe it is hard to think of how to ask that. Let's take a minute and think of some ways Mary might ask her dad about his perspective. Who has an idea?

JESSICA: Could you say something like, "Dad, I really want to understand where you are coming from, but I am having a hard time with that. Can you explain why you feel that way?"

MARY: Yeah, I could say something like that. He would probably think it was pretty cool that I am interested in hearing what he has to say. A lot of times, I walk away while he is talking, and he hates that.

LEADER: I agree, I think parents really appreciate it when teens listen to them, so that makes a lot of sense. Let's practice quickly so you can become comfortable. Give us an example of a time when you might not understand where your dad is coming from, and we can set up a quick role play to help you ask him.

Address barriers to using interpersonal strategies. It is also helpful to talk about barriers to using interpersonal strategies. Some barriers have to do with the teen herself, such as reluctance to express feelings using *I statements* or difficulty taking others' perspectives as discussed previously. Another common barrier for teens to communicating effectively in relationships is not bringing up a topic because it feels uncomfortable to bring something up out of the blue. Teens learn to **Strike while the iron is cold** during group and not to say something when they are angry or upset. However, they sometimes struggle with whether it is a good idea to bring up an issue at a later date, worrying that doing so will create conflict when things are calm. It can be helpful for the group to talk through this concern and to think about the best way to balance the strategy of **Strike while the iron is cold** and the need to communicate about important topics that have an impact on their mood.

Other barriers relate to problems the other person in the relationship might be having, such as a parent who is depressed, a boyfriend or girlfriend who is unwilling to talk about certain things, or a friend who is too busy to have a conversation or spend more time together. The group can brainstorm ways of overcoming these barriers, such as introducing a conversation in a way that acknowledges to the other person that it may feel a little out of the blue, or conducting a decision analysis about who else teens can speak with if someone does not have the time or interest to talk about a problem. In addition, it may be helpful to initiate small role plays to see how these new approaches feel for the group members and to encourage them to try them out in their own relationships before the last group session. To increase motivation to overcome these barriers, it can be helpful to discuss how the teens' current ways of interacting in relationships may be contributing to sad or negative mood. The hope is that the new ways of handling relationships will be more effective, leading to an improvement in mood. This can be motivating for certain adolescents. An example of how the leader can facilitate a discussion of barriers to using interpersonal strategies is provided next.

Example: Barriers to using interpersonal strategies

LEADER: *We talked about communication strategies that were helpful and also some that were more difficult for each of you. For all of us, there can be other things that get in the way of communicating with people in our lives. Did any of you notice any barriers to giving these new ways of communicating a try?*

JESSICA: *Well, I was really worried that my friends wouldn't care or they wouldn't listen if I tried to talk to them, so it was hard to even bring things up.*

LEADER: *That is a common worry people have. What was it like when you finally did talk to your friend about wanting to spend more time together?*

JESSICA: *It actually went better than I thought. Even though we still aren't hanging out as much as I'd like, I was glad I said something.*

LEADER: *I'm glad to hear that it felt worth it in the end. How did you get yourself to have the conversation despite the worry?*

JESSICA: *I knew I was coming in here to group, so that motivated me to do it. I also wanted to make things better with my friend.*

LEADER: *What about for other people? Does that kind of worry get in the way of starting conversations for anyone else?*

MICHAEL: *Yeah, that's hard for me, too. I don't think I can tell my brother how much he bugs me. He would just get on my case more and think it was funny.*

LEADER: *It is tough when the other person won't listen, and unfortunately sometimes you can communicate in the best way possible and the other person still won't change what they are doing. What can Michael do if he tries talking to his brother and his brother reacts by think-ing it is funny or bugging him more?*

FARRAH: *He could try again another time or talk to his parents about it.*

MICHAEL: *I don't think I want to try talking to my brother again after last time, but maybe I could talk to my parents about it to see if they can help.*

LEADER: *That's a great idea. What about other people? Are there other things that get in the way for the rest of you?*

Closing tasks: emphasize importance of attending the last session, plan last group activi-ties, and assign interpersonal work at home. Group members should be encouraged to attend the final group session so that everyone can have a chance to wrap up and say good-bye. The leader can discuss with group members if they would like to have a special snack to celebrate the group ending and obtain teens' preferences for what they would like that to be. Sometimes, group members might like to do a special activity during or after the last group to celebrate. For instance, in one of our groups, teens asked to stay after group and listen to music and talk casually as a way of marking the end of the group. Other groups might decide that a special snack is enough.

If interpersonal issues were discussed at the start of the group session, teens should be encouraged to have planned conversations before the final group meeting. If particular barriers to using the communication strategies were addressed in the session, the leader can ask group members to try ways of overcoming these barriers so they can report back on these attempts in the final group session.

Group Session 8

Session goals and tasks. Session 8 provides teens with an opportunity to reflect on their own interpersonal accomplishments and to consider ongoing issues both in their use of commu-nication skills and in their relationships. The group begins somewhat differently, with teens reflecting on changes in mood ratings and symptoms over the course of the entire group, rather than sharing changes in mood over the past week. Because the group will discuss changes in mood and symptoms, it is helpful for the leader to review mood ratings and symptoms from prior weeks to guide how this discussion will proceed. For example, if teens endorsed many symptoms that decreased over time, the leader may choose to frame the discussion differently than if most teens had few symptoms to begin with and this remained stable over time.

Throughout the session, the leader seeks opportunities to highlight group members' ability to use communication strategies and problem-solving skills on their own to address relationship issues. The final activity is meant to help teens consider characteristics to look for in a friend or confidant. The leader should keep in mind that this activity can take a sig-nificant amount of time (approximately 30 minutes) and plan accordingly. At the end of the group, teens can take their binders home as a reminder of what they have learned.

Distribute binders and have adolescents complete depression checklist and mood rating. Teens complete the depression checklist and mood rating. The leader should review symp-toms and mood ratings.

Group Session 8 Checklist:

☐ Distribute binders and have adolescents complete depression checklist and mood rating

☐ Review changes in mood ratings and depression symptoms since the start of the group

☐ Identify warning symptoms and what adolescents should do if they experience these symptoms in the future

☐ Review interpersonal work at home assigned in the previous session (if needed)

☐ Identify the most significant interpersonal issue(s) each group member worked on

☐ Discuss how teens can maintain skills learned in the group

☐ Encourage continued interpersonal work on teens' goals as well as in future situations

☐ Using a group activity, discuss characteristics to look for in important people in teens' lives

☐ Discuss teens' experience of being in a group and elicit feedback

☐ Closing tasks: plan for booster sessions and have a graduation ceremony

Materials Needed:

☐ Binders and pens

☐ Communication strategy cue cards (see Appendix)

☐ Paper for teens to write down characteristics of group members

☐ Graduation certificates (see Appendix)

Review changes in mood ratings and depression symptoms since the start of the group. The verbal check-in at the start of this session is different from that in prior sessions, as the focus is on changes in mood and symptoms over the course of the entire group, rather than in the prior week. After teens have completed the checklist and mood ratings, they should be asked to look over their depression checklists for the past 8 weeks, paying attention to any changes that they notice. Group members can note changes in their symptoms and mood ratings and engage in a discussion about their observations. This discussion will look different depending on the level of symptoms endorsed during the group. If most teens have been circling Yes to at least a few symptoms, which is the case in most indicated prevention groups and some selective prevention groups, the leader can ask teens to focus on changes in mood ratings and symptoms, including which symptoms have changed and which have stayed the same, if any. If most teens in the group have not been endorsing symptoms over the course of the intervention, the leader can ask the teens to focus on changes in mood ratings over the eight sessions.

It is possible that some teens may experience a worsening of symptoms or may report fluctuations over the course of the group. The leader acknowledges each teen's experience and, if possible, helps link fluctuations in mood to events in relationships. For example, some teens may notice that worsening mood corresponded to weeks when they had more arguments with a parent. This information can be used to encourage continued work on the interpersonal relationships that are most closely linked to sad mood. To best facilitate this conversation, it is helpful for the leader to review each group member's weekly mood ratings and depression checklists before the start of the last group session. However, it is also important to continue to protect teens' privacy, being careful not to share anything that a teen does not discuss him- or herself.

Example: Discussing changes in mood and symptoms

LEADER: *This week we are going to start group a little differently. Instead of focusing on your mood this past week, I want you to take a minute and think back to the start of group. You can all use your binders to help you, too. What changes have you noticed in your mood and in your symptoms since the start of group?*

FARRAH: *My mood mostly stayed the same. I was feeling kind of okay when group started, and it is still kind of okay. I do see a week where my mood was worse though, about a month ago.*

LEADER: *Do you remember what was going on in your relationships around that time?*

FARRAH: *I think that was when I got into that fight with my mom about my grade in math, so that makes sense.*

LEADER: *You can see how that really affected your mood that week. But, once you addressed that and things got better, your mood improved pretty quickly. What about for other people?*

MICHAEL: *My mood got better at first, but for the past few weeks it actually got a little worse again.*

LEADER: *I'm sorry that you haven't seen your mood continue to improve. What do you think has been going on that has affected your mood more recently?*

MICHAEL: *Well, I have been pretty bummed that things haven't gotten too much better with my dad.*

LEADER: *That's something we can talk about later on in terms of what you'd like to keep working on after group ends, but I am glad you were able to make that connection. Once you know what is affecting your mood, it is easier to start thinking about what to do next.*

Identify warning symptoms and what adolescents should do if they experience these symptoms in the future. It is important to talk with group members about recognizing warning signs of depression so they are aware if they need help in the future. It is often helpful to use a metaphor, such as a check engine light in a car. If the check engine light goes on, the driver should not keep driving until the engine breaks down. Instead, it is important to get the car checked and get any needed repairs. This metaphor helps teens understand the importance of recognizing depression warning signs, which can be a signal to each person that he or she should check out what might be going on and take steps to resolve the problem, rather than waiting for the problem to go away on its own or get worse.

For indicated prevention groups or selective prevention groups in which teens endorse some symptoms, the leader should help teens identify which symptoms (based on their review discussed previously) are the best indicators for them that they might be developing depression. It is helpful to normalize that everyone has times when they feel down or sad for a couple of days, and this does not mean they are experiencing depression. It becomes more concerning when these feelings last longer than a couple of weeks or when a number of symptoms occur together. Teens should be encouraged to take notice of this if it happens so that they can address the problem.

For universal prevention groups or selective prevention groups where teens endorse relatively few symptoms, the leader should review the symptoms of depression with the group and discuss how these symptoms can be thought of as warning signs for depression. Teens can be asked if there are changes that they tend to notice when they feel down. Most teens can relate to this idea even if they have not had symptoms of depression per se. For example, some teens might report that they tend to sleep less when they feel down, while others might report that they get into more arguments with family members. If teens notice these symptoms in the future, that can be a sign for them that they should address whatever is bothering them.

For all types of groups, the leader should discuss with teens what they can do if they begin to experience these symptoms in the future. This should be an interactive discussion, so that teens generate ideas with the help of the group leader. During this discussion, the leader highlights the following steps that teens can take if they start to notice some of these warning signs: think about what is going on in their lives and whether it would be helpful to talk to someone to address an interpersonal problem or get support; think about how the interpersonal strategies may be helpful; or use other problem-solving or coping strategies if the issue is not best addressed by talking to someone directly (e.g., spending more time with friends, listening to music, etc.). If the symptoms persist despite these efforts, teens should be encouraged to tell a parent or another appropriate adult who can get them help before the symptoms become more severe and impairing. This can be a school counselor, teacher, coach, or other trusted adult if teens do not feel comfortable talking to their parents. Again, it is helpful for the leader to emphasize that it is normal to feel sad at times, and everyone can have a bad day or a bad week. However, if low mood or other symptoms of depression persist (i.e., for 2 weeks or more) or if symptoms are severe (i.e., suicidality or self-harm), it is important to talk to an adult.

Example: Warning symptoms

LEADER: *Now that you have all reviewed your symptoms and mood ratings over the course of the group, I want everyone to think about which symptoms you tend to notice most when you are feeling down. This will give you a good idea of what to look for in the future. Jessica, looking back to when group started, what symptoms of depression did you tend to circle Yes for?*

JESSICA: *Well, I didn't want to hang out with friends anymore. They would call and ask me to do something, and I'd say no. I just wanted to be in my room.*

LEADER: *So, for you, wanting to be by yourself was a real sign that something wasn't right. What else?*

JESSICA: *I felt like crying, even about little things.*

LEADER: *Your warning signs included not wanting to be with friends and crying a lot. That means that, in the future, if you start crying a lot and feel like you want to be alone, it would be a sign for you that perhaps you are becoming depressed. It would be a sign that it might be time to get help. What are other people's warning signs? [After a discussion of each group member's warning signs, the leader should move to a discussion of what group members can do when they notice warning signs.]*

LEADER: *Each of you has identified at least one warning sign for depression. It is normal for everyone to feel sad sometimes, and even to have some of these other symptoms, like having trouble concentrating. But, if that goes on for a while, like more than a week, that might be a sign that there is something more going on than just a bad day or a bad week. You can think of this like a check engine light on a car. Does anyone have an idea of what you should do when the check engine light comes on?*

RYAN: *You should make sure your car is okay, probably.*

LEADER: *Exactly. You don't want to ignore the check engine light, because the problem could get worse. Rather than waiting for things to get worse, it's always a good idea to do something about it right away, like bringing it to a mechanic. I want to help you all think of the steps you can take if your check engine light goes on and you start to notice symptoms of depression in yourself. What might be the first thing you should do if you start experiencing symptoms?*

MARY: *You could talk to someone.*

LEADER: *That's a great idea! So, one thing you could do is think about your relationships and figure out if something is going on with someone important to you that may be affecting your mood. You might want to talk to them or come up with some ways to solve the problem. Or, you could talk to another person who could help you solve the problem. What if you do all that, and you still feel down?*

RYAN: *I like to listen to music when I'm upset. That usually helps.*

LEADER: *That's another good point. Sometimes if you are having a bad day, doing something on your own to boost your mood can help. For some people, that is listening to music; for other people watching a movie, seeing friends, or doing something active like playing a sport or going for a walk outside can help. What if that also doesn't help enough?*

FARRAH: *You could talk to a friend; that usually helps me.*

LEADER: *Yes, that is true; friends can definitely help. What if that doesn't help enough? Is there an adult that you can each talk to if you continue to feel down after trying some of these other ideas?*

JESSICA: *I could talk to my mom.*

MICHAEL: *I don't know; I don't think I would talk to my parents about how I feel. They wouldn't understand.*

LEADER: *What about someone at school, maybe a counselor or a teacher?*

MICHAEL: *I don't know the counselor too well, but my Spanish teacher is really nice. I think she would listen.*

Review interpersonal work at home assigned in the previous session (if needed). It is important to review any interpersonal work at home so that group members have a chance to share accomplishments or difficulties, and so they can receive feedback from the group to help them continue improving their relationships. Given that this is the last session and there are termination-specific tasks that need to be completed, this review should be briefer than in previous sessions and should focus on the group members' ability to do this work independently. There will likely not be time to talk at length about next steps or to consider how a teen could have communicated differently in a given situation.

Identify the most significant interpersonal issue(s) each group member worked on. The leader asks each teen to share the most significant issue that they worked on during the group. This includes specifying the problem, the steps or strategies the adolescent used to solve the problem, and the teen's successes. It is important to emphasize the significance of the successes, helping teens to recognize how they contributed to changes in relationships through their utilization of communication skills outside the sessions, without the immediate presence of the leader or other group members. This will bolster group members' sense of mastery if teens have truly made progress in their communication and their interpersonal goals.

In a group where teens have been engaged and have made significant changes, the group leader may begin this discussion by asking teens to share aloud what they have accomplished during the group. This is more difficult to do in groups where some group members have been reluctant to try out new strategies or where there have been fewer obvious successes. In this case, it is useful to point out smaller accomplishments that adolescents have made in communicating with certain people, adjusting expectations about a situation, or modifying their behavior so that they do not make a situation worse. The leader can also underscore strategies or specific relationships that group members can continue to work on. The following example highlights how the language is different for a group member who made significant changes in relationships as compared to an adolescent who made smaller changes:

Example: Review of changes in interpersonal relationships

LEADER: *Ryan, what do you think has changed the most about your relationships since you started group?*

RYAN: *Well, my mom and I have stopped fighting all the time. She doesn't annoy me as much as she used to, and because I am going to school more, she has stopped getting mad at me for skipping school.*

LEADER: *How have these changes affected your mood?*

RYAN: *I've been feeling better. I am not in a bad mood all the time. I can pay attention in school, too, maybe because I'm sleeping better.*

LEADER: *So, things have gotten better with your mom, and you have been feeling better. Partly this is because you are going to school, which helps you get along better with your mom. Ryan, of the strategies we learned, which was most useful for your relationship with your mom?*

RYAN: *I am not really sure.*

LEADER: *One thing you really worked on in here is finding the right time to talk to your mom when you can talk calmly.*

RYAN: *Yeah. I used to yell at her and say things I regretted. Now, I wait until I feel calmer before I try to talk to her.*

LEADER: *That's right. That is a big change. Michael, what have you noticed that has changed since the start of group?*

MICHAEL: *Well, not much has really changed with my dad. I still don't get to see him too much, even though I tried to talk to him about it.*

LEADER: *I know it was disappointing to you that your dad hasn't followed through on some of the plans you made. One thing I noticed that was a change for you, though, was that you were able to tell your dad how you felt and that you want to spend more time with him.*

MICHAEL: *That's true; I never did that before.*

LEADER: *How did you feel after you talked to him that time?*

MICHAEL: *I did feel better, knowing that at least I tried. But, then I felt upset later when he didn't follow through.*

LEADER: *That is frustrating. But, I remember you saying in here that it felt good to let him know how you felt. Sometimes, one or even two conversations isn't enough to change a relationship, and sometimes other people don't follow up on their end even if you say everything you want to say. We talked a couple of weeks ago about some ways you could follow up with your dad. Now that you have all of these communication skills under your belt, I am confident that you can try some of those strategies on your own.*

MICHAEL: *Yeah, I guess I can try talking to him one more time and see what happens.*

LEADER: *Who could you talk to that might be able to help you think through what you want to say?*

MICHAEL: *Well, maybe my mom. She knows how he is, and she has seen how upset I've been, so I think she would help.*

If the target relationship is more difficult, use of the communication strategies and interpersonal problem-solving skills may not have resulted in actual changes in the relationship. However, the teen may have changed how he or she coped with the relationship, such that it no longer leads to negative feelings. This is an important point to emphasize, given that teens who have more difficult relationships might feel discouraged as they hear about more significant changes in others' relationships. The leader can help these teens to recognize important gains they made in terms of their own reactions to difficult relationships or increasing support from other people in their lives.

The group can also discuss how adolescents' participation in the group may have resulted in changes in the behavior of other people in their lives. The leader can help teens to recognize how making changes in their interpersonal behavior or in the way they communicated led to changes in other people's behavior, which led to further changes in how the group members behaved and felt. In cases where significant others did not change their behavior, emphasize that teens learned how to cope better with these difficult situations and as a result feel better.

Example: Making connections to changes in others' behavior

LEADER: *Ryan, do you remember saying at the beginning of group that there was no way your mom was going to change?*

RYAN: *Yeah, I remember.*

LEADER: *You were just telling us about how things have changed between the two of you. It sounded like your mom was acting differently toward you, too, as a result of some of the changes you made. Is that right?*

RYAN: *Yeah, she has seemed more interested in what is going on with me, in more of a good way. And, she doesn't assume that I didn't do my homework like she used to. Now, she asks me instead of starting to yell at me right off the bat.*

LEADER: *That is a pretty big change! This is an example of how we can change how other people act toward us by first changing how we act toward them. Ryan, it is great that the changes you made also really affected your mom's behavior. You all have the skills to continue this work after group ends.*

Discuss how teens can maintain skills learned in the group. The leader should help teens identify ways to maintain what they learned during the course of group. For instance, some teens have talked about role playing in front of a mirror, writing down what they want to say, or planning a conversation as they would in group. It might also be helpful for teens to identify a family member, friend, or someone else who can be a source of encouragement for their continued work on improving their relationships. Depending on the setting, it might be appropriate to suggest that group members continue to be a resource for each other to remember interpersonal skills or plan a conversation in advance. The leader can suggest using binders and cue cards, which teens will be taking home as a reminder of how to communicate differently. The leader can ask group members if they can anticipate any potential obstacles to continued use of the communication strategies and problem-solving skills and how these might be overcome.

Encourage continued interpersonal work on teens' goals as well as in future situations. Group members can also identify how they can continue working on their interpersonal relationships, either by continuing to work on the relationships related to their interpersonal goals or by generalizing these skills to other relationships or future interpersonal challenges. For some groups, teens have only begun to work on their interpersonal goals. In this case, the discussion can focus on how group members have the tools to continue this work on their own. It is useful to frame this as a beginning rather than an ending of the interpersonal work.

For groups where there has been more interpersonal work accomplished, the leader can ask teens to identify future situations that might be difficult for them interpersonally or emotionally. This is often difficult for teens to do unless the group leader provides guidance. Often, teens relate to future difficulties framed in terms of transitions, such as summer vacation, transitioning to a new grade or a new school, changes in friendships, breakups, or siblings leaving the home. The group can then discuss how the strategies learned may be helpful for these future situations. The leader should emphasize that because of their new skills, group members can successfully apply new approaches to problems without the help of the group.

Example: Future situations

LEADER: *We talked about what you all have accomplished in group and how you can continue to work on your relationships after group ends. Let's think through any future situations*

*that might be difficult. For example, some of you are starting high school next year, and that
can be a challenge. Can anyone think of something coming up that might be hard?*

MICHAEL: *I'm going to high school next year, but I'm not worried about it.*

LEADER: *What about over the summer, any worries about that?*

FARRAH: *Yeah, I am worried that things will get worse with my mom because we will be spending a lot of time together. She really gets on my nerves sometimes, especially if I have to see
her a lot.*

LEADER: *What do you think you can do to make this situation better?*

FARRAH: *I don't know.*

LEADER: *Do any of you have ideas?*

JESSICA: *You can schedule things to do so you're not home the whole day.*

RYAN: *If you get upset with your mom, you should let her know what's bothering you and maybe
the two of you can work it out.*

LEADER: *Those are both good ideas. I like the idea of addressing problems early when they come
up so that they don't get worse. What do you think, Farrah?*

Discuss characteristics to look for in important people in teens' lives using a group activity.
An important discussion during the last group session concerns recognizing what makes
a person a good friend or someone teens would want to confide in. The leader should help
teens recognize how they developed relationships in the group and how group members can
use these same skills to develop new relationships outside the group. Part of this discussion is
identifying the characteristics of group members that made them supportive, which can lead
to a conversation about qualities to look for in new friends or when deciding which friend
might be a source of support.

One way to initiate this conversation is by using an exercise where teens are asked to
write down a positive characteristic of each group member (including the leader). To facilitate this, the group leader can give each teen a stack of papers with the names of each group
member on top. Teens should be instructed to write something on each person's piece of
paper that made that person a good member of the group, in order to elicit the types of
characteristics they would look for in a friend. The leader should also write something about
each group member to provide meaningful positive feedback about the work each teen has
done in group. It can also be helpful to have teens write something positive about themselves
to facilitate acknowledgment of their positive contributions. This can be a powerful exercise
for the adolescents in terms of recognizing the connections they have made to other teens in
the group, as well as identifying their own strengths.

The leader should collect all of the papers and read the characteristics written about
each group participant aloud to the group. This provides each group member with individualized positive feedback, without identifying who wrote each comment. It is advisable for
the leader to review what group members wrote in advance in case there is critical or inappropriate content. If this happens, the leader can instead choose only a few comments to read
aloud for each teen rather than reading all of the comments that were written about each
group member. This way, only the most positive and helpful statements are shared. Another
option, if the leader anticipates that people will not have enough to say about a quiet or

disruptive group member, is for the leader to read a subset of the statements anonymously, without identifying who each statement is about or who wrote it. For instance, the leader might say the following: "You've all written some really nice things about the other group members. Some of the characteristics you listed include 'gave good advice,' 'has a good sense of humor,' 'listened to my problems,' 'was thoughtful,' 'helped me out,' and more. Those are some really important qualities that you have all brought to the group." This should only be done if the leader notices large discrepancies in comments made about different group members, as it removes the element of specific positive feedback from the activity.

This activity helps bolster group members' self-esteem and provides group members with positive feedback. It also helps the leader to initiate a discussion about important characteristics to look for in a friend. In reflecting on this exercise, the leader highlights common characteristics that group members identified during the activity. These will likely include good listening skills, emotional availability, physical proximity, trustworthiness, and the ability to maintain privacy or keep secrets. The group can then discuss how teens should look for these qualities in the people they choose to confide in or become close with in the future.

Discuss teens' experience of being in a group and elicit feedback. Teens can be asked to reflect on both positive and negative aspects of being in the group, with a focus on (a) getting enough attention for their own problems; (b) learning by hearing about others' experiences; (c) learning to role play different ways of interacting and communicating; (d) making friends with other teens; (e) dealing with the time-limited nature of the group; and (f) sharing personal feelings or experiences with peers. The leader should encourage teens to talk about what it might be like not to have the group every week and how they might use this time when the group ends.

It is important to normalize both positive and negative reactions to the group ending. While some teens are likely to feel ready for the group to be over, others might be nervous about handling certain interpersonal issues on their own. The leader can assure teens that having negative feelings is normal and remind them of the earlier discussions in group about their ability to continue the work outside the group. This is also a good time to ask adolescents for feedback or suggestions of things they would have liked to have been different in the group to inform any changes to the group the next time it is offered.

Closing tasks: plan for booster sessions and have graduation ceremony. If booster sessions will be offered, the leader can remind all of the group members about this and describe the timeline as well as any important details about where and when these will take place. It is helpful to provide teens with a brief description of these sessions so that they know what to expect. In particular, the leader should let teens know that each group member will meet with the leader individually, rather than in a group format. The session will begin by reviewing the adolescent's depression symptoms and mood rating and then talking about how the teen's relationships have been going, particularly those relationships that are related to the teen's goals for group. The bulk of the session will be spent working on any ongoing interpersonal issues. The leader should provide a rationale for booster sessions to increase motivation to attend. The leader conveys that booster sessions are intended to help teenagers to continue working on their relationships. By continuing to improve their relationships, the preventive effects of this program are more likely to persist. In addition, booster sessions can be used to apply the communication strategies to new situations that might arise after the group has ended. This provides opportunities for teens to generalize the skills they learned in the group to new situations that might differ from those they worked on during the group.

A positive way to end the group is with a graduation-type ceremony, where the leader hands out certificates (see Appendix) for completing the group to reward teens for their attendance and hard work. This can be emphasized as much or as little as the leader feels is appropriate for a particular group. One way to elaborate on this ceremony is to give out personalized awards to each teen, based on their strengths or accomplishments in the group (e.g., one group member could receive a coaching award for being a helpful volunteer to coach other group members during role plays; another might receive the best actor award for his or her role-playing abilities). Having some type of graduation ceremony serves to end the experience on a positive note and recognizes the effort that the teens put into the group. Before saying good-bye to group members, the leader should give group members their binders and cue cards to bring home to remind them of the skills that they learned.

Summary of the Termination Phase

The termination phase prepares teens to end the group with the knowledge that they are capable of continuing interpersonal work on their own. The leader helps group members to both reflect on accomplishments and consider areas for continued work. The leader emphasizes that while the group is coming to an end, this is a starting point for continued growth in the adolescents' relationships. Given their knowledge of the communication strategies and problem-solving skills, the adolescents have the ability to continue this work independently (with help from the leader during booster sessions if these will be offered). The leader can also begin to consider issues that might be helpful for teens to work on during booster sessions.

IPT-AST Booster Sessions

9

Booster sessions are offered to extend the effects of the group and individual sessions of Interpersonal Psychotherapy – Adolescent Skills Training (IPT-AST) and to help teens apply interpersonal strategies to new situations. Three or four individual booster sessions are recommended in the 6 months following completion of the group. The frequency and number of sessions are flexible, based on the adolescent's needs and the availability of the leader. For instance, although we typically suggest three to four booster sessions, the leader may decide to offer additional booster sessions or may decide to check in with the adolescent periodically to assess the need for additional services. We recommend that booster sessions be conducted individually both for ease of scheduling and to allow adolescents to do targeted work on interpersonal issues. However, the leader may decide to hold booster sessions in a group format instead if this is desirable in a particular setting. If booster sessions are offered in a group format, we recommend adapting the outline that follows to facilitate group-based work on interpersonal goals, as described in the middle phase in Chapter 6.

As discussed in Chapter 13, studies of IPT-AST have found strong immediate effects of the program on depressive symptoms, anxiety symptoms, overall functioning, and social functioning, but the benefits are not consistent beyond 6 months following the intervention. This suggests the need for booster sessions to lengthen the effects of IPT-AST. Based on these findings and the recommendations of others (e.g., Merry, 2007), we have added booster sessions in our most recent studies of IPT-AST. We do not yet have data on whether these booster sessions lengthen the effects of the program, but our clinical experience indicates that these sessions are beneficial, particularly for the subset of adolescents who report ongoing interpersonal difficulties.

The purpose of the booster sessions is to check how the adolescent is doing, identify any current interpersonal problems, review the communication strategies and interpersonal problem-solving skills learned in group, and discuss how these strategies generalize to current interpersonal difficulties. Some teens have done their most significant interpersonal work during booster sessions, either because they were not yet ready to address some issues during the group phase or because they were not comfortable discussing certain topics with the group. Other teens may have accomplished a great deal during the group and have difficulty identifying additional issues to work on during boosters. Given that the original goals might not be relevant for the teen by this point, it can be useful for the leader to review notes from the interpersonal inventory and mid-group session in advance to identify relationships that the leader might ask about other than those related to the adolescent's interpersonal goals for group. This will make it easier for the leader to probe for other interpersonal issues if the teen does not spontaneously identify something to work on.

Booster Sessions

> **Booster Session Checklist:**
> ☐ Assess mood rating over the past month
> ☐ Assess depression symptoms over the past week
> ☐ Review progress made on interpersonal goals and discuss emerging interpersonal issues
> ☐ Discuss how communication strategies and interpersonal problem-solving skills from group can be used to address interpersonal problems and script and role play a conversation if applicable
> ☐ Closing tasks: assign interpersonal work at home and discuss the possibility of worsening symptoms
>
> **Materials Needed:**
> ☐ Communication strategy cue cards (see Appendix)

Session goals and tasks. The primary task of each booster session is for the leader to help the adolescent work on a current interpersonal issue. The booster sessions are not intended to consist of the adolescent recounting everything that has happened in the past month, as this will be much less beneficial for the teen than targeted work on an interpersonal issue. Thus, it is important that the leader structure the booster sessions to be most productive. Some adolescents will continue working on their interpersonal goals for group, while others will have resolved those issues and will instead work on other interpersonal relationships.

The format of the booster sessions closely resembles the middle phase sessions. The leader begins by assessing the adolescent's depressive symptoms and getting a mood rating and then reviews the adolescent's significant interpersonal relationships to identify an interpersonal problem to work on in the remainder of the session. If a specific issue is identified, the leader asks questions to learn more about the situation and then proceeds to work on the identified problem using a combination of IPT-AST techniques (e.g., communication analysis, decision analysis, scripting, and role playing). If a specific issue is not identified, the leader and teen review the communication and problem-solving strategies from the group and then discuss the application of these strategies in the past month, to future interactions, or with hypothetical situations that are particularly relevant for the adolescent.

Assess mood rating over the past month. The leader should begin by asking the teen to rate his or her mood, assessing the average mood rating over the past month as well as over the past week using the 1–10 scale described in Chapter 4. The following questions can be used to assess variations in mood over those two time frames: Was there a period of time when the teen felt significantly worse than the average? What was the mood rating then? Can the teen relate the worsening of mood to any specific interpersonal event? This discussion not only allows the leader to assess the teen's mood over the past month but also provides the first opportunity to note any interpersonal issues that might be relevant to discuss in more depth later in the session.

Assess depression symptoms over the past week. Next, it is important to assess current symptoms of depression that the teen has experienced in the past week. The leader takes note of any significant symptoms and asks follow-up questions about any areas of concern. This should take no longer than 5–10 minutes to complete, unless the teen is experiencing significant symptoms and more time needs to be spent assessing the need for crisis intervention or additional noncrisis services. If the teen reported having a time when he or she felt much worse than currently, it may also be helpful to briefly assess the teen's symptoms at that time, particularly assessing any suicidal ideation. More information on assessing symptoms of depression is provided in Chapter 3. We include a list of symptoms here for the leader's reference. Symptoms of depression include the following:

- Feeling sad, bored, or irritable most of the time
- Not being interested in things you used to like doing
- Difficulty sleeping or sleeping too much
- Feeling slowed down or restless
- Increase or decrease in appetite
- Feeling tired
- Difficulty concentrating or making decisions
- Feeling worthless or guilty
- Thoughts of death

Review progress made on interpersonal goals and discuss emerging interpersonal issues. The next step is to check in with the teen about changes in the teen's relationships since the last meeting. The leader should ask the teen to remember his or her interpersonal goals for the group and ask about progress related to these goals. In many cases, particularly when a long time has lapsed since the final group session, the teen will need to be reminded of interpersonal goals. The leader and the adolescent should collaboratively decide whether there are issues related to the original interpersonal goals that the teen would like to work on.

During later booster sessions, it is likely that the teen's original goals will no longer be relevant. If this is the case, the leader can help the teen identify other interpersonal issues that would be useful for the teen to discuss. This can be accomplished by asking open-ended questions, targeted questions about any issues the adolescent brought up during the mood check-in, or questions about relationships the leader is aware of from either the pre-group sessions or the group sessions that might be relevant for the teen to work on.

Example: Reviewing progress on goals

LEADER: *Jennifer, do you remember what your goals were for the group?*

JENNIFER: *To feel better.*

LEADER: *You are right; that was the overall goal for the group. Do you remember more specifically what goals you had related to your relationships?*

JENNIFER: *I remember I wanted to work on telling my mom how I was feeling, especially about how tough it was to start high school.*

LEADER: *That's right; that was one of your goals. How has that been for you since the group ended?*

JENNIFER: *Well, I really like high school now.*

LEADER: *That's great to hear. Did you end up talking to your mom at all about that since the end of group? I know that you had planned a conversation with her, but last time we checked in, you hadn't spoken to her about that.*

JENNIFER: *Well, I didn't end up saying anything, because things started just getting better.*

LEADER: *Okay, that makes sense. Have you noticed other situations where it has been difficult to tell your mom or anyone else about how you are feeling?*

JENNIFER: *Well, I have been having a problem with my one friend, Lily. She started dating this guy, and now she doesn't spend as much time with us. I want to be happy for her, but at the same time, I miss her. I haven't really talked with anyone about it.*

LEADER: *That sounds like a tough situation. It might be something we can talk more about today if you think that would be helpful. Before we do that, I wondered if things had changed at all with your mom, in terms of being able to talk to her.*

JENNIFER: *No, that's been pretty much the same.*

LEADER: *Okay, so we can think about whether that is still an important goal for you. Do you remember your other goal for group?*

JENNIFER: *I think it was about my friend, Sarah, but I don't remember what I wanted to work on exactly. Things are good between us now.*

LEADER: *That is great to hear that things are good. When we first met, you felt like you had drifted apart and wanted to spend more time with her. Have you been able to see her more since then?*

JENNIFER: *Yeah. We actually have started talking more, and I get to see her sometimes on the weekend.*

LEADER: *That is great to hear. So, it sounds like the two things that are going on at this point is that you still find it hard to talk to your mom about feelings, and you also have this issue with your friend Lily where she started dating this guy. Are either of those things something you would want to work on today, or is there something else that we haven't talked about yet that would be even more helpful?*

JENNIFER: *This thing with Lily is really bothering me now, and I don't know about talking to my mom. So, maybe we can talk about Lily today.*

LEADER: *We can certainly talk about your friend Lily today if that would be most helpful, but I know that things with your mom have been on your mind for a long time. What makes you hesitate to talk about your mom today?*

JENNIFER: *Well, I do want to work on talking to my mom about things that bother me. But, lately I have been pretty happy. I'm getting along okay in my new school. So, I guess it just hasn't felt so important to talk to her.*

LEADER: *I can understand how it might seem like less of a priority right now because you don't feel like you need your mom's support as much at the moment. Would it be helpful to talk to your mom about wanting to be able to open up to her more in general?*

JENNIFER: *I don't know; it might be. I was really hoping to talk about Lily, though; that has really been on my mind.*

LEADER: *Okay, let's start there. If we have time, we can also talk a bit about how to apply some of our communication strategies to help you talk to your mom. What are your thoughts about what you want to do about your friend Lily?*

JENNIFER: *Well, I guess I could talk to Lily, but I'm worried she'll just think I am jealous or tell me that I should be happy for her. I am happy for her, but I don't know why she has to spend all of her time with Jim. I don't think it is worth talking to her about it. She's so excited about this new relationship that I am not sure she is even interested in spending time with anyone other than Jim.*

LEADER: *It sounds like you are not sure you are ready to talk to Lily. What else could you do?*

JENNIFER: *I think that my friend Connie is upset about it, too. It used to be the three of us hanging out all of the time. So, I think she would understand how I am feeling. Maybe I can talk to her.*

LEADER: *That sounds like a good place to start. Let's think through what you can say to Connie. Do you remember the strategies we talked about in group?*

JENNIFER: *Yeah, I think so:* **Strike while the iron is cold***;* **Have a few solutions in mind***;* **I statements***;* **Don't give up***;* **Put yourself in their shoes***; and . . .*

LEADER: *The last one was "Be . . ."*

JENNIFER: **Be specific***?*

LEADER: *Exactly. Great memory! Do you think any of these might be helpful as you think about having a conversation with Connie?*

Discuss how communication strategies and interpersonal problem-solving skills from group can be used to address interpersonal problems and script and role play a conversation if applicable. If the adolescent has something specific to work on, the leader can help the teen identify appropriate strategies to address the interpersonal problem, script what the teen might say in a conversation, and then role play the interaction. When appropriate, the leader can encourage the teen to have a conversation with the other person as practiced during the role play as a work-at-home assignment. This discussion should follow the same framework used in the middle phase group sessions and individual mid-group sessions:

1. Identify an interpersonal situation to work on
2. Conduct a communication analysis to learn more about relevant prior interactions
3. Use decision analysis (if needed) to consider how best to resolve the interpersonal situation

4. Help the teen clarify the goals for a future conversation, as well as the main message the teen wants to convey

5. Discuss how the communication strategies can be used to increase the likelihood of a successful interaction

6. Script the conversation in detail

7. Role play the conversation and debrief about how it went

8. Assign the teen work at home to have the conversation

Some teens may avoid working on their interpersonal goals, even though the leader believes they would benefit from working on those relationships. In those cases, the leader can initiate a discussion about barriers the teen might face in using interpersonal strategies in their relationships. After helping the teen identify ways to overcome those barriers, the leader can transition into talking in depth about an interpersonal issue to address. For instance, some teens may be reluctant to communicate their feelings to others in their lives, believing that it will not make a difference. It may be helpful for the leader to conduct a decision analysis with the teen about continuing the way he or she has been interacting in relationships or trying something new. During the decision analysis, the leader should help the adolescent recognize the cons of the status quo, including highlighting how this pattern of interaction is contributing to sad mood and other symptoms of depression. This can help motivate the teen to work on these relationships in the remaining booster sessions.

In other cases, teens may have no pressing interpersonal issues to discuss. There are several options to maximize the time when the adolescent does not identify an interpersonal situation to work on. One option is for the leader to review the communication strategies with the adolescent. It is helpful to first ask the adolescent to name the skills he or she learned during the group. This can be presented in a fun, game-like fashion, and leaders should help the teen if the teen cannot remember some of the skills. Next, the leader can ask the teen to explain what each of the strategies means and then whether the adolescent has used the skills since the last group meeting or the previous booster session. If so, it is helpful to elicit examples from the teen, both to help the teen recognize times when he or she has used the communication strategies successfully and to provide opportunities for the leader to correct misunderstandings about any of the skills. For teens who had difficulty understanding the skills or applying them, this individualized review can be productive. Another useful discussion is whether any of these strategies might be helpful in upcoming interpersonal situations. This provides opportunities to help the teen think about how these skills apply to particular situations relevant to the teen.

During this discussion, the leader should make use of any opportunities the adolescent presents to initiate a more detailed discussion of ways that the teen has already made use of the skills or ways that the teen can apply the skills to a current or future interpersonal situation. If both opportunities arise, it is best to focus on a current or future interpersonal situation as this allows the leader and teen to script and role play a proactive conversation. This provides useful practice even if the teen is unsure whether or not he or she will have the conversation outside the session.

Example: Detailed skill review with transition to relevant situation

LEADER: Because things are better with your mom and there aren't any other issues you'd like to discuss, let's spend some time reviewing the communication skills you learned in group. First, let's see how many you can name.

JENNIFER: I remember most of them, I think. There was **Strike while the iron is cold** *. . .* **Be specific . . . I statements . . . Put yourself in their shoes** *. . .*

LEADER: That's great! There are two more to go.

JENNIFER: Something about having some ideas before you start the conversation.

LEADER: That's right. **Have a few solutions in mind and remember to compromise.** *Just one more left. It started with "Don't."*

JENNIFER: Hmm, I can't quite remember it.

LEADER: That's okay; you did a great job. The last one is **Don't give up.** *Let's review what those mean. What does* **Strike while the iron is cold** *mean?*

JENNIFER: That one was about talking to someone when they're not too mad or upset.

LEADER: That's right. We also talked about making sure that you are not too mad or upset and making sure both of you aren't busy or distracted. Since our last meeting, when have you thought about using **Strike while the iron is cold?**

JENNIFER: Well, I did have to ask my mom if I could bring a friend with me when we went to the beach for the weekend over the summer. I was nervous about it, so I waited until she was in a really good mood to ask. So, I guess I thought about it then.

LEADER: That's a great example! Did it make a difference when you used **Strike while the iron is cold?**

JENNIFER: Yeah, I think so, because she said yes and I had a great time because I didn't have to just hang out with my brother the whole time.

LEADER: That's great. Thinking about things that are coming up now that you started school again, are there any times you think this skill will be useful for you in the next month or so?

JENNIFER: Well, I have been thinking about trying out for basketball, but I know my mom is really worried about me focusing on schoolwork now that I'm in high school. I want to ask her, but I think she might say no, so I should probably try to find a time when she's in a good mood for that, too.

LEADER: That sounds like a good idea. Because you're nervous about the conversation, would it be helpful to think about how you could use the other skills to make that conversation also go better?

JENNIFER: Okay.

LEADER: Great. First, let's think of what you want to accomplish in this conversation. What do you hope to get out of the conversation?

JENNIFER: I want her to let me try out. But, for now, I'd be happy if she would agree to think about it. I have a month before tryouts so she doesn't have to agree right away.

LEADER: That's great. So, that brings us back to **Strike while the iron is cold**. *When might be a good time to talk to her, knowing your mom?*

JENNIFER: Well, I guess I would want to wait for her to be in a good mood again. Maybe this weekend because I know she has some free time on Saturday.

LEADER: Great. That sounds like a good idea. What else do you think would be important in this conversation with your mom?

JENNIFER: Well, because I know that she is worried about me focusing on school, maybe I can put myself in her shoes to let her know I get that, and then I can think of some ways to make sure I keep my grades up during basketball season.

LEADER: Those are two great ideas. So, you want to use **Put yourself in their shoes,** *and then it sounds like you want to* **Have a few solutions in mind**. *Let's think of where you can start and how you want to phrase those ideas.*

Another option is to review skills as described previously and then ask the adolescent to script and role play a conversation that applies to a hypothetical situation. This is most effective when the hypothetical situation is closely related to a current or anticipated future interpersonal issue for the adolescent. Scenarios from group session 2, which are provided in the Appendix, can be used as guides, but situations should be customized to be most relevant for the adolescent. It is useful for the leader to offer two or three options of hypothetical situations to discuss, reminding the teen that this is a chance to practice applying skills, and the teen will not be expected to necessarily have the conversation in real life if it is not currently relevant. The process of planning and practicing the conversation will be the same as for other types of conversations. Again, the leader can maximize the effectiveness of the session by listening for opportunities to move the discussion to a current interpersonal situation that the adolescent might bring up during the conversation. An example of this situation is provided next:

Example: Transitioning from a hypothetical to a real interpersonal situation

LEADER: Because things have really improved with the two goals you set at the start of group, and there isn't any other issue you want to work on right now in your relationships, let's think of something we can work on together so we can make this session the most helpful for you today.

MICHAEL: Okay. That sounds all right.

LEADER: So, I have two ideas for things that I know aren't big problems now, but maybe we can think about one of them together for the sake of practice. One idea would be to think about how to ask your mom for permission or a ride to see friends because the school year is almost over and you might want to get together with people once you aren't seeing them at school every day. Another idea I have is thinking about how you could speak up if you feel left out by your friends in the future, say, if they end up going out and doing something and don't invite you. Which of those situations sounds like it would be most helpful to talk about today?

MICHAEL: Hmm, I don't know. I guess we can talk about that kind of situation with friends.

LEADER: So, let's imagine that your friends went out and did something and didn't invite you. Which friends might do that, and what might they do?

MICHAEL: *Well, sometimes that happens with my friends Joseph and Eric. Actually, last weekend I found out Joseph went over to Eric's house to play video games and neither of them called me.*

LEADER: *I can imagine that didn't feel very good. How did you feel about that? How did you find out that happened?*

MICHAEL: *Well, they were talking about how they reached a higher level on this game we all play on Monday. I didn't say anything to them about it, but it kind of bothered me a little.*

LEADER: *Okay, because this really happened this week, would it be okay if we focus on that situation today? Maybe we can think of some ideas of what you could do to address it, and then you can decide whether you want to use any of those ideas to talk to Joseph or Eric.*

MICHAEL: *Yeah, that would be okay. I'm not sure if I want to say anything to them, but we can talk about it.*

LEADER: *Before we think about what you might want to do next, help me understand the situation better. What are you most concerned about?*

Closing tasks: assign interpersonal work at home and discuss the possibility of worsening symptoms. If the teen worked on a particular interpersonal issue in the booster session, the leader should encourage the teen to have the planned conversation in the next couple of weeks, before the next booster session. The leader informs the teen that he or she will be excited to hear about the work at home in the next session. Even if the adolescent did not work on an interpersonal issue, the teen should be encouraged to use the strategies in between sessions and to continue to pay attention to how relationships affect mood and vice versa. Toward the end of the session, the leader reminds the adolescent when the next booster session will be and what to do in between sessions if the teen notices a worsening of symptoms. This can include a reminder about his or her particular warning signs and who the teen can talk to if the teen starts to notice those warning signs before the next booster session.

Closing tasks for the final booster session. If this is the last booster session, the leader should again review the symptoms of depression that might signal to the teen that he or she is feeling worse. The leader reminds the teen to talk to a parent or school counselor if he or she notices symptoms of depression, so that the teen can get help before the symptoms become more severe. This is also a time to consider offering more booster sessions or referrals if the leader thinks the adolescent would benefit from additional services. Teens should generally be reminded that they have learned interpersonal problem-solving and communication strategies that will allow them to solve interpersonal problems on their own.

An empowering way to end the final booster session is to review the teen's accomplishments, in terms of both improved communication skills and any changes the teen made in relationships. This helps the adolescent feel confident that he or she can continue interpersonal work without the support of the leader. The leader should also leave some time to discuss what it will be like to no longer meet with the leader and what the teen's experience has been like with the prevention program as a whole.

Example: Final booster session closing tasks

LEADER: *Because this is our last session together, I wanted to take some time for us to think back to what you've worked on and accomplished over the course of the group and our meetings together. What do you remember that you learned or accomplished?*

JENNIFER: *I did talk to my friend about wanting to spend more time together, and now we see each other a lot more, which is really nice.*

LEADER: *That is right, I know that you weren't sure if it was a good idea to say something to her, but it made a big difference once you did, so that was great. Anything else you noticed?*

JENNIFER: *Well, I didn't end up talking to my mom more about stuff, but I think I have been using some of the skills more, like* **Strike while the iron is cold**, *and that's helped.*

LEADER: *That's great also. Do you think in the future, you might want to think about expressing your feelings to your mom more? Is that still something you would want to work on?*

JENNIFER: *I'm not sure. I think it would be nice to be able to tell my mom more about what's going on with me. I just don't want to make her upset.*

LEADER: *I know you haven't been ready to work on that so far, but I also know you have learned communication strategies that can help you work toward that goal if you decide to try. Are there any other things you'd like to still work on?*

JENNIFER: *I'm going to talk to my friend Lily, and then I guess just whatever comes up later.*

LEADER: *Okay, that makes a lot of sense. And, like I said, you have some great ideas about how to communicate differently with people now, so I am confident you have the tools to work on things that come up in your relationships in the future. I also wanted to talk about what it will be like for us not to meet anymore. Some people are glad that they don't have to come in and they have time for other things, and other people are sometimes sad or nervous that it might be hard not to have someone to talk to anymore. What do you think?*

JENNIFER: *Well, it has been really helpful to get to talk to you about stuff and think about what I want to say. I think I am okay with stopping though, too, especially because things have gotten better with high school and everything.*

LEADER: *Well, that's good. I'm glad that you got a lot out of this, and I agree that you can handle a lot of things on your own, too. I know lately you have been feeling pretty good, but let's briefly talk about what to notice and what to do in case your mood gets worse or you notice some of your warning signs. Do you remember what the warning signs are for you to notice if you start to feel down?*

JENNIFER: *I remember when my mood was worse, I didn't want to talk to people; it was kind of hard to get into things, and I also had trouble sleeping.*

LEADER: *That's right. So, if you notice those things again, what are some things you can do?*

JENNIFER: *I can talk to my friends—they can help cheer me up.*

LEADER: *That is a great idea. If you still feel down after that, are there any adults you could talk to who might be able to help more and even find someone like me for you to talk to if you needed to do so?*

JENNIFER: *Well, I guess I could tell my mom. It might feel weird, but then I know she would want to help. Or, I could talk to my counselor at school; she is pretty nice.*

LEADER: *Great, those are two good people to talk to in case you don't feel better on your own or by talking to friends. It has been so nice to get to know you over the past several months, and I hope you have a good rest of your school year!*

Summary of the Booster Sessions

Booster sessions are a chance to solidify gains in knowledge and skills that teens made over the course of the group. They also provide opportunities for teens to generalize their communication skills to new interpersonal situations or to talk about interpersonal issues that they were unable or unwilling to address during group sessions. While not all settings will be able to offer booster sessions, they are an important way to help teens continue the interpersonal work that they started in the group. The booster sessions also provide teens with more challenging interpersonal goals and additional time to work on these goals with the support of the leader.

10

Conducting IPT-AST in Schools

Given that schools offer a natural venue for delivery of mental health interventions, in particular prevention programs such as Interpersonal Psychotherapy – Adolescent Skills Training (IPT-AST), this chapter discusses the delivery of IPT-AST in school settings. First, we briefly review the literature on school-based mental health programs, focusing on the advantages of delivering preventive interventions in schools. Despite these advantages, there are several challenges that often present themselves when implementing prevention programs in schools. In the remainder of the chapter, we discuss ways to address these challenges, including obtaining agreement from school personnel and boards of education; identifying personnel who will take the lead in implementing IPT-AST; assessing capacity to implement IPT-AST; identifying adolescents who will be appropriate for these services; explaining IPT-AST to adolescents and parents to engage them in the program; and managing logistical and scheduling issues within the schools.

The Advantages of School-Based Prevention Programs

School-based mental health services have shown promise in increasing access to services for youth who otherwise would likely not receive any intervention (Weare & Nind, 2011). Schools address many of the logistical barriers to care, including transportation, scheduling, and financial limitations. Youth are also less likely to perceive services offered in schools as stigmatizing (Masia-Warner et al., 2006; Ryan, 2003). For all of these reasons, children and adolescents diagnosed with a psychiatric disorder are more likely to receive services in a school setting than in any other single setting, according to a recent review of data from the National Comorbidity Survey (Costello, He, Sampson, Kessler, & Merikangas, 2014). Schools are particularly well suited to offer preventive interventions, which are intended to reach a wider population of youth than interventions for those who have a diagnosable mental health problem.

Schools are increasingly being asked to recognize and address the social and emotional development of their students, in addition to focusing on academic learning and achievement. In a survey of schools conducted by the Department of Health and Human Services, it was found that approximately 20% of students received mental health services in the 2001–2002 academic year (Foster et al., 2005). The most commonly occurring psychosocial problems were social, interpersonal, and family problems, indicating a need for programs that address interpersonal issues. The school setting also offers opportunities for teens to apply new skills and strategies in a more realistic environment. When prevention programs, such as IPT-AST, are offered in schools and are integrated into the school environment, adolescents can be encouraged to use what they have learned with peers, teachers, and others in the school. The leaders can effectively partner with teachers to reinforce the skills being taught in the programs and provide ample opportunities to apply the skills while school personnel further support and shape their use. For example, school personnel can be trained to encourage use of communication strategies when students have conflict with other students or teachers. These skills can also be incorporated into existing peer mediation programs, particularly when IPT-AST is used as a universal prevention program for all teens in a school.

In addition, prevention of mental health problems such as depression can improve adolescents' school functioning, as depression is likely to affect school performance. A recent meta-analysis of school-based interventions aimed at enhancing students' social and emotional functioning found that these programs were successful in improving academic performance (Durlak, Weissberg, Dymnicki, Taylor, & Schellinger, 2011). IPT-AST has specifically been found to improve school engagement and retention in adolescents (Young, Kranzler, Gallop, & Mufson, 2012). Finally, the school as a whole is likely to benefit, as more serious problems (i.e., depression and accompanying difficulties with school attendance and performance, crises related to suicidal ideation or nonsuicidal self-injury) may be prevented through provision of prevention services. Through the process of implementing a prevention program such as IPT-AST, the hope is that the school community will also become more aware and accepting of mental health issues.

Obtaining Agreement From Key Stakeholders

Despite the advantages of implementing IPT-AST in schools, there are several challenges that need to be overcome to ensure the success of the program. The first hurdle that someone seeking to implement IPT-AST in the schools must face is obtaining agreement from school personnel to conduct IPT-AST groups. Key stakeholders include members of the district's school board, the school principal and other administrators, school counselors and members of the school's Child Study Team, and teachers. In our experience working with schools to implement IPT-AST, we have encountered both enthusiasm for the possible benefits of the program and doubts about feasibility and worries that the program might be cumbersome for personnel who are already stretched to their limits with other responsibilities. School administrators might worry about bringing up topics such as depression in the school district due to concerns over parent objections or about the school's liability.

There are several ways to begin to address these concerns. School administrators can be encouraged to consider offering IPT-AST in their schools based on evidence that this prevention program works (see Chapter 13, which describes the evidence base for IPT-AST). Research indicates that IPT-AST is likely to benefit the individual adolescents involved. IPT-AST might also benefit the student body as a whole as both students and school personnel become more aware of how depression can affect teenagers and what resources are available to help those teenagers. A depression prevention program such as IPT-AST may allow schools to identify adolescents in need of services before problems become severe and therefore may improve the school climate significantly. As parents become increasingly concerned about issues such as bullying and school violence, they also want schools to provide services to support their children not only in terms of their education but also in terms of mental health. These benefits of IPT-AST can be emphasized to school administrators, who may be initially reluctant to support implementation in their schools.

Some administrators and other school personnel may believe that talking about depression and suicide with teens might increase their risk for these problems. Information can be provided in these cases to assure them that research does not support this assertion. Gould and colleagues (2005) found that teens who were asked about suicide were no more likely to experience distress immediately after questioning and no more likely to report suicidal ideation 1 week later than teens who were not asked about suicide. In fact, among teens at higher risk (i.e., teens with more elevated symptoms), those who were asked screening questions about suicidal ideation and behavior reported less distress and less suicidal ideation than teens who were not asked those questions. Speaking about issues related to depression and suicide in the context of a preventive intervention is therefore not likely to increase risk for adolescents. In fact, encouraging teens to ask for help appropriately is likely to reduce their risk, as they are able to access support more quickly. School personnel can be coached on how to present IPT-AST to parents and adolescents to obtain buy-in and reduce any worries that they may have.

School personnel who would be asked to implement IPT-AST are likely to have concerns about the amount of time that this endeavor might take, above and beyond the responsibilities that they already have in the school. While this is something that individuals in each school will have to consider, personnel who already provide counseling or mental health services in schools are likely to find that providing a group-based prevention program such as IPT-AST will be a natural extension and complement to the work that they already do. While time must be committed in both preparation and execution, it is likely to enhance their work with students and provide an avenue for them to reach adolescents who might not otherwise be identified as being in need of services. In many cases, teachers and counselors may already have concerns about a number of students who may be at risk and may be providing some support to those teens either individually or in a group format. Those teens could instead be served as part of a group-based prevention program, which may improve outcomes for these adolescents without substantially increasing the workload of school personnel.

In other cases, adolescents participating in IPT-AST groups may not have been identified as in need of services before the program is implemented. Over the long term, it is hoped that reaching adolescents through a prevention program will make it less likely that those teens will need further, perhaps more intensive, services in the future. In that way, implementation of a depression prevention program such as IPT-AST might reduce the burden on counseling and mental health service providers over the long run.

To implement IPT-AST in a school, it is desirable to identify one or two key people who will be responsible for overseeing the process. They should be experienced in school mental health promotion and feel comfortable assessing adolescents to determine whether a prevention program is a good fit or if more intensive intervention is required instead (see Chapter 3). The overseer of the program should also be prepared to refer students for emergency services in the event that a student discloses suicidal ideation. As schools are likely to have their own policies in place that determine how to proceed in these situations, personnel involved with the IPT-AST program should be familiar with school policies.

While the person overseeing the implementation of IPT-AST in the school should have a background in a mental health or school counseling field, those who act as group leaders can be school counselors, members of the Child Study Team, social workers, school nurses, or other school personnel who are routinely responsible for the emotional well-being of students. Teachers may also be appropriate group leaders, particularly for universal prevention groups or when they are supervised by someone with a mental health background. While there is currently no research to support the effectiveness of teachers as IPT-AST group leaders, teachers have delivered other depression prevention programs successfully (Gillham et al., 2007).

Assessing Capacity to Implement IPT-AST

Often, the next challenge for a school that commits to implementing IPT-AST is deciding how best to identify adolescents who would be appropriate for the program and developing the capacity to serve those adolescents who are identified. As discussed in Chapters 1 and 2, IPT-AST can be delivered as an indicated or selective prevention program for adolescents at risk for depression. It can also be delivered as a universal prevention program to teenagers who may have no particular risk for depression but may still benefit from the program. Given the resources that schools have available, they may decide to limit access to the program based on adolescents' risk for developing depression. Schools would benefit from conducting a needs assessment in their district to estimate how many students are likely to be identified by a particular method, as well as the resources that would be required to provide this prevention program to all identified teens.

A variety of methods are available to identify adolescents at risk (described in the next section). In prior studies of IPT-AST conducted in schools, 20% to 30% of students screened for depression had elevated scores on a standardized measure of depression. This is likely to vary across districts but may provide a starting point for schools to consider. Whatever method is chosen to identify appropriate adolescents, it is important to consider whether the school will have the ability to provide services to all identified teens and what sources of support are available to ensure access to services for those adolescents who will not be included in the IPT-AST program.

Identifying Adolescents to Participate

If schools wish to deliver IPT-AST to adolescents at risk, how should they determine who these students are? There are several options available. For schools that want to implement IPT-AST as an indicated prevention program, one method is to screen students in the target age range for symptoms of depression and to follow up with those adolescents who endorse symptoms of depression to assess their interest in and appropriateness for participating in IPT-AST, as described in Chapter 3.

Mental health screenings in schools have been the source of some controversy. While this is a relatively rare practice in schools, a survey of schools published in 2005 found that approximately 15% of schools provided mental health screenings in the 2002–2003 academic year (Foster et al., 2005). Screening for mental health issues in schools has the potential to offer great advantages, identifying students who could benefit from intervention before they would otherwise come to the attention of school personnel or other adults. Mental health screening has also been recommended by several professional and government organizations as part of a broader public health approach to prevention and early intervention for behavioral health problems (Weist, Rubin, Moore, Adelsheim, & Wrobel, 2007). At the same time, concerns have been raised about issues of privacy and government overreach, as well as concerns about being sure that intervention resources are available to any students who are identified as part of a screening initiative. Screening may be feasible in some school districts but not others, depending on the particular community and state and local laws.

Concerns about mental health screening can be addressed by requiring adolescents to have active parental consent to participate in the screening (thereby making it a voluntary process) and by making sure that any adolescents with more severe symptoms are referred for treatment. Before adolescents are screened, parents and teens should be provided with initial information about both the benefits and any potential risks of participating. As discussed in Chapter 3, screening instruments such as the Center for Epidemiological Studies Depression Scale (CES-D; Radloff, 1977); the Child Depression Inventory (CDI; Kovacs, 2003); or the Reynolds Adolescent Depression Scale (RADS; Reynolds, 2002) can be used, with appropriate threshold cutoffs set to identify adolescents who are experiencing elevated levels of symptoms.

This screening process serves the dual purpose of helping to identify adolescents who are appropriate to participate in IPT-AST and those who are in need of more intensive services. In our experience conducting these types of screenings in schools, we have found that a substantial number of identified adolescents were not previously known to school personnel, and the screening helped these teens get linked with appropriate prevention or treatment programs.

Another option is to offer IPT-AST as a selective intervention to adolescents who share a common experience that might put them at risk for depression, such as teens who are new to the school and are having difficulty adjusting to a new setting or teens whose parents have recently divorced. It is important to note that we do not yet have data on the effects of IPT-AST as a selective intervention (a study of IPT-AST as a selective prevention program is ongoing), but we are hopeful that these groups would be beneficial. Teens may be identified for inclusion in a selective prevention group based on referrals by teachers or counselors, or teens and parents can be given the option to self-refer. In this case, leaders may want to send out a description of the types of groups that they will be running in the coming semester so teens and parents are aware of the options and can sign up to participate. This approach has the benefit of creating a group with a common theme, where group members share similar experiences. If a school has a substantial population of adolescents with a common issue and would like to provide support around that issue, this can be a helpful option. A third option is to refer adolescents to the program if they have been identified through informal or formal channels as needing extra support by school personnel. Adolescents might be identified through a committee or group of teachers, school counselors, members of the school's Child Study Team, and school administrators. Adolescents might also be identified on the basis of frequent referrals to the guidance or counseling department.

Some schools might give students the option to self-select for participation in IPT-AST groups. This can be achieved either informally (e.g., adolescents requesting meetings with school counselors can be offered the group program as an alternative) or more formally (e.g., all students can be asked to fill out a form indicating whether they would like to participate in IPT-AST groups and other types of services offered at the school). The advantage of this approach is that adolescents who become involved in the prevention program this way are more likely to be invested in it, as they decided for themselves that this sounded like a good fit for them. When this strategy is used, school personnel overseeing the program will still need to evaluate whether each adolescent who requests to be involved in a depression prevention group is an appropriate fit for that type of program, as opposed to more intensive services.

However adolescents are identified as possible IPT-AST group members, it is important for the leader to conduct a brief clinical assessment prior to group to determine whether each adolescent is appropriate for a prevention program such as IPT-AST or would be better served by more intensive services. More information is provided in Chapter 3 about conducting a clinical interview before the pre-group sessions to determine whether an adolescent is suitable for IPT-AST. In addition, it is important that the group leader monitor adolescents for worsening of symptoms throughout the course of IPT-AST using the weekly depression checklists so that teens can be referred for more intensive treatment if needed.

Discussing IPT-AST With Adolescents and Parents

After schools decide which youth would be most appropriate for IPT-AST, school personnel must discuss this opportunity with adolescents and their parents. This process may differ depending on which school personnel are responsible for implementing the program; how adolescents are identified as eligible for the program; and what the relationships are like between the school and the teens' parents. If adolescents are selected based on risk for depression, it is important to let parents know why their child in particular might benefit from IPT-AST, while reassuring them that there is no evidence that their child is depressed at this time. Many parents will welcome the offer of services for a child they may have already been worried about and may be relieved that a program is available at the school. In other cases, parents might feel unduly singled out and may question why their child was selected. In those cases, it is often helpful to explain that the program is intended for adolescents who are not depressed and is designed to provide teens with skills and resources that may prevent them from experiencing depression in the future. When parents are informed that IPT-AST is a prevention program, they are less likely to see it as a source of stigma. Parents should also be informed of the policy regarding what information will be shared with them over the course of the program and what information is kept private. This will help reduce any misunderstandings that could arise later.

Teens may have different concerns about participating in an IPT-AST group. Some teens may worry about other adolescents in the group hearing about their problems or may be shy about speaking in a group more generally. Teens and parents should be informed of the policy related to privacy in the setting in which IPT-AST groups are offered. While no guarantees can be made that other teens in the group will not share information outside group meetings, teens can be informed that the leader will encourage group members to keep information private. Teens are usually motivated to keep information private, because they also do not wish for their information to be shared, and we have never encountered a breach of confidentiality from group members.

Adolescents may also worry that they will not be similar to other teens in the group. Depending on how adolescents were selected, they can be reassured that teens are likely to be similar to them in many ways, and that teens who are depressed or have other serious mental health concerns would not be included in the group. Teens can further be informed that often the most helpful part of IPT-AST is getting a chance to talk about issues with peers, who can give valuable feedback and advice given that they often have similar experiences.

Teens may also ask who specifically will be in the group with them. It is important to avoid sharing this information with teens before the first group meeting, as some potential members may decide not to participate and would not want their names to be shared with others. This policy can be explained to teens, and general information about group composition can be provided (e.g., about five other students from your grade will be there; the group will include both boys and girls; etc.).

Logistical Concerns for Implementation

A number of logistical considerations also come into play when IPT-AST is implemented in schools. Scheduling can be difficult with all the other obligations that adolescents and school staff have to fulfill. One frequent concern is that the length of sessions recommended often does not match the length of school class periods, which can vary widely from approximately 30 minutes to over 90 minutes (when block scheduling is used). IPT-AST group sessions are ideally 60 to 90 minutes in length. However, they have been conducted in periods as short as 45 minutes. When possible, it is helpful to offer extra sessions when only 45 minutes at a time is available. For example, groups might be held twice per week for 45 minutes instead of once per week for 90 minutes. Another option is to hold group meetings once per week, but add on a few extra weeks of group to make up for the time that is lost with shorter sessions. If this option is chosen, we recommend lengthening the middle phase of the intervention so there are more sessions for the teens to work on relationships related to their interpersonal goals. In this case, the group would consist of 3 initial phase sessions, 5 middle phase sessions, and 2 termination phase sessions, for a total of 10 group sessions. We have successfully used these modified formats to conduct groups that fit into various school schedules. These constraints need not prevent schools from implementing IPT-AST successfully.

Given the many other commitments that both teens and school personnel have to fulfill, schools should consider when the best time to provide IPT-AST groups might be. Many schools prefer to have adolescents attend groups during the school day. If this is the preferred option, will groups take place during a regular class period, lunch, or an activity/ elective period? It may also be possible to alternate the class period during which group will take place each week, so that teens do not miss the same class every week. Alternatively, does it make more sense to offer groups after school, so that they do not conflict with academic learning? The time that a school selects may have an impact on teens' attendance and engagement in the prevention program. We have implemented IPT-AST groups both during the school day and after school, with success in both situations dependent on the particular school setting and the schedules of the teens involved. There will often be no perfect time for all teens involved in an IPT-AST group. Schools, teens, and parents often do not agree about which classes or activities adolescents should be able to miss for IPT-AST group meetings. However, given the potential benefits and the short duration of the program, it is likely that a compromise can be reached.

As schools offer an accessible venue for the provision of preventive mental health services, we encourage school personnel to strongly consider delivering IPT-AST in their schools. While many potential obstacles to implementation are discussed and addressed in this chapter, those wishing to offer IPT-AST in school settings will likely find unique ways to address implementation issues specific to their communities. Flexibility and problem-solving, in consultation with other professionals, can help this process go as smoothly as possible.

11

IPT-AST With Different Populations and in Diverse Settings

While Interpersonal Psychotherapy – Adolescent Skills Training (IPT-AST) was initially developed for use with an indicated prevention population and has primarily been implemented in schools, the program can also be implemented with populations of varying levels of risk and in a number of different settings. In this chapter, we discuss modifications that can be made when offering IPT-AST to adolescents at varying levels of risk. We also describe a number of settings where IPT-AST can be implemented and discuss associated benefits as well as challenges. Finally, we discuss logistical considerations when IPT-AST is offered in these diverse settings.

Conducting IPT-AST With Adolescents at Varying Levels of Risk

As discussed in Chapters 1 and 2, IPT-AST was initially developed as an indicated prevention program for adolescents with elevated symptoms of depression. However, it can also be used as a selective prevention program for adolescents with known risk factors for depression or as a universal prevention program for adolescents who have no current symptoms of depression and no known risk factors for depression. When implementing IPT-AST with selective or universal populations, some of the language used with adolescents should be modified, particularly in the initial and termination phases of the intervention. While most aspects of IPT-AST remain similar for indicated, selective, and universal prevention populations, language pertaining to the rationale for and expected benefits of this prevention program are likely to differ across these groups (e.g., this program is intended to reduce vs. prevent onset of symptoms). In the termination phase, teens are asked to reflect on changes in their symptoms and mood ratings observed throughout group, and these should be addressed differently depending on how symptomatic teens were initially.

Universal prevention. For a universal prevention population as opposed to an indicated prevention population, the primary difference will be in the way that the group leader frames the purpose of the group and the skills to be learned. While teens with elevated symptoms may be told that they are attending an IPT-AST group because they all have some symptoms of depression, teens in a universal group would be told about the benefits of this type of preventive intervention for all teens. During the individual pre-group sessions as well as the first few group meetings, explanations about the concept of prevention and the links between relationships and mood will look similar for teens without any symptoms of depression as they do for teens with some elevated symptoms. However, in the context of universal prevention, the group leader can explain that the program is meant to prevent teens from developing depression later, rather than emphasizing any particular risk for depression that the adolescent might currently be experiencing. Rather than focusing on a goal of symptom reduction, the leader should focus on helping teens to either improve or maintain positive mood and relationships by working on interpersonal goals. Symptoms of depression should still be assessed, as these can change over time. An example of how a group leader can explain the focus and purpose of IPT-AST to teens in a universal prevention group is provided next.

Example: Introduction to group for universal prevention group

LEADER: You are all in this group with the hope that it will prevent you from developing depression. As you know from your pre-group sessions, we are going to spend a lot of time in group learning new ways to communicate with important people in our lives. We believe that improving your relationships will help you to handle problems better as they come up, and this will help keep your moods positive over time. As group progresses, you'll see that a lot of you are dealing with similar issues with family or friends. We are going to use the group to address these problems.

In the termination phase, language can again be adjusted when working with adolescents without symptoms of depression. Rather than helping teens to reflect on changes in their depression symptoms, the review of depression checklists will focus primarily on mood ratings. Mood ratings are more likely to fluctuate than reported symptoms for teens in a universal prevention program. Just as in indicated prevention groups, teens can be encouraged to notice links between fluctuations in mood and interpersonal events, particularly when those events are related to their goals for the group. Individual warning signs should be discussed regardless of the level of risk of teens in the group. Even teens without significant symptoms of depression should be able to recognize particular signs that they might be feeling down or upset, such as difficulty sleeping or withdrawal from friends or family. Although adolescents might not have had significant symptoms of depression at the time of the group, they can be encouraged to take note of the types of symptoms they might experience in the future that are indicative of low mood for them. Group members should also be encouraged to pay attention to how they are feeling and to think of ways to address a problem or reach out to someone for help or support if they notice sad mood or other depression symptoms in the future.

Example: Review of mood ratings and warning signs with a universal group

LEADER: *This week we are going to start group differently. Instead of reporting on your mood over the past week, I want you to think about your mood over the entire group. Take a minute and look back over your mood ratings. Have you noticed any changes in your mood ratings over the eight group sessions? [At this point, group members can take turns sharing patterns in their mood ratings and the leader can help link this to changes in relationships.]*

LEADER: *Great! Thank you for sharing everyone. I want to help you all think about what you tend to experience when you feel down, so that you can be aware of these potential warning signs if you experience them in the future. We talked about symptoms of depression at the start of group, and you just looked through your depression checklists as we were talking about changes in mood. Take a minute to think about the symptoms of depression. Have you noticed any of those symptoms or changes at times when you have felt down? For example, some people get really irritable when they are down and get into more arguments with friends or family members. Other people notice that they sleep a lot. What about for each of you?*

Selective prevention. Language should be altered in different ways for teens who are referred to an IPT-AST group due to an identified risk factor for depression (e.g., for teens with a depressed parent). Adolescents may or may not have any symptoms of depression at the time that they begin the group program, but they will all have something in common that puts them at increased risk for developing depression at some point in their lives. When explaining IPT-AST in the initial phase to a selective prevention group, it might be desirable to point out the commonalities that the adolescents share, without breaking confidentiality. For example, if a group is formed that includes only children of parents who have divorced, and families are aware of that, it makes sense to bring this up in the first group as part of the introduction to the IPT-AST program. Throughout a selective prevention group, the leader might refer to commonalities between group members, both to encourage teens to help each other by offering feedback and advice and to normalize teens' experiences. The following is an example of how a group leader might introduce a selective IPT-AST group during the initial phase:

Example: Introduction to group for a selective group

LEADER: *You are all in this group because you have experienced your parents' divorce, and you and your parents made a really smart decision to participate in this group so you can learn some different ways to deal with that and with other situations that come up in relationships. As you know from your pre-group sessions, we are going to spend a lot of time in group learning new ways to communicate with important people in our lives because we believe that improving your relationships will help you to feel better. As group progresses, you'll see that a lot of you are dealing with similar problems. Some of you are fighting with your parents a lot; others have withdrawn from family and friends. We are going to use the group to address these problems.*

Similarly, because selective prevention groups may have youth with a range of symptom levels, leaders should tailor conversations in the termination phase to best reflect the experience of teens in the group, choosing to emphasize changes in symptoms when appropriate or changes in mood when that makes the most sense.

Implementation of IPT-AST in Diverse Settings

Interpersonal Psychotherapy – Adolescent Skills Training can be implemented in many other settings in addition to schools, including primary care, mental health, and community organization settings. Medical and mental healthcare settings offer the advantage of access to other services and professionals should more intensive services become necessary. Community settings, such as afterschool programs, religious organizations, and youth leadership organizations, offer the advantage of increasing access to prevention.

Primary care settings. As youth are likely to see a pediatrician or family physician on a regular basis throughout childhood, pediatric primary care providers are in a good position to screen for mental health problems and to provide access to preventive interventions as well as mental health treatment when indicated (Knapp & Foy, 2012). Because families typically have a relationship with their child's primary care provider already, it may be easier for them to accept a recommendation from the pediatrician regarding the importance and possible benefits of this preventive intervention (Brown, Wissow, Zachary, & Cook, 2007). Some primary care settings already partner with psychologists, psychiatrists, social workers, psychiatric nurses, and other providers of behavioral health services to facilitate access to mental healthcare. These mental health providers can be fully integrated into a medical practice, can be co-located but administratively separate, or can be affiliated without sharing a common administrative structure or physical space. The benefits of integrating mental health in primary care settings have been recognized by both the medical and mental health communities as a way to improve both physical and mental health outcomes (Vogel, Malcore, Illes, & Kirkpatrick, 2014). As physicians are increasingly called on to address issues related to depression, anxiety, and other mental health concerns, many have called for coordinated, co-located, or fully integrated primary and behavioral healthcare (Hine, Howell, & Yonkers, 2008). Offering prevention services, such as IPT-AST, may be one way for pediatricians and other physicians serving youth to enhance the social and emotional health of their patients.

Primary care providers may decide to offer IPT-AST to youth in several ways. One option is for physicians to routinely screen youth for emotional disorders, as has been recommended by the American Academy of Pediatrics (Knapp & Foy, 2012) and the National Association of Pediatric Nurse Practitioners (NAPNAP, 2013). Based on these mental health screenings, teens with elevated depression symptoms could be referred for IPT-AST either on site or at an affiliated location. Youth with more significant symptoms of depression could be evaluated for more intensive services, either on site or by an affiliated mental health provider. Alternatively, primary care doctors and nurses might offer IPT-AST on a case-by-case basis when they feel that a teen is particularly at risk for depression (due to the presence of known risk factors, such as maternal depression) or when a parent or teen expresses concerns about the teen's emotional well-being. However, a challenge with this approach is identifying enough teens at any one time to form an IPT-AST group. Primary care settings may also choose to offer IPT-AST as an optional service for all teenage patients, as a way to promote the emotional health of their patients and families.

Mental health settings. Community mental health centers, outpatient clinics, and therapists and counselors in private practice may wish to offer IPT-AST as a way to address relationship difficulties and social and communication skill deficits in the adolescents they serve who may be at risk for depression. Offering preventive services such as IPT-AST allows mental health providers to reach a wider population than they would otherwise be able to reach. Provision of prevention services is likely to reduce the burden on overtaxed community agencies, as it is hoped that teens who have participated in evidence-based prevention programs will be less likely to require more intensive services later. Offering a prevention program, such as IPT-AST, provides a way for agencies to respond in an effective and cost-efficient manner to the needs of adolescents at increased risk for depression. Providers and agencies will have to decide how these services will be funded, whether by obtaining grants, billing patients directly, or finding other means of support.

For example, adolescents who have siblings or parents receiving mental health services for depression or other emotional disorders may not qualify for a diagnosis themselves but are likely at increased risk for depression (Rice, 2010). While these teens may not require their own individual treatment, they could benefit from learning how to navigate difficult relationships and how to access increased support from important people in their lives. Mental health providers could offer IPT-AST as a selective preventive intervention to these adolescents while their parents or siblings attend treatment appointments. While we think this has great potential, it may be challenging to find enough teens who can attend group at the same time.

Community organizations. Community organizations offer another venue where a large number of adolescents may be able to access prevention services. Afterschool programs, religious organizations, and other settings where youth gather for recreational, leadership-building, or other purposes could incorporate a program such as IPT-AST into their programming. Community organizations would be best equipped to provide a universal prevention group, where the program is offered to all teens in the appropriate age group. However, a selective prevention group may also be offered, particularly when the organization caters to a population at particular risk for depression (e.g., an afterschool program in a homeless shelter). By offering IPT-AST to the youth they serve, community organizations can allow many adolescents to access prevention services without requiring families to take additional time for travel to other sites.

Community organizations may face challenges similar to those faced by schools when they seek to implement IPT-AST. First, it will be necessary to obtain agreement from administrators and staff and to decide who will be in charge of implementing the program. Administrators and staff may have concerns about fitting IPT-AST into the schedule when other activities and programs are already in place. However, many may welcome the opportunity to provide an evidence-based program to improve the social and emotional functioning of the youth they serve. In deciding who should lead IPT-AST groups, program administrators should consider staff members' professional backgrounds as well as level of comfort discussing social and emotional issues with teens. It is also important that someone involved in implementation have the skills to handle any crises that might come up involving suicidal ideation or threats of violence toward others (see Chapter 3). While teens in IPT-AST do not have a depression diagnosis, they can experience crises that would require the skills of an experienced mental health clinician; therefore, the settings should have plans in place for managing such situations before initiating the group program.

Once programs decide that they will implement IPT-AST and identify staff who will be in charge of that implementation, they will need to decide how best to fit IPT-AST in with the programs and services already offered. IPT-AST may be incorporated as one of many activities within a broader set of programs, or it may be offered as a separate program that teens can attend without broader participation in the community organization. For example, in an afterschool program, teens who already spend time there every day could be asked to participate in IPT-AST once per week while they are there. In programs where there is some unstructured time available (e.g., time for homework, reading, or unstructured recreation), this may be a good time to fit IPT-AST into the weekly schedule. In contrast, a youth organization may decide to offer IPT-AST as a stand-alone program, where adolescents from the community are invited to participate in a short-term prevention program without committing to any other involvement with the organization. In either case, it is recommended that the once-per-week structure of IPT-AST be maintained so that teens have time between group sessions to practice implementing what they have learned at home.

Logistical Concerns for Implementation

Once a plan has been put in place to implement IPT-AST, the organization can approach parents and teens about participating in the program. When parents and teens already have a positive relationship with the organization, they may be more open to participation in a prevention program such as IPT-AST. Parents and adolescents should be approached sensitively, and the preventive nature of IPT-AST should be emphasized to avoid teens and their parents feeling that they are being told there is a problem. See Chapter 10 for a detailed discussion of how to address the concerns of parents and adolescents at this stage.

Some modifications to the original intervention format might be needed or desired in a setting where families travel long distances to receive services. For example, it may be necessary to combine the two pre-group sessions into one session to reduce the travel burden on families. If this is done, we recommend that a full 90 minutes be devoted to that session to allow ample time to assess important relationships and set goals for the group. When one pre-group session is used, the leader will have to think quickly about appropriate interpersonal goals, as there will not be time between the first part of the interpersonal inventory and the goal-setting phase for more careful reflection and planning. However, we have found that it is possible to complete an interpersonal inventory and establish meaningful interpersonal goals successfully in one 90-minute session. To facilitate this, the leader can ask the teen to identify which relationships are most important to talk about to best understand what relationships or interactions affect the teen's mood. It is recommended that eight weekly group sessions be offered to allow adolescents time to practice newly learned communication skills outside group meetings. While we recommend 90-minute group sessions, these can be shortened to as few as 60 minutes depending on the size of the group, as long as content can be adequately covered in that time.

Although having two coleaders is preferable, when this is not feasible, organizations may choose to have one leader for each group. When only one group leader is available, it is important to keep in mind that this leader will also be responsible for all individual pre-group, mid-group, and booster sessions (if offered). Weeks when pre-group or mid-group sessions occur will be particularly busy when there is only one leader.

Funding

In mental health clinics, primary care settings, and community organizations, funding for prevention programs such as IPT-AST may be an issue of concern. Currently, insurance companies do not typically provide reimbursement for preventive services provided to youth who do not have a mental health diagnosis. However, parents or caregivers may wish to pay for these services if they are made aware of the potential benefits they offer their children. Some settings may be able to apply for grants or seek other sources of funding to provide preventive services to the populations that they serve. Grant-based funding may be more feasible for hospitals, clinics, and large community organizations than for individual physicians or mental healthcare providers in private practice. Given the potential benefits of offering IPT-AST in these various settings, organizations are encouraged to explore different options for funding these programs.

12

Common Clinical Issues

This chapter addresses common clinical issues that Interpersonal Psychotherapy – Adolescent Skills Training (IPT-AST) group leaders have encountered over the years. These issues include absences, engaging reluctant adolescents in group activities such as role plays, difficult or defiant adolescents, breaches to confidentiality within the group, challenging family situations, and crises, including disclosures of suicidal thoughts and suspected abuse. We discuss ways that we have addressed these common clinical situations in IPT-AST groups.

Missed Sessions

We recommend that the importance of regular attendance be emphasized from the very beginning of each teen's involvement in IPT-AST. Given the short-term nature of the intervention, it is particularly important to minimize absences from the group. However, despite the leader's best efforts to encourage regular attendance, some teens will miss sessions. A teen not only may miss sessions due to genuine emergencies or scheduling conflicts but also may miss sessions due to avoidable miscommunications with parents, prioritizing another activity over the IPT-AST program, or avoidance due to low mood or beliefs that the teen does not need the group.

In the first group session, the leader should forecast fluctuating motivation to attend sessions and encourage teens to attend weekly despite the fact that they might feel less motivated to come to group on some days. Teens can be encouraged to attend both so that they can receive the maximum benefit from the program and so that they can be helpful to other group members. By predicting that teens might not always feel like coming to group meetings, the leader can often help teens to avoid acting on impulses to skip sessions.

Another way to reduce the likelihood of missed sessions is to make reminder calls the day or evening before group. This can serve two purposes. First, the leader can remind teens about the group and encourage them to attend, which may increase their motivation. Second, in the middle phase of the group, these calls also provide an opportunity to obtain a brief update on whether the teens have been able to complete any work-at-home assignments and, if not, to encourage them to do so before group. This information is useful for setting an informal agenda for the next group session. For instance, the leader may choose to review work at home earlier in the session if a teen has had a successful encounter that would be helpful to highlight. Making reminder calls to all group members might not be feasible in some settings. Instead, the leader might choose to make reminder calls only to those group members who missed the previous group session to encourage attendance.

Whenever a teen misses a group session, it is important for the leader to discuss this absence with the teen and the teen's parent to find out more about barriers to attendance. The leader can help the family problem-solve so the adolescent attends as many sessions as possible. When teens have difficulty attending individual mid-group and booster sessions, we have in some cases allowed them to complete these sessions over the phone. While this is often preferred by families, it tends to result in less productive sessions, so we have used it only as a last resort when a teen has moved away and is no longer able to attend in person.

If teens miss certain group sessions, particularly in the initial phase, the leader should catch them up on what they missed. In the initial phase, a few minutes can be set aside at the start of the group session to review the previous session for anyone who did not attend. Other group members can be asked to briefly explain to the adolescents who were not at the previous session what they missed. Alternatively, if there is not enough time during the next group session for this type of review, the leader can meet with a teen individually for 15 minutes before the start of group to review important content. This would need to be scheduled in advance so that the teen and leader arrange their schedules to meet before the start of group.

The importance of review for the individual teen as well as the effects on the group as a whole might vary depending on which group session(s) a particular teen misses. If a teen misses the first meeting, the leader should allow time in group session 2 for abbreviated introductions to facilitate a cohesive group dynamic. If time permits, the leader may decide to conduct a second icebreaker activity as well. It is particularly important to review communication skills with a teen if the teen misses group session 3, as this provides the foundation for work in the middle phase. This can be a helpful review for all group members in session 4 and can also serve as an opportunity for the leader to correct any misunderstandings other group member may have about the communication strategies. However, if there are more pressing interpersonal issues that come up during the mood check-in at the beginning of session 4, the leader might decide to meet with the adolescent who missed the prior group individually to review the communication strategies after group session 4 or before the next group meeting.

When a teen misses several group sessions, the leader should be aware of how this might affect the group process. For example, if a teen is absent when the other group members are building connections with each other and starting to share personal information, the remaining group members may become uncomfortable when that teen returns to group. In this situation, the leader should sensitively try to integrate that group member while maintaining a focus on the interpersonal work that the other adolescents have been doing. Depending on the group dynamic, the leader might decide to specifically ask a group member who has been absent a few times to contribute thoughts or ideas, particularly if it seems that the teen is likely to feel excluded otherwise. Conversely, if a teen has missed several sessions and then comes in with an interpersonal issue to discuss, the leader might decide to prioritize other group members who have been attending more regularly. The leader can encourage the teen to come to the next session so the group can help address the interpersonal problem. With more regular attendance, the teen and other group members are likely to be more comfortable.

Engaging Reluctant Teens

Often, group members become engaged in role plays easily during group session 2, when role plays are based on hypothetical scenarios and do not place demands on teens to communicate effectively. These role plays are meant to be a fun introduction to those conducted in group session 3 and in the middle phase, when teens are asked to apply newly learned communication skills to conversations that group members plan to have with important people in their lives. Some teens (and group leaders) are reluctant to participate in role plays. Until teens gain familiarity with role plays, they can feel awkward or anxiety provoking. It is important to encourage teens to participate anyway because we believe that role plays are one of the most effective tools that we have to help teens improve their communication skills and therefore improve their relationships and mood. Part of what makes role plays effective is that they do evoke anxiety. The conversations that teens plan to have will be anxiety provoking in real life, and experiencing that anxiety in the context of a role play is an important part of preparing for the real thing. When teens are nervous about role plays, simply explaining this rationale can be a helpful way to convince teens to give them a try.

There are several strategies that the group leader can use to increase participation in role plays. By involving all teens in role plays from the second session of the group, the leader sends the message that this is an expected part of what teens will do together. The leader should be careful not to frame group activities as optional, as this gives teens an easy out. For example, after planning a conversation, the leader can introduce a role play as the expected next step (e.g., "Okay, you all did a great job helping Susan plan what she will say to her mother. Now, let's help Susan practice the conversation. Who wants to play the role of Susan's mother?"). This is likely to result in a role play taking place. In contrast, teens are more likely to reject a role play if they think it is optional (e.g., "Okay, you all did a great job helping Susan plan what she will say to her mother. Susan, do you want to practice the conversation?").

While in our experience the progression from hypothetical to realistic role plays typically makes this less intimidating, there are some adolescents who continue to have difficulty engaging in role plays. The most common reason that teens have difficulty with this activity is social anxiety. Teens with social anxiety are likely to have difficulty participating in role plays, because it puts the spotlight on them for an uncomfortable period of time. For some teens, participation can be facilitated by first assigning them a smaller role, such as coach, and then helping them gradually work toward discussing their own interpersonal issue, which might lead to a role play.

When the leader knows that a teen is nervous about speaking in front of the group, it is helpful to provide extra support and encouragement as needed, so that the experience of forgetting what to say or freezing in the moment does not make the activity too aversive. This might mean jumping in to remind the teen what the teen planned to say if he or she seems stuck or simply interjecting to let a teen know he or she is doing a great job if the teen knows what to say but is nervous or hesitant to continue. Another strategy is for the leader to initially accept that a teen is not willing to do a role play after planning a conversation. The leader can encourage the teen to try the planned conversation at home. If the teen is able to have the planned conversation and implement the strategies successfully, it may not be necessary for the teen to role play in subsequent groups. However, if the teen reports that he or she did not have the planned conversation or if the teen attempted the conversation but had difficulty, the leader can use this as leverage to encourage the teen to role play in the next session as a tool to improve his or her communication. Some shy teens can use the group as a way to practice speaking in front of others. While this is not a primary function of IPT-AST groups, it can provide the side benefit of helping teens to feel more comfortable speaking in front of a small group of peers. This is something that the leader can discuss with a teen individually during a mid-group session if speaking up in group is a particular concern.

Difficult or Defiant Adolescents

As discussed in Chapter 3, we recommend that teens with severe behavioral or conduct problems be excluded from IPT-AST groups. These teens are likely to require more support than the leader can provide and might have a negative impact on the experience of other group members. However, teens with mild behavior problems or who have difficulty staying on task or following adult instructions (e.g., teens with attention deficit hyperactivity disorder [ADHD] but without comorbid behavioral problems) can be productively included in IPT-AST groups. Teens who present as difficult or defiant may do so across settings or may exhibit difficulties exclusively in individual sessions or exclusively in group sessions. We describe strategies to manage difficult behaviors in each of these settings separately.

When a teen is defiant or difficult to engage in individual sessions, it often helps to provide options so that the teen feels he or she has some control over what will happen in the session. For example, in a pre-group session, the leader might allow the teen to choose which relationship to talk about next, rather than directing the conversation toward particular people on the teen's closeness circle. It may also be helpful to start by focusing on factual questions, such as how often the teen sees the other person and what activities they do together, rather than on more process- or feeling-related questions.

Another strategy is to spend more time in rapport-building, allowing the teen to warm up to the leader. When a teen shows clear resistance to participating in the session, the leader can gently point this out and ask what might be contributing to this resistance (e.g., "It seems like this is a little tough for you. How do you feel about meeting today? Is there something else you wanted to talk about instead?"). The leader should be mindful to balance completing important session tasks with helping the teen have a positive experience. When a teen has a positive experience with the leader, he or she is more likely to commit to the group and might engage with the tasks of the group more over time. For this reason, it is important to avoid responding to difficult behavior or lack of engagement with criticism. An example of how to engage a reluctant teen in the first pre-group session is provided next.

Example: Engaging a reluctant teen in the first pre-group session

LEADER: I notice that it seems a little tough for you to talk about these relationships.

BRIAN: I can talk about them, I just don't see what the point is of all this.

LEADER: I am glad you asked about that. I know it might seem kind of strange that I'm asking all these questions about the people in your life. The reason I'm doing that is so that I can get to know who the important people are in your life and what those relationships are like for you. The idea is that we will talk about some of these people today and the next time we meet. Then, toward the end of our time together next time, we are going to figure out which relationships you want to work on while you're in the group. So, talking about all these relationships will help us figure out what some helpful goals could be for you. Does that make a little more sense?

BRIAN: I don't think there's anything for me to work on. Everything is fine. I don't get why I am even doing this.

LEADER: Well, I am glad to hear that things are going well for you; that is a good thing. In fact, this program is not just for kids who have a lot of problems. Remember when we talked about prevention?

BRIAN: Yeah.

LEADER: Well, this is a prevention program, so we think that by working on improving our relationships, even if they are mostly okay, we can help prevent kids from getting depressed later. I don't think you have lots of problems or things to work on. But, everyone has trouble with communication sometimes, and everyone has some things that aren't so great about some of their relationships. Because our relationships and our mood are so related, like we talked about before, it can help us to feel better if we can make our relationships stronger and resolve any issues we might have going on. Do you think it would be okay for you and me to think about that together so you can get the most out of this program now that you are here?

BRIAN: Yeah. I guess that would be okay.

LEADER: Okay, so who do you think we should talk about first?

If a teen is reluctant to engage in either the mid-group session or in booster sessions, the leader can provide several options of interpersonal issues to discuss during the session, rather than relying on the teen to identify something to work on. These ideas should be related to the teen's interpersonal goals for the group but can include relevant hypothetical situations if the teen is resistant to discussing personal issues. During the booster sessions, the leader may decide to cut the session short if the teen is unwilling to engage in a discussion. It is still worthwhile to review the teen's depression symptoms, briefly discuss his or her interpersonal relationships, and review the communication strategies. If the teen reports a worsening of depression symptoms, the leader may be able to engage the adolescent in an examination of factors that are contributing to these symptoms, which may result in a more productive session.

The leader is faced with a different set of challenges when a group member displays difficult behavior within the context of group. Here, the entire group process must be considered. Often, teens may be silly or distracted when they are with a group of peers. To some degree, this is a good thing because it is helpful for the group dynamic if teens have a good time together. Typically, it is effective simply to redirect teens to the task at hand after a reasonable period of time. When this does not work, the leader might have to specifically redirect the adolescent who is being disruptive. Again, it is important not to be overly critical in order to maintain a positive group atmosphere. Sometimes, an adolescent who is having a hard time staying on task can be asked to sit next to the group leader to minimize distractions. Some teens respond to being given a special role in the group that can maintain their attention (e.g., observer, note taker, coach during role plays, etc.). Taking a break halfway through the group session can also help teens to stay engaged during the group.

When a group member does not respond to gentle reminders in the group sessions, the individual mid-group session is an opportune time for the leader to address issues of group behavior. This provides a private setting for the leader to express any concerns and to find out from the teen if there are particular issues affecting the teen's behavior in group. The leader can work with the teen to come up with strategies to help him or her to stay on task and to improve the way the teen communicates with other teens in the group. The leader may decide to help the teen set a secondary or tertiary goal aimed at improving behavior in the group. As the teen's group interactions are a microcosm of interactions with peers more generally, this is likely to be helpful for the teen outside the group as well.

If a group member says or does something that directly affects other group members, the leader should take more decisive action. For example, if a teen insults another group member, the teen should be reminded of the group rules, which will include a statement about being respectful of others. If this does not put either person on the spot too much, the group member who received the insult can also be asked to use the communication skills to let that teen know how the other teen's behavior made him or her feel. Before using this technique, the leader should consider how able the adolescent who made the offensive comment is to hear this type of feedback from a peer. Sometimes, communication from peers has a more powerful effect than any redirection or reprimand from a group leader can have. However, care should be taken not to place an undue burden on other group members or to produce a shaming environment for the teen with behavioral difficulties.

Example: Handling difficult behavior in the group context

TAYLOR: I think that's dumb to ask your parents for something like that. That's just really spoiled, to expect them to give you a new phone just because you lost yours.

LEADER: I want to interrupt you for a second, Taylor. It is okay for us to disagree in here, but do you all remember what we talked about in the first group session, when we set some group rules?

TAYLOR: Yeah, we talked about being nice to each other.

LEADER: Right, that is part of it. John, can you read rule 3 for us, from the rules in your binder?

JOHN: *Sure, it says, "Be respectful of other group members: say kind things and give feedback in a respectful manner."*

LEADER: *Thanks, John. Taylor, how could you rephrase the feedback that you gave to Farrah in a more respectful way?*

TAYLOR: *I don't know. I just think the way she wants to go about it would make her mom mad.*

LEADER: *Okay, that is much more respectful already. Thank you for giving that a try. Farrah, can you use an* **I statement** *to let Taylor know what it was like to hear her say that just now?*

FARRAH: *The way she just said it or what she said before?*

LEADER: *Let's start with what she just said.*

FARRAH: *I felt okay when you said it that way. I can understand that maybe some people's moms would be mad about that. It made me really mad, though, when you called me spoiled.*

LEADER: *Thank you for sharing that, Farrah. Everyone in the group is going to have a different take on what might work in a certain situation, and that is okay. The important thing is that we can disagree with each other and share different ideas in a helpful, respectful way. Just like we talked about when we learned these communication strategies, it is much harder for people to listen if they feel insulted or blamed. So, let's get back to helping Farrah with this conversation. Farrah, how do you think your mom would respond to your last statement, when you said you wanted a new phone?*

Typically, we do not recommend removing a teen from the group. Exceptions to this include times when a group member is physically violent or times when a teen consistently disrupts the group to the point it feels too uncomfortable or unsafe for other group members to receive a benefit from the group. This should rarely occur in the group, and can be prevented by careful screening of adolescents before the group begins, as is described in Chapter 3.

Breaches to Confidentiality

In the first group session and throughout the group, the leader emphasizes the importance of group members protecting each other's privacy by refraining from sharing any personal information about others outside the group. Although we have not encountered this issue personally, it is possible that an adolescent might disclose others' information, either by gossiping to peers at school or via social media. If the leader becomes aware that an adolescent has shared information with others about another group member, it is important to consider how this should be addressed both individually and within the group. Some settings may have existing policies regarding use of social media to bully or harass others, and these policies should be followed.

At the least, the leader should discuss the matter with the adolescent who disclosed information outside the group, as well as with any group members whose information was shared. It may also be advisable to discuss the breach in confidentiality with the entire group, so that all group members can discuss their concerns. It is likely that teens will know that something has happened, particularly if the group takes place in a school setting where rumors spread rapidly. By openly discussing what happened in the group, the leader can prevent further speculation. The leader may decide that an adolescent must be removed from the group if the issue cannot be resolved in a way that ensures group members feel safe talking about interpersonal issues. In other instances, it may be possible for the adolescent to stay if he or she agrees to make some reparation toward the other group member (e.g., an apology, removing statements from social media) and if the teen can assure others that nothing similar will happen again.

Challenging Family Situations

A number of difficult family situations can come up during IPT-AST, and this becomes particularly relevant during the mid-group session, when parents are invited to attend. Issues that we have encountered in the past include parents' separating or divorcing; conflictual relationships between teens and parents; parents' own mental health problems; and parents who have unrealistic expectations of the teen (from the group leader's perspective). It is important to take a neutral stance, providing support for the adolescent as the teen learns new ways to communicate with people in his or her life about difficult subjects, while respecting different families' perspectives. Often, teens have not attempted to communicate with parents about topics that have been bothering them for a long time. The leader is in a position to facilitate communication about these topics, either directly during mid-group session with parents or indirectly by helping teens to plan these conversations in the context of group meetings. Even with challenging family situations, we have seen significant positive changes in teens' relationships with their parents. Thus, we first encourage teens to try new ways of communicating in these relationships, as even small changes can have a significant impact on an adolescent's mood. If attempts to change communication are not successful, work can be done in group to help teens find ways to minimize the impact of these relationships on their mood and to seek other supportive relationships in their lives.

When parents are divorced or separated, the leader should consider how best to approach parent involvement in the program. In our work, we typically include one parent who is most involved, usually the custodial parent. It is advisable for the leader to gather some information about guardianship and custody for the adolescent to ensure that permission to participate in the program is granted by the proper legal guardian. In some situations, both parents will want to be involved and informed of issues related to their child's participation. These requests should be honored when possible and legally permitted. Involvement of both parents is useful from a clinical perspective to ensure that they both support the adolescent's work on interpersonal goals throughout the program. However, when noncustodial parents are not in regular contact with the adolescent, or when there is a hostile relationship between the adolescent and a noncustodial parent or between the parents, involvement may not be possible or desirable.

Some teens will be reluctant to have parents attend the mid-group session as a result of a difficult situation or relationship. In general, we believe that including parents in the mid-group session is helpful for teens, even if this is a difficult session. There are some cases when the teen (and the leader) might believe that inviting the parent to the mid-group session is counterproductive. For example, when a parent has his or her own mental health difficulties, a teen might worry that the parent will react poorly, leaving the teen to feel hurt or embarrassed. Alternatively, a teen might feel that a parent will be unduly burdened or stressed by having to attend the session. It is important to discuss these feelings and determine the best course of action. It is helpful for the leader to remember that the teen interacts with this parent on a regular basis; an opportunity to communicate about an issue in a mid-group session with the leader there to mediate might be helpful and is unlikely to make the situation worse.

There may be times when the leader should think about who should invite the parent to the mid-group session. When relationships between teens and parents are very tense, teens might frame the session in a misleading way that makes parents reluctant to attend. Some teens may also not relay the invitation to attend the mid-group sessions. In those cases, the leader might reach out to the parent by phone to discuss the purpose and structure of the mid-group session. This can help to remove the burden for teens of inviting a parent to the mid-group session and allows the leader to help alleviate any anxiety the parent might have about the meeting.

When guiding teens to bring up difficult topics with their parents, either at home or in a mid-group session, it is important to emphasize that a single conversation is unlikely to lead to significant or lasting change. This should not discourage teens from broaching difficult subjects, but the group leader can remind teens not to be disheartened if a single conversation does not result in the desired outcome. For example, a parent with a strict rule that her daughter cannot sleep over at a friend's house is not likely to change her mind in a single conversation. However, she might be willing to let her daughter invite a particular friend over, and once she gets to know this friend, she might over time be willing to let her daughter go over to her friend's house for dinner. Eventually, she might be more open to allowing a sleepover. When teens' expectations are realistic, they are less likely to become discouraged, give up, and decide that communicating with people is not productive.

Sensitive Topics

Adolescents should be encouraged to discuss interpersonal issues related to their goals in the group setting in most cases to help them get the most out of IPT-AST. However, some teens will have goals that they are unwilling to discuss in the presence of their peers. For example, we have had group members who are concerned about issues surrounding parental divorce; parents' infidelity; parents' incarceration; bullying by peers at the same school where groups take place; sexual orientation; as well as other sensitive topics. Some teens have chosen to share these issues with the group, often with positive results. Sharing with peers in the context of a group such as IPT-AST can be a powerful experience for teens, allowing them to get needed support from peers and helping to reduce feelings of shame when they find that peers do not judge them harshly based on what they share. However, while the leader can let teens know that others have benefitted from discussing many different issues in these groups, teens should never be forced or unduly pressured to share information with the group if they do not feel comfortable. Instead, a teen who chooses not to talk about her feelings about her parents' recent divorce can be encouraged to talk instead about her second goal (e.g., conflict with a parent about chores). The divorce-related goal can be discussed in individual mid-group and booster sessions.

Often, a teen who told the leader that he or she would not discuss a certain issue with the group might decide to do so as the teen becomes more comfortable with group members. The mid-group session provides a good opportunity for the leader to encourage an adolescent to reconsider talking about a sensitive issue in group. This discussion can take place in the context of reviewing goals and progress in group. It can be helpful for the leader and teen to conduct a brief decision analysis about the pros and cons of sharing with the group and can discuss whether there is an aspect of the problem that feels safer to discuss. For instance, we have had teens who were unwilling to talk about the infidelity that contributed to a parents' divorce but were able to talk with the group about the divorce, specifically obtaining assistance on planning a conversation with one of their parents. Two sensitive topics that have come up in IPT-AST groups in the past are discussed next.

Sexuality. Sexuality and issues regarding sexual orientation and gender identity are often difficult for teens to discuss. Teens may be at varying stages in their own process of exploring and communicating about sexual orientation or gender identity. In many cases, teens are not yet ready to discuss their sexuality with anyone, including the group leader. Relatedly, teens who have same-sex parents may or may not choose to share this with peers and might be anxious about what others might think about their family if they find out.

To help teens feel comfortable, the leader should be careful not to assume a particular sexual orientation for teens or parents. One way to avoid making assumptions is to use gender-neutral terms when appropriate. For example, rather than asking an adolescent girl if she has a boyfriend, the leader can ask if she is dating anyone or is in a romantic relationship. Similarly, in the group context, the leader can avoid assuming that a female character in a hypothetical scenario is talking to a boyfriend and can instead say "boy- or girlfriend" or "romantic partner." This careful use of language sends the message to teens that the leader is open to talking about both same-sex and opposite-sex relationships.

Some teens who are ready to talk about sexuality might use the group to think about how to come out to family members or peers. The leader can support the teen in this process by being open and accepting and by helping the teen think about how he or she might use the new communication strategies to talk to important others about sexuality. Other group members are likely to be supportive, particularly when the group has developed a good rapport. However, the leader should be alert to negative reactions from other group members, arising from either negative biases or their own discomfort with the topic of sexuality or sexual orientation.

Bullying. Teens might also be reluctant to discuss bullying with their peers, fearing that they will be judged and perhaps revictimized. Teens might not even recognize an incident as an example of bullying without the help of the leader or other group members. The leader can encourage the teen to discuss bullying with the group, to the extent that the teen is willing to do so. It can be helpful for teens who have experienced bullying to obtain support and validation from peers. The group can also help a teen figure out what to do if he or she is bullied. Typically, this will involve a decision analysis: the group works to identify and evaluate multiple options for how the teen can approach the problem. When a bully is involved, the best solution is often to seek support from a friend or an adult, as confronting the bully directly is not always useful. If a teen decides that talking to a third party might be helpful, communication skills can be applied as they would in other interpersonal situations.

Self-Harm and Suicidality

Although IPT-AST is a preventive intervention, over the course of the program the leader may learn that a teen either has thought about or has engaged in self-harm. Similarly, the group leader may learn that a teen has had thoughts of suicide. It is important to take all of this information seriously to ensure the safety of adolescents participating in IPT-AST. Chapter 3 provides an overview of how to assess teens to determine whether the IPT-AST program is likely to be a good fit. Here, we focus on what the leader can do when suicidality or thoughts of self-harm are disclosed after the group program has already begun. In these instances, the leader should refer to Chapter 3 for guidance on how to ask detailed questions about self-harm and suicide to determine the need for more intensive services.

One way that thoughts of suicide or self-harm may come to the group leader's attention is through the weekly written depression checklist and mood rating that group members complete at the start of every group session. Whenever a group member endorses Yes or Sometimes about item 14 ("Have you wished you weren't born or you could just disappear?") or 15 ("Have you thought about hurting yourself?") on the depression checklist (included in the Appendix), the leader should set time aside to meet individually with that teen after the group session is over to further assess the teen's level of risk. This should be done sensitively to avoid breaking the group member's confidentiality. Another way that these thoughts can come to the leader's attention is when a group member shares this information verbally during an individual or group session. In an individual session, the leader should assess for risk as described in Chapter 3.

When issues of self-harm or suicide are raised in a group session, the leader has to decide the best course of action both for the individual raising the topic and for the other adolescents in the group. It is important for the entire group that the leader conveys concern and takes seriously any indication that a teen is thinking about hurting him- or herself. The leader should acknowledge a disclosure about self-harm or suicidal thoughts and let the entire group know that the leader will follow up with the group member individually (e.g., "Jill, I am sorry to hear you have been feeling badly, and I'm concerned about the thoughts you've had about hurting yourself. You and I should talk more about that after the group. For now, do you want to talk more about the fight you had with your mom? It sounds like that really affected your mood last night, and I think the group could be really helpful as you try to figure out what to do next."). However, any detailed probing about suicidal thoughts or self-harm should take place after the group session when the leader and teen can meet alone. Once the leader can meet with the teen privately, the leader should thoroughly assess the level of risk to the teen and determine the best course of action. The leader should document this discussion and the protective measures that were implemented.

In most cases, we believe that the teen should be allowed to continue to participate in the IPT-AST group if there is disclosure of suicidal thoughts or nonsuicidal self-injury.

This is because removal of a teen from the group can be disruptive both for the teen and for the rest of the group. There are a few exceptions to this. Of course, if a teen is judged to be at imminent risk and requires hospitalization, the teen will be unable to attend group sessions. If the teen's symptoms are severe enough to warrant other intensive treatment in an outpatient or day treatment setting, it may be difficult for the teen to also attend prevention groups. However, if thoughts of death are fleeting or any ongoing self-injury is minor, teens can continue to address interpersonal issues through IPT-AST groups. The leader should continue to monitor the teen closely and should determine whether the teen would benefit from a referral for additional treatment while completing the IPT-AST program or after the program is over.

Suspected Abuse

The IPT-AST group leader should be familiar with the policies in place within his or her organization as well as state and federal laws pertaining to child abuse reporting. In the United States, a leader is likely to be considered a mandated reporter and would therefore be legally mandated to report any suspected abuse to the child protective service agency within the state where IPT-AST groups are conducted and to document the action taken. When an adolescent discloses information that leads a group leader to suspect abuse in an individual pre-group, mid-group, or booster session, other tasks of the session will likely have to be set aside to ask further questions about the suspected abuse.

When an adolescent discloses information that causes the leader to suspect abuse in the context of a group session, the leader should weigh the needs of the individual with the needs of the group as a whole to come to a decision about how to proceed. Several considerations should be taken into account, including the need for the teen disclosing what the leader might consider abuse to feel heard and accepted by peers and the leader; the need for the leader to assess the situation further to determine whether it should be reported; protection of confidentiality for the teen (in terms of abuse reporting); and helping all teens in the group to feel protected by the leader. It is important that the leader speaks privately with the teen to determine whether a particular situation needs to be reported. This will likely take place after the group session is over or could possibly take place during a break in the middle of the group session if the leader typically takes a break.

The leader must also decide how to handle the conversation in the moment during the group session. If the disclosure is on topic (e.g., in the context of a teen talking about a relationship he or she wants to work on) and the adolescent is asking for support or advice, it is likely advisable to allow the conversation to continue. For example, in the context of talking about how upset she feels when she and her parent argue, a teen may disclose that her parent has used corporal punishment that might be considered reportable as physical abuse. Other teens are likely to be able to empathize with the teen and support her in feeling upset about this. If the content becomes too upsetting or difficult to reasonably expect other teens to hear without adverse effects (i.e., very violent or sexual content), the leader can interrupt and let group members know that, given the situation, the leader plans to discuss this individually with the teen after the group session is over.

In the unlikely event that a teen discloses severe physical abuse or any type of sexual abuse to the group, it will be difficult for the other teens in the group to know how to respond in a helpful manner. Allowing other teens to hear more about the situation is likely to be inappropriate as it might cause them significant distress. However, it is important that the leader take care to avoid a stigmatizing or blaming response that might heighten the teen's feelings of embarrassment or shame. The group leader should convey that he or she will follow up regarding the issue, so that other teens do not worry that the leader will not address the fact that their fellow group member may be experiencing abuse.

In this chapter, we highlighted several common clinical issues that can be challenging for a group leader and provided guidance about how best to address these issues within the context of IPT-AST. If needed, the leader should also consult with other professionals, including supervisors, in settings where IPT-AST is offered. This is especially important in school settings where it might be prudent for the school administration to be involved to ensure that sensitive situations are handled in a manner consistent with school policies. The IPT-AST group leader may also encounter other challenging situations not discussed in this chapter. However, we hope that this discussion provides a useful starting place for the group leader as the leader begins to conduct IPT-AST groups.

13

Review of Empirical Evidence for IPT-AST

Since Interpersonal Psychotherapy – Adolescent Skills Training (IPT-AST) was developed 12 years ago, there have been a number of studies on the efficacy of IPT-AST for the prevention of depression in adolescents. In addition, there has been increasing recognition of the promise of IPT-AST for other populations, including adolescent girls at risk for obesity. This chapter provides an overview of the past decade of research on IPT-AST and a look at current and future directions.

Efficacy Research

In the first pilot randomized controlled trial of IPT-AST, 41 adolescents in the 7th to 10th grades with elevated depression symptoms were randomized to receive either IPT-AST or usual school counseling (SC) (Young, Mufson, & Davies, 2006). The study took place in single-sex and coeducational parochial schools in New York, which served primarily Hispanic communities. IPT-AST in this study consisted of two pre-group sessions and eight group sessions; there were no mid-group or booster sessions in this initial trial. Adolescents in SC were referred to the school counselor or social worker to be seen for individual counseling at a frequency determined by the adolescent and the clinician. School counselors could also refer the adolescent for additional treatment if the problems worsened or the adolescent requested more services. We chose usual SC as the comparison group because it approximates what normally occurred in the schools when an adolescent was identified as having mild symptoms of depression, and this allowed us to examine whether IPT-AST was more effective at addressing depression symptoms than usual counseling.

Adolescents in the two intervention conditions were compared on depression symptoms, overall functioning, and depression diagnoses postintervention and at 3-, 6-, and 12-month follow-up. Adolescents who received IPT-AST had significantly fewer depression symptoms and better overall functioning postintervention and at 3- and 6-month follow-up assessments. Adolescents in IPT-AST also reported fewer depression diagnoses than adolescents in SC in the 6 months following the intervention. More specifically, 3.7% of adolescents in IPT-AST had a depression diagnosis at any time during the 6-month follow-up period compared to 28.6% of adolescents in SC (Young et al., 2006). Although the article only reported on results through the 6-month follow-up, the diagnostic rates remained the same through the 12-month follow-up.

In secondary analyses of this pilot trial, we examined the impact of IPT-AST on parent-child conflict, a known risk factor for depression and a focus of IPT-AST. Adolescents in IPT-AST had a significantly greater decrease in mother-child conflict than SC adolescents during the intervention and follow-up (Young, Gallop, & Mufson, 2009). This finding is noteworthy because it provides preliminary evidence that IPT-AST reduces parent-child conflict, an important risk factor for depression and one of the targets of IPT-AST.

While the initial indicated study of IPT-AST was under way, a group of researchers at Vanderbilt University became interested in conducting a randomized controlled trial comparing IPT-AST to a cognitive-behavioral preventive intervention, the Coping With Stress program (CWS; Clarke & Lewinsohn, 1995). In this universal prevention study, participants were 380 high school students randomly assigned to CWS, IPT-AST, or an assessment-only control group (Horowitz et al., 2007). Both CWS and IPT-AST consisted of eight 90-minute weekly sessions held during ninth-grade wellness classes. There were no individual pre-group or mid-group sessions because of study constraints.

As briefly described in Chapter 1, CWS is a cognitive-behavioral prevention program that focuses on modifying negative and irrational thoughts believed to contribute to depression. CWS has been shown to be an effective intervention for adolescents with elevated depressive symptoms (indicated prevention) and for adolescents who are at risk for depression because they have a parent with a history of depression (selective prevention). This study examined the efficacy of IPT-AST and CWS in a universal sample of ninth-grade students; all adolescents regardless of their risk for depression participated in the study.

At postintervention, students in both the CWS and IPT-AST groups reported significantly lower levels of depressive symptoms than did those in the no intervention group; the two intervention conditions did not differ significantly from each other. Both CWS and IPT-AST were particularly effective, relative to the no intervention group, for a high-risk subset of adolescents who reported elevated depressive symptoms at baseline (Horowitz et al., 2007). This is in line with prior research that has found stronger effects of indicated prevention programs than universal programs (Horowitz & Garber, 2006; Merry et al., 2011; Stice et al., 2009). The findings from this study indicate that both IPT-AST and CWS equivalently reduce depressive symptoms in the short term for the overall sample and the high-risk subset of adolescents. But, unlike the study by Young et al. (2006), the benefits of IPT-AST and CWS did not persist at 6-month follow-up. This study lends further support to the efficacy of IPT-AST, as well as CWS, but suggests that the effects of these prevention programs are more notable and long lasting in adolescents at risk for depression, rather than in a universal sample.

In 2010, Young and colleagues published results from the second indicated prevention study of IPT-AST. In this study, we hoped to replicate the findings of Young et al. (2006) and examine the feasibility and potential benefits of including parents in IPT-AST in a school setting. To answer these questions, we conducted another randomized controlled trial comparing IPT-AST and usual SC in adolescents with elevated symptoms of depression (Young, Mufson, & Gallop, 2010). The study was conducted with 9th and 10th graders in three single-sex parochial schools. Each of the schools in the study was randomized to include parents in IPT-AST during either the first or the second year of the study. IPT-AST without parent involvement consisted of two pre-group sessions and eight weekly group sessions. In IPT-AST with parent involvement, referred to as Enhanced IPT-AST, the parents participated in one of the pre-group sessions (similar to pre-group session 1 as described in Chapter 4), a mid-group parent-adolescent session to work on a particular interpersonal issue (similar to mid-group sessions with parents as described in Chapter 7), and a post-group parent-adolescent session to review progress made during the intervention. If a parent was unable to attend a session, the adolescent met alone with the leader. Similar to our prior study, SC consisted of individual counseling sessions with the school counselor, with adolescents in SC receiving an average of 3.76 sessions over the 10-week course of the study.

Adolescents completed assessments at baseline and postintervention and at 6, 12, and 18 months postintervention. For the purposes of our primary analyses, we grouped all of the IPT-AST adolescents together. From baseline to postintervention, IPT-AST adolescents showed significantly greater improvements than SC adolescents on self-reported depression symptoms, clinician-rated depression symptoms, and overall functioning (Young et al., 2010). Regarding mean differences between the groups, IPT-AST adolescents had significantly lower depression symptoms and higher overall functioning at postintervention and 6-month follow-up. Although teens in IPT-AST continued to demonstrate lower levels of depression and higher overall functioning than teens in SC at the 12- and 18-month follow-ups, these differences were no longer significant. By the 6-month follow-up, 19.1% of SC adolescents met criteria for a depression diagnosis as compared to 0.0% of IPT-AST adolescents. By the 18-month follow-up, no additional adolescents in SC developed a depressive diagnosis (cumulative percentage 19.1%), while three IPT-AST adolescents reported an onset of a diagnosis (cumulative percentage 8.3%). These findings demonstrate a preventive effect of IPT-AST on new diagnoses of depression in the first 6 months following the program, with effects on diagnoses persisting over time, albeit at a nonsignificant level.

Regarding the question of the feasibility and benefits of including parents in IPT-AST, parents attended an average of 62.2% of the sessions (84.6% of parents attended a pre-group session, 46.2% attended the mid-group session, and 53.9% of the parents attended the post-group session). Although the study was not designed to compare the effects of IPT-AST with and without parental involvement, we examined mean differences across the two IPT-AST groups to explore the possible benefits of including parents in IPT-AST. Adolescents in Enhanced IPT-AST reported significantly lower depression scores (on both the self-report measure and the clinician-administered measure of depression) postintervention than adolescents in IPT-AST without parental involvement. There was no significant difference on overall functioning postintervention and no significant differences on depression or functioning at any of the follow-up assessments. Thus, there was some evidence of the short-term benefit of the Enhanced IPT-AST program over regular IPT-AST, but we were not able to disentangle whether it was the parental involvement or additional adolescent attention (adolescents received a mid-group session and a post-group session that adolescents in regular IPT-AST did not) that contributed to these benefits.

Based on these findings, the variable attendance of parents, and our clinical experiences conducting IPT-AST and Enhanced IPT-AST groups, we made the decision to retain the mid-group session in our more recent iterations of IPT-AST. We believed the mid-group session would be useful for all adolescents as it offers an important opportunity for individualized work on adolescents' interpersonal goals. In addition, we hoped that by reducing the number of sessions that we asked parents to attend, it would be more feasible for parents to attend the mid-group session, which would give the teens the opportunity to apply the communication strategies in a conversation with their parents. Our experiences conducting IPT-AST over the past 5 years have confirmed the clinical utility of the mid-group session, both with and without parents. As described in Chapter 4, we also invite parents to attend part of the pre-group session when it is feasible, as we believe this provides an important opportunity to orient parents to the IPT-AST program. However, in settings where it is challenging to get parents to attend sessions, we prioritize parent attendance at the mid-group session.

In secondary data analyses of the Young et al. (2010) study, we examined the effect of IPT-AST on school and social functioning (Young, Kranzler, et al., 2012). We believe it is important to examine diverse outcomes in prevention studies, rather than focusing exclusively on symptoms. IPT-AST teens experienced significantly greater improvements than SC teens in overall social functioning and functioning with friends from baseline through postintervention. Adolescents in both conditions also demonstrated significant improvements in school, dating, and family functioning, although there were no significant differences between IPT-AST and SC in rates of improvement. However, there was evidence that IPT-AST led to significant improvements in emotional engagement in school, whereas SC did not result in changes in teens' engagement in school. Finally, and perhaps most important, IPT-AST adolescents were less likely than SC adolescents to be asked to leave school for academic or behavioral reasons (9.1% vs. 28.6%) in the 18 months following the intervention. Taken together, these findings indicate that IPT-AST improves overall social functioning and functioning specifically in the peer domain, supporting our theory that IPT-AST improves interpersonal functioning. In addition, the results suggest that prevention programs that target depressive symptoms may also positively affect school engagement and school success. We believe these findings are important and augment the rationale for implementing depression prevention programs in schools. We are continuing to collect school-related outcomes (grades, attendance, and disciplinary incidents) in our ongoing studies of IPT-AST, as we recognize these data provide further support for the value of implementing prevention programs in schools.

More recently, we pooled the data from the two indicated prevention studies to examine the effects of IPT-AST on anxiety symptoms. Given that so many children and adolescents experience elevations in both depression and anxiety, we were interested in examining the effects of IPT-AST on anxiety symptoms. Adolescents who received IPT-AST demonstrated significantly greater reductions in total anxiety symptoms than SC adolescents from baseline through postintervention. Teens in IPT-AST reported significantly lower levels of anxiety symptoms at postintervention and 6-month follow-up. They continued to report lower levels of total anxiety at the 12-month follow-up than teens in SC, but these differences were no longer statistically significant (Young, Makover, et al., 2012). Importantly, the effects of IPT-AST on anxiety symptoms were generally larger than those reported in the depression prevention and treatment literature and suggest that IPT-AST is an effective prevention program for both depression and anxiety.

In 2010, we embarked on the Depression Prevention Initiative (DPI) project. DPI is a larger randomized controlled trial that compares IPT-AST delivered by research staff to group counseling (GC) delivered by school counselors in both middle and high school settings. We enrolled 186 adolescents in 7th to 10th grades with elevated symptoms of depression in the study. They have been evaluated at baseline, midintervention, postintervention, and up to 24 months following the intervention to examine the effects of IPT-AST on depressive symptoms, depressive disorders, overall functioning, interpersonal functioning, other mental health problems, and school-related indices.

This study builds on the prior IPT-AST findings in a number of ways. First, prior studies showed strong immediate effects on depression, but the benefits were not consistently maintained beyond 6 months following the intervention, suggesting the need for booster sessions to lengthen the effects of the program. In DPI, both IPT-AST and GC included four booster sessions in the 6 months following the group with the aim of enhancing the long-term effects of these programs. Second, in the prior studies, IPT-AST was compared to individual counseling, delivered at a frequency determined by school counselors. DPI compared IPT-AST to counseling groups that were run by school counselors and were matched on frequency and duration of sessions, providing a more rigorous test of the efficacy of IPT-AST. Both interventions included pre-group sessions, eight group sessions, a mid-group session, and four booster sessions in the 6 months following the intervention. Because we wanted GC to approximate normal practices in the schools, we did not provide any limitations on the content or techniques used in GC. Some GC groups were manual based, while others were more open ended. The comparison of IPT-AST and GC allows us to examine whether IPT-AST is more effective than groups that can be delivered by school counselors without additional training or supervision.

To date, we have analyzed the main outcomes, specifically depression symptoms, overall functioning, and depression diagnoses, from baseline through the 6-month follow-up. Although both IPT-AST and GC led to significant improvements in depressive symptoms and overall functioning, teens in IPT-AST showed significantly greater improvements in depressive symptoms and overall functioning than teens in GC from baseline through 6-month follow-up. However, there were no significant differences between the two conditions in onset of depression diagnoses from baseline through the 6-month follow-up (Young et al., 2015). These results indicate that IPT-AST has modest benefits over groups run by school counselors that were matched on frequency and duration of sessions, in particular in the reduction of depressive symptoms and improvements in overall functioning. It is important to note that the effect sizes (a metric used to quantify the difference between two conditions) in this study were smaller than those in our earlier IPT-AST studies. This is not surprising given that GC was a powerful comparison condition, and many GC groups utilized a number of cognitive techniques shown to be effective in preventing depression.

Although smaller than in prior studies of IPT-AST, the effect sizes are similar to or larger than those reported in meta-analyses of other depression prevention studies, many of which did not include an active comparison condition (Horowitz & Garber, 2006; Merry et al., 2011; Stice et al., 2009). Merry at al. (2011) examined the few depression prevention studies with an active control condition and found no effects on depressive symptoms or diagnoses in these studies. In the context of this literature, we are excited about the initial results from the DPI study. We are in the process of analyzing the data from later follow-up assessments to examine the long-term impact of these prevention programs on depressive symptoms, overall functioning, and depression diagnoses, as well as other outcomes, such as social functioning, school functioning, and internalizing and externalizing symptoms.

For Whom Is IPT-AST Effective?

An important step in depression prevention and intervention research is to identify factors that moderate the impact of these programs (Gillham, Shatté, & Reivich, 2001). Moderator analyses answer the question of whether an intervention is particularly helpful for a subset of the population, as well as whether there are certain types of adolescents who do not benefit from an intervention. Over the past several years, we have examined a number of possible moderators of IPT-AST, focusing both on demographic characteristics (age, gender, race/ethnicity, and income) and risk factor variables (baseline depressive symptoms, baseline anxiety symptoms, parent-child conflict, and sociotropy). To date, none of the demographic variables have moderated intervention outcomes (Horowitz et al., 2007; Young et al., 2015). We think this is encouraging as it suggests that the benefits of IPT-AST on depressive symptoms, overall functioning, and depression diagnoses are robust across gender, age, race/ethnicity, and income.

On the other hand, there is some evidence that some of the risk status variables moderate outcomes. In our first pilot randomized trial, adolescents in IPT-AST with high baseline mother-child conflict showed the greatest decreases in depressive symptoms during the course of the program, suggesting IPT-AST may be particularly effective for adolescents with high parent-child conflict (Young et al., 2009). In the Horowitz et al. (2007) study, higher levels of sociotropy, which refers to a person's tendency to value interpersonal relationships, were related to lower depressive scores in IPT-AST but were unrelated to depressive scores in the other conditions. This suggests that adolescents who value relationships may benefit from an interpersonally focused prevention program. In addition, the study by Horowitz and colleagues found that baseline level of depressive symptoms moderated intervention outcomes. More specifically, there was greater evidence of the benefits of IPT-AST and CWS, relative to a no intervention control group, in the subset of adolescents with elevated depressive symptoms. This suggests that teens with elevated depressive symptoms, those who value interpersonal relationships, and those with parent-child conflict may experience greater benefits from participating in IPT-AST than teens without these characteristics; this knowledge may guide leaders' decisions about group makeup.

Finally, in secondary analyses that combined data from the Young et al. (2006) study and the Young et al. (2010) study, we examined whether baseline levels of anxiety symptoms had an impact on depression outcomes. We examined this question given the high comorbidity between depression and anxiety symptoms in children and adolescents, as well as evidence from depression treatment studies that comorbid depression and anxiety may lead to worse outcomes. In both IPT-AST and SC, adolescents low in baseline anxiety experienced more rapid reductions in depressive symptoms than adolescents high in baseline anxiety. In other words, the presence of baseline anxiety predicted rates of improvement for adolescents in both conditions. This suggests that, for adolescents with comorbid symptoms of depression and anxiety, there may be slower rates of improvement than in adolescents who only present with elevated depression symptoms. However, it is important to note that by postintervention, there were no differences in depression symptom levels between teens with and without elevated anxiety symptoms. Thus, baseline anxiety symptoms do not mean worse long-term outcomes, but rather delayed intervention effects (Young, Makover, et al., 2012). Anxious adolescents may be initially more hesitant to use the skills learned from prevention programs, and this may contribute to delayed effects. Over time, as these adolescents begin to implement more of the IPT-AST strategies, they experience fewer depressive symptoms. Given this finding, IPT-AST leaders may want to encourage anxious adolescents to experiment with the interpersonal strategies both within and outside group to ensure that the program is effective.

Satisfaction and Attendance

While the published research on IPT-AST has focused on the efficacy of the program and possible moderators of these effects, we have also collected data on attendance and satisfaction with the IPT-AST program. We briefly review these data here as we think they speak to IPT-AST's appeal as a preventive intervention. In all three studies of IPT-AST, we had good attendance at IPT-AST sessions regardless of whether the groups were held during the school day or after school hours. In the first two studies, we held individual sessions during students' free periods or after school, and group sessions were held after school. In the first study by Young and colleagues (2006), adolescents in the 7th to 10th grades attended an average of 2.0 pre-group sessions and 6.9 of 8 group sessions. In the second study, with high school students, there were more missed sessions (adolescents attended an average of 1.9 pre-group sessions and 5.2 of 8 group sessions), but attendance levels were still better than those reported in other prevention studies. Finally, in the DPI project, individual and group sessions occurred either during the school day or after school. Adolescents attended an average of 2.0 pre-group sessions, 0.98 mid-group sessions, 6.8 group sessions, and 3.6 of 4 booster sessions. This means that the average teen in IPT-AST attended 89.5% of the group and individual sessions. Of note, attendance in the IPT-AST condition was significantly better than attendance in the GC condition (Young et al., 2015) and better than reported in other school-based prevention studies. We believe the attendance data speak to the appeal of IPT-AST to adolescents and points to the feasibility of implementing IPT-AST in schools, whether during the school day or after school.

We have also collected intervention satisfaction data in our studies that indicate that adolescents enjoy participating in IPT-AST and find it helpful. In the first study, 92.6% of adolescents in IPT-AST rated the intervention as very helpful (66.7%) or helpful (25.9%) compared to 76.9% of adolescents in SC (very helpful: 23.1%; helpful: 53.8%). In the second study, 94.0% rated IPT-AST favorably (very helpful: 66.7%; helpful: 27.3%) and 70.0% rated SC favorably (very helpful: 15.0%, helpful: 55.0%). Thus, in both of these studies, teens reported that IPT-AST was more helpful than the individual counseling typically provided in these schools.

In the DPI project, we assessed satisfaction with both programs: IPT-AST and groups delivered by school counselors (GC). In IPT-AST, 88% of teens rated the intervention as very helpful (58.7%) or helpful (29.3%). In GC, 91% of teens rated the groups as very helpful (51.7%) or helpful (39.3%). Thus, adolescents in both conditions viewed the groups favorably, speaking to the relevance and promise of conducting groups in schools. Despite similar ratings of intervention satisfaction across the two conditions, significantly more IPT-AST adolescents (83.5%) than GC adolescents (67.0%) reported feeling confident that they did not need additional services after completing the group. This suggests that, although teens liked both prevention programs, teens who participated in IPT-AST felt more confident that they could continue to apply the IPT-AST strategies and therefore did not need additional services. We believe the attendance and satisfaction data provide a compelling rationale for running IPT-AST groups.

IPT-AST Adaptations

Over the past several years, other researchers have become interested in studying the implementation of IPT-AST to prevent other health problems. Specifically, Dr. Marian Tanofsky-Kraff and her colleagues have developed a modification of IPT-AST for the prevention of weight gain (IPT-WG) in adolescent girls at risk for obesity. IPT-WG is based on the theory that interpersonal problems contribute to loss of control eating, which leads to weight gain; IPT-WG can break this cycle by addressing interpersonal difficulties that result in negative affect and loss of control eating, thereby averting excessive weight gain (Tanofsky-Kraff et al., 2007). The IPT-WG program is based on IPT-AST and interpersonal psychotherapy (IPT) for eating disorders (Wilfley, MacKenzie, Welch, Ayres, & Weissman, 2000) and includes one 90-minute pre-group session, twelve 90-minute group sessions, and a brief individual mid-group and post-group check-in. In two randomized controlled trials, IPT-WG has been compared to a health education (HE) control for overweight adolescent girls. In the first study, adolescents who participated in IPT-WG experienced greater reductions in loss of control eating episodes than adolescents in HE and were less likely to gain excessive weight during the 1-year follow-up (Tanofsky-Kraff et al., 2010). In their second study, both IPT-WG and HE led to decreases in expected weight gain, but IPT-WG adolescents reported fewer binge-eating episodes at 1-year follow-up than adolescents in HE (Tanofsky-Kraff et al., 2014). These findings point to the impact of programs based on IPT-AST on other important health domains, besides depression.

Current and Future Directions

We are continuing to analyze data from the DPI project to better understand the effects of IPT-AST on a variety of outcomes and to examine the mechanisms through which IPT-AST affects depression symptoms and overall functioning. We have some evidence from prior studies that IPT-AST improves parent-child conflict, overall social functioning, and functioning in the peer domain. However, because of the size of these studies, we have been unable to examine whether changes in these interpersonal domains lead to (or mediate) change in depression and functioning. The DPI sample is large enough to examine this important question. We also plan to examine whether various risk factors (e.g., parent-child conflict, interpersonal functioning, parental depression) moderate intervention outcomes so we can continue to determine for whom IPT-AST is most effective. In addition, these analyses will guide the further development of IPT-AST to ensure that the program is beneficial for a wide range of youth from diverse backgrounds. Finally, we are interested in better understanding the types of groups that counselors led in the GC condition and the techniques utilized in these groups, as many of these groups had powerful and positive effects on depression symptoms and functioning. We hope to determine which types of groups were associated with better outcomes, as this can inform future prevention programs in schools, as well as the IPT-AST trainings we conduct with school counselors.

In addition to work on the DPI project, we are in the early stages of the Personalized Depression Prevention (PDP) project. The PDP project is a two-site study that is examining whether the effects of prevention programs can be maximized by matching youth with different risk profiles to interventions that more specifically address their needs. For example, IPT-AST, which focuses on interpersonal issues, may be particularly helpful for adolescents high on parent-child conflict or who have other interpersonal difficulties, but may be less relevant for adolescents with positive relationships. To boost effects of depression prevention programs, there may be value in developing strategies to match adolescents to prevention programs based on their risk factors for developing depression.

In the PDP project, teens with high cognitive and interpersonal risk profiles are being randomized to two interventions that are designed to address distinct risk factors for depression: CWS, a cognitive-behavioral prevention program; and IPT-AST, an interpersonal prevention program. This will allow us to determine whether we can identify which adolescents would benefit most from a particular prevention program. To date, much progress has been made developing and studying depression prevention programs. Moderator analyses, such as those described in our IPT-AST studies, provide useful information about which individuals are most likely to respond to an intervention. However, studies, such as PDP, that include two different prevention programs that target different risk factors for depression provide prescriptive information about what type of prevention program would be of most benefit to a given adolescent.

So far, research on IPT-AST has supported its efficacy in reducing depressive symptoms, improving functioning, and preventing depression diagnoses in adolescents. These effects appear to be robust across gender, ethnic, racial, and socioeconomic lines, supporting the use of this intervention with diverse populations. Ongoing research is being conducted to investigate ways to lengthen the effects of IPT-AST and examine whether teens with different risk factors for depression might benefit from different types of prevention programs. Our hope is that this ongoing research and future research efforts will continue to lead to improvements in IPT-AST and other prevention programs and will provide clinicians and counselors with a method to determine which program would be most beneficial for each adolescent who presents in their offices.

Appendix

Pre-Group Session 1 Outline   177

Pre-Group Session 2 Outline   178

Group Session 1 Outline   179

Group Session 2 Outline   180

Group Session 3 Outline   181

Group Session 4 Outline   182

Mid-Group Session With Parent(s) Outline   183

Mid-Group Session Without Parents Outline   184

Group Session 5 Outline   185

Group Session 6 Outline   186

Group Session 7 Outline   187

Group Session 8 Outline   188

Booster Session Outline   189

Closeness Circle   190

Interpersonal Inventory: How to Query About Relationships   191

Depression Checklist   192

Depression Vignettes   193

Communication Notecards   198

Interpersonal Scenario Notecards   204

Communication Strategy Cue Cards   215

Communication Strategy Descriptions   225

Certificate of Participation   226

The materials in the Appendix are available online. You may download and print these reproducible materials. To access these items online, please visit http://www.oxfordclinicalpsych.com/, search for the book's title, and click on the Appendix section.

Pre-Group Session 1 Outline

With Teen and Parent:

1. Introduce concept of prevention and provide a rationale for the interpersonal focus of IPT-AST.
2. Orient adolescent and parent(s) to the group program, providing information on the number and duration of sessions and parent involvement in the mid-group session.

With Teen Alone:

3. Assess for depression symptoms in the past week.
4. Introduce and complete mood rating using 1–10 scale and help the teen link mood to events in relationships.
5. Complete a closeness circle interactively with teen to identify important relationships that will be discussed in the interpersonal inventory.
6. Begin the interpersonal inventory with the goal of assessing four to six key relationships across both pre-group sessions.
7. Summarize what was discussed and prepare teen to continue to work on the interpersonal inventory in the next session.

Materials Needed:

1. Copy of depression checklist for leader's reference
2. Closeness circle
3. List of questions to ask during interpersonal inventory for leader's reference

Pre-Group Session 2 Outline

1. Assess for depression symptoms in the past week and complete a mood rating.
2. Complete the interpersonal inventory, focusing on relationships that have the greatest impact on teen's mood.

   a. If potential goals are unclear based on review of individual relationships, ask additional questions about difficulties making friends, recent transitions, and other interpersonal events that have an impact on mood.

3. Provide a summary and feedback about the interpersonal inventory, highlighting what you have learned about challenges and strengths in teen's relationships.
4. Collaboratively set two goals for teen to work on based on the interpersonal inventory; ideal goals are specific and target problems that have an impact on the teen's mood.
5. Introduce teen to the group program, explaining that the group is an interpersonal lab where teens can experiment with new ways of interacting with others.
6. Address any concerns the teen may have about participating in the group.

Materials Needed:
1. List of depression symptoms for leader's reference
2. Completed closeness circle from pre-group session 1
3. List of questions to ask during interpersonal inventory for leader's reference
4. Written group schedule to give to teen at end of session (optional)

Group Session 1 Outline

1. Distribute binders with weekly depression checklists, description of communication strategies, and communication strategy cue cards.
2. Have adolescents complete depression checklist and mood rating.
3. Conduct group introductions and icebreaker activity so teens begin to feel comfortable.
4. Collaboratively establish group rules; guide teens to discuss the following:

    a. Confidentiality
    b. How group members will interact outside group
    c. Mutual respect for others
    d. Giving feedback to others in a constructive manner
    e. Time commitment to group and policies regarding lateness or cancelling

5. Discuss that in the group teens will learn new ways to communicate in relationships and outline the role of group members and the group leader.
6. Discuss signs and symptoms of depression using depression vignettes, highlighting the differences between normal sadness and depression.
7. Discuss issues and problems that teenagers face and explain how the group can help teens handle the interpersonal issues that were raised.
8. Summarize discussion and encourage consistent attendance at remaining sessions.

Materials Needed:

1. Binders and pens
2. Materials for icebreaker activity (e.g., candy)
3. Printed depression vignettes

Group Session 2 Outline

1. Distribute binders and have adolescents complete depression checklist and mood rating.
2. Distribute and review a printed list of rules.
3. Discuss links between mood and interactions with others, utilizing a personal example.
4. Use a hypothetical situation to illustrate how interactions affect mood and relationships.
5. Conduct activity to illustrate impact of teens' communication on others and discuss how people interpret statements based on both the words used and nonverbal cues.
6. Conduct activity to illustrate impact of teens' communication on interpersonal interactions, where leader and teens role play interpersonal scenarios.
7. Introduce communication analysis to dissect the role plays, discussing questions such as the following:

   a. What did you say?
   b. What did he/she say?
   c. Then what happened?
   d. How did you feel? How do you think it made _____ feel?
   e. Could you tell him/her how you felt?
   f. Was that the message you wanted to convey?

8. Encourage adolescents to think about the link between their relationships and mood over the next week.

Materials Needed:

1. Binders and pens
2. Printed group rules
3. Communication notecards
4. Interpersonal scenario notecards

Group Session 3 Outline

1. Distribute binders and have adolescents complete depression checklist and mood rating.
2. Role play additional interpersonal scenarios and conduct communication analysis, emphasizing turning points in the conversations.
3. Interactively teach six communication strategies:

    a. Strike while the iron is cold
    b. I statements
    c. Be specific
    d. Put yourself in their shoes
    e. Have a few solutions in mind and remember to compromise
    f. Don't give up

4. Practice applying these communication strategies by redoing the role plays from earlier in the session; this involves having group members:

    a. Brainstorm how each strategy can apply and then script the conversation in detail.
    b. Role play the conversation.
    c. Debrief about the interaction, focusing on how this differed from the initial role play.

5. Highlight transition to middle phase sessions, where the sessions will focus on addressing interpersonal problems related to group members' goals.
6. Describe and discuss mid-group sessions.

Materials Needed:

1. Binders and pens
2. Interpersonal scenario notecards
3. Communication strategy cue cards

Group Session 4 Outline

1. Distribute binders and have adolescents complete depression checklist and mood rating.
2. Remind group members of transition to middle phase group sessions.
3. Model and complete mood ratings aloud, having teens share if mood was better, worse, or the same as the previous week; help teens link changes in mood to interpersonal events.
4. Discuss group members' interpersonal situations:

    a. Identify an interpersonal situation to work on.
    b. Conduct a communication analysis to learn more about relevant prior interactions.
    c. Use decision analysis (if needed) to decide how to resolve the interpersonal situation.
    d. Help teen clarify goals and the main message the teen wants to convey in the conversation.
    e. Discuss how communication strategies can be used to increase the likelihood of a successful interaction.
    f. Script the conversation in detail, considering how the other person will likely respond.
    g. Role play the conversation and debrief about how it went.
    h. Help the teen revise the plan if needed.

5. Assign and prepare for interpersonal work at home, helping teen to anticipate barriers to a successful conversation.
6. Remind group members about upcoming mid-group sessions and mark the midpoint of the group.

Materials Needed:

1. Binders and pens
2. Communication strategy cue cards

Mid-Group Session With Parent(s) Outline

With Teen Alone:

1. Discuss and address any concerns about the group.
2. Review progress toward interpersonal goals, helping teen revise goals if needed.
3. Collaboratively decide what the teen will discuss with his or her parent and script conversation using communication strategies.
4. Discuss what will be shared with parent, including general information about the group and positive feedback about teen's participation.

With Teen and Parent:

5. Provide information about the group so far, review the teen's progress in the group, and elicit parent feedback and concerns.
6. Facilitate communication between the teen and parent, coaching teen actively during the interaction as needed to encourage effective communication; if teen does not want to discuss an issue with parent, prompt teen to teach parent communication strategies.
7. Discuss their reactions to this way of communicating and encourage continued use of the strategies if the interaction was successful.

With Teen Alone:

8. Debrief regarding conversation with parent, identifying successes and challenges.
9. Discuss what the teen will share with the group; encourage teen to disclose what was talked about so that the group can provide further support and learn from the teen's experience.

Materials Needed:

1. Communication strategy cue cards

Mid-Group Session Without Parents
Outline

1. Discuss and address any concerns about the group.
2. Review communication strategies if the teen missed session 3 or if the teen seems to have difficulty understanding the strategies.
3. Review progress toward interpersonal goals, helping teen revise goals if needed.
4. Identify an issue related to the teen's interpersonal goals to work on in session.
5. Discuss the teens' interpersonal issue:

   a. Identify an interpersonal situation to work on.
   b. Conduct a communication analysis to learn more about relevant prior interactions.
   c. Use decision analysis (if needed) to decide how to resolve the interpersonal situation.
   d. Help teen clarify goals and the main message the teen wants to convey in the conversation.
   e. Discuss how communication strategies can be used to increase the likelihood of a successful interaction.
   f. Script the conversation in detail, considering how the other person will likely respond.
   g. Role play the conversation and debrief about how it went.
   h. Help the teen revise the plan if needed.

6. Assign and prepare for interpersonal work at home related to what was discussed in mid-group, helping teen to anticipate barriers to a successful conversation.
7. Discuss what the teen will share with the group; encourage teen to disclose what was talked about so that the group can provide further support.

Materials Needed:

1. Communication strategy cue cards

Group Session 5 Outline

1. Distribute binders and have adolescents complete depression checklist and mood rating.
2. Complete mood ratings aloud and help teens link mood to interpersonal events.
3. Discuss mid-group sessions completed before session 5; ask teens to share what they worked on and reflect on strategies that were effective or ineffective.
4. Review interpersonal work at home assigned in the previous session or in mid-group sessions and conduct communication analyses if appropriate.
5. Discuss group members' interpersonal situations:

   a. Identify an interpersonal situation to work on.
   b. Conduct a communication analysis to learn more about relevant prior interactions.
   c. Use decision analysis (if needed) to decide how to resolve the interpersonal situation.
   d. Help teen clarify goals and the main message the teen wants to convey in the conversation.
   e. Discuss how communication strategies can be used to increase the likelihood of a successful interaction.
   f. Script the conversation in detail, considering how the other person will likely respond.
   g. Role play the conversation and debrief about how it went.
   h. Help the teen revise the plan if needed.

6. Assign and prepare for interpersonal work at home, helping teen to anticipate barriers to a successful conversation.

Materials Needed:

1. Binders and pens
2. Communication strategy cue cards

Group Session 6 Outline

1. Distribute binders and have adolescents complete depression checklist and mood rating.
2. Complete mood ratings aloud and help teens link mood to interpersonal events.
3. Discuss mid-group sessions completed between session 5 and session 6; ask teens to share what they worked on and reflect on strategies that were effective or ineffective.
4. Review interpersonal work at home assigned in the previous session or in mid-group sessions and conduct communication analyses if appropriate.
5. Discuss group members' interpersonal situations:

   a. Identify an interpersonal situation to work on.
   b. Conduct a communication analysis to learn more about relevant prior interactions.
   c. Use decision analysis (if needed) to decide how to resolve the interpersonal situation.
   d. Help teen clarify goals and the main message the teen wants to convey in the conversation.
   e. Discuss how communication strategies can be used to increase the likelihood of a successful interaction.
   f. Script the conversation in detail, considering how the other person will likely respond.
   g. Role play the conversation and debrief about how it went.
   h. Help the teen revise the plan if needed.

6. Assign and prepare for interpersonal work at home, helping teen to anticipate barriers to a successful conversation.

Materials Needed:

1. Binders and pens
2. Communication strategy cue cards

Group Session 7 Outline

1. Distribute binders and have adolescents complete depression checklist and mood rating.
2. Complete mood ratings aloud and help teens link mood to interpersonal events.
3. Mark the transition from the middle phase to the termination phase of the group, where the sessions will focus on reviewing main themes and preparing teens for continued work on their interpersonal relationships after the group ends.
4. Review interpersonal work at home assigned in the previous session and conduct communication analyses if appropriate; if work at home was not completed, help teen address any barriers.
5. Discuss any pressing interpersonal situations; identify which skills would be helpful to address the interpersonal problem, drawing on group members' experiences utilizing the strategies in similar situations.
6. Discuss communication strategies that were most helpful/challenging for group members and how group members can address any challenges to successful application of the strategies.
7. Address barriers to using interpersonal strategies, such as reluctance to express feelings or not wanting to initiate a conversation that feels out of the blue.
8. Emphasize importance of attending the last session, plan last group activities, and assign interpersonal work at home if appropriate.

Materials Needed:

1. Binders and pens
2. Communication strategy cue cards

Group Session 8 Outline

1. Distribute binders and have adolescents complete depression checklist and mood rating.
2. Ask teens to review changes in mood ratings and depression symptoms since the start of the group, linking changes in mood to events in relationships.
3. Identify warning symptoms and what to do if teens experience these symptoms in the future; options include talking to someone to address an interpersonal problem or get support, using other coping strategies, and talking to an adult if symptoms persist.
4. Review interpersonal work at home assigned in the previous session (if needed).
5. Identify the most significant interpersonal issue(s) each teen worked on and discuss if this resulted in changes in the relationship or how the teen coped with the relationship.
6. Discuss how teens can maintain skills learned in the group, either on their own or with the help of others.
7. Encourage continued interpersonal work on teens' goals as well as in future situations.
8. Discuss characteristics to look for in important people in teens' lives using a group activity where teens write down positive feedback about each other.
9. Discuss teens' experience of being in a group and elicit feedback.
10. Discuss and plan for booster sessions if offered.
11. Have graduation ceremony to recognize teens' work in the group.

Materials Needed:

1. Binders and pens
2. Communication strategy cue cards
3. Paper for teens to write down characteristics of group members
4. Graduation certificates

Booster Session Outline

1. Assess mood rating over the past month, identifying fluctuations in mood, linking these to interpersonal events, and noting any interpersonal issues that might be relevant to discuss in more depth later in the session.
2. Assess depression symptoms over the past week.
3. Review progress made on interpersonal goals and discuss emerging interpersonal issues.
4. Discuss how techniques from group can be used to address a current interpersonal problem; this would include conducting a communication analysis or decision analysis, reviewing communication strategies and discussing how they can increase the likelihood of a successful interaction, and scripting and role playing a conversation.
5. If teen does not identify an interpersonal situation to work on:

   a. Review the communication strategies, asking whether the teen has utilized the skills and whether these skills might be helpful in upcoming interpersonal situations.
   b. Script and role play a conversation related to a hypothetical situation that is closely related to a current or anticipated future interpersonal issue for the teen.

6. Assign and prepare for interpersonal work at home, helping teen to anticipate barriers to a successful conversation (if appropriate).
7. Discuss the possibility of worsening symptoms and strategies teen can use to address them.

Materials Needed:

1. Communication strategy cue cards

Closeness Circle

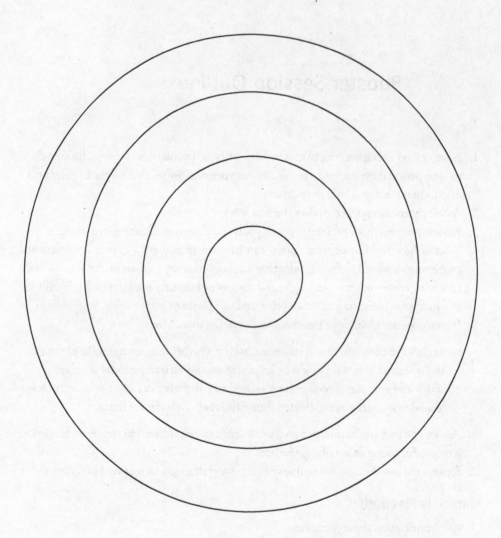

Interpersonal Inventory: How to Query About Relationships

Questions to Ask All Adolescents About Each Relationship:

- How often do you see this person?
- How often do you communicate by phone, text, or email?
- What do you do together?
- How do you get along with _____ ?
- What do you like about _____ ?
- What don't you like about _____ ?
- What can you talk about with this person?
- Can you confide in this person? Can you talk about your feelings?
- Are there any things you cannot or would not talk about with this person?
- If you do not talk about your feelings with this person, what stops you?
- Are there things you don't agree on? What are they?
- How often do you argue with this person?
- When you have an argument with _____ , how does it get resolved?
- How do arguments with this person affect your mood?
- Have you noticed times when your mood has affected how you act toward this person?
- How does being with this person affect your mood?
- Are there things about the relationship that you would like to change?
- How would you feel if those things were different?

Additional Questions to Consider:

- Do you have difficulty making friends? In what way?
- How do you feel about meeting new people?
- How do you feel in new social situations?
- Can you confide in anyone? Who?
- Have there been any changes in your family recently?
- Have you had to adapt to anything new, like a new school or new neighborhood?
- What has been difficult about the change(s)?

Note: Closeness Circle and Interpersonal Inventory adapted from Mufson, L., Dorta, K. P., Moreau, D., & Weissman, M. M. (2004). *Interpersonal psychotherapy for depressed adolescents* (2nd ed.). New York: Guilford Press.

Name:_____ Date: _____/_____/_____

Depression Checklist

During the past week . . .

1. Have you felt sad a lot?	Yes	Sometimes	No
2. Have you felt hopeless that things will never get better?	Yes	Sometimes	No
3. Have you gotten mad easily, sometimes over little things?	Yes	Sometimes	No
4. Has it been difficult to have fun doing things you used to enjoy?	Yes	Sometimes	No
5. Have you felt guilty about little things that may not be your fault?	Yes	Sometimes	No
6. Have you felt more or less hungry than you used to?	Yes	Sometimes	No
7. Have you had trouble falling asleep or staying asleep?	Yes	Sometimes	No
8. Have you taken lots of naps or felt like sleeping all the time?	Yes	Sometimes	No
9. Have you had less energy than you used to?	Yes	Sometimes	No
10. Have you felt bad about yourself?	Yes	Sometimes	No
11. Has it been difficult to pay attention in school?	Yes	Sometimes	No
12. Has it been hard to make decisions?	Yes	Sometimes	No
13. Have you had headaches or stomachaches a lot?	Yes	Sometimes	No
14. Have you wished you weren't born or you could just disappear?	Yes	Sometimes	No
15. Have you thought about hurting yourself?	Yes	Sometimes	No

RATE YOURSELF ON A SCALE OF 1–10, WHERE 1 IS THE **BEST** YOU'VE EVER FELT AND 10 IS THE **MOST DEPRESSED** YOU'VE EVER FELT.

----

1   2   3   4   5   6   7   8   9   10

Depression Vignettes

Anna is a 15-year-old girl. For the past month, she has been feeling sad. She's not sure why, but thinks maybe it has to do with starting a new school and not knowing a lot of people. She has been having trouble falling asleep. Sometimes, she lies in bed for 2 hours before she finally falls asleep. During the day, she feels really tired, and, although she is going to school, she finds that her mind wanders in her classes. As a result, she failed her last three quizzes. Anna feels really guilty about this and worries that her mom will be disappointed. Anna used to love going out with friends, but lately she doesn't feel like it. Instead, she goes home and sits in front of the television by herself.

Jose is a 13-year-old boy. He has been getting in a lot of arguments with his mom and brother since the school year started. It seems that whatever Jose's brother does, it bothers Jose. In addition, Jose has been having a lot of headaches, and he has lost his appetite. He went to the doctor, but the doctor said that nothing was wrong. Lately, Jose has been thinking about his dad, who died when he was younger. Sometimes when he thinks about this, he feels like life is not worth living anymore. All Jose wants to do is sleep. If he could, he would sleep all day. In addition, he has been having a hard time making decisions, such as what to do after school or what to wear in the morning.

George is a 16-year-old boy who feels sad almost every day. He's not sure what happened, but in the past few months, he just hasn't felt like himself. He has been spending time alone a lot and can't pay attention in class. When he does hang out with friends, he has a good time and feels better.

Carla is a 12-year-old girl who feels sad a couple of times a week. The sadness lasts for about an hour or two and then goes away when Carla finds something to do. Some of the sadness is related to the fact that Carla hasn't been getting along with her best friend, Marie. Ever since they started seventh grade, Marie has been hanging out with a new group of girls, and Carla feels left out. On Sundays, Carla has a hard time falling asleep because she thinks about the upcoming week at school and wonders whether Marie will include her.

Communication Notecards

✂ ....

<u>Say the following in a *quiet* voice</u>
<u>while looking down:</u>
"I'm fine. Nothing's wrong.
Really, I'm fine."

Say the following in a regular, _calm_ voice:

"I'm fine. Nothing's wrong. Really, I'm fine."

✂ ┄┄

Say in a _loud_ voice:

"What do you want from me? No matter what I do, nothing is okay with you!!!
I'M SICK OF THIS."

Say in a _calm_ voice:
"Maria, I feel sad when you talk
about me behind my back. It hurts
my feelings."

✂ ···

Say with your arms crossed:
"You always do that. You say we'll
play basketball and then you
don't show."

Say in a *calm* voice:
"Dad, I don't think it's fair that I have to take care of my brother every weekend."

✂ ···

Say in a *sad* voice:
"I can't believe you gave me an F. My parents are going to freak out."

<u>Say in an *angry* voice:</u>
"I can't believe you gave me an
F. My parents are going to
freak out."

✂ ....

<u>Say in a *quiet, sad* voice:</u>
"Mom, I hate you.
You are ruining my life.
I wish I had a different mother."

Interpersonal
Scenario Notecard

Say with your arms crossed:
"You always do that. You say you are going to hang out with me after school, and then you go off with Wendy instead."

✂ ....

Say in a *loud, angry* voice:
"Mom, I hate you.
You are ruining my life.
I wish I had a different mother."

Interpersonal
Scenario Notecards

You heard that someone in your
class was spreading rumors about you.
You want to approach this classmate.
What do you say?
**_Pick someone to play your
classmate._**

✂ ···

You are upset with your friends because
they didn't ask you to go to the movies.
You want to talk to two of your friends
about this.
What can you say to your friends?
Pick two people to play your friends.

Every time you go out with your friends,
your mom or dad calls you every
5 minutes on your cell phone.
***What might you say to
your mom or dad?***
**Pick someone to play your mom
or dad.**

✂ ....

Your parents have told you that you are
not allowed to date anyone until you are
18. You don't agree with this and decide
to talk to your parents about it.
What would you say?
**Pick two people to play your
parents.**

Your brother teases you and calls you fat all the time. You decide it's time to talk to him about it.
What would you say?
Pick someone to play your brother.

✂ ....

Your friend is flirting with someone you like.
What can you say to your friend?
Pick someone to play your friend.

You are in a fight with your friend because your friend started spending a lot of time with other classmates. You feel left out and want to talk about it.
What would you say?
Pick someone to play your friend.

✂ ···

You are upset because your parents won't let you talk on the phone with friends. You decide to talk to them about it.
What can you say?
Pick someone to play your parents.

You think your parent makes you clean
up more than your brother or sister, and
it doesn't seem fair.
What can you say?
Pick someone to play your parent.

✂ ....

You would like to spend more time
with your mom or dad.
What can you say to him/her?
**Pick someone to play your mom
or dad.**

A friend told you that he saw your girlfriend talking to another guy.
What can you say to your girlfriend?
Pick someone to play your girlfriend.

✂ ....

You are annoyed. There is a basketball game on TV and your sister wants to watch something else.
What can you say to her?
Pick someone to play your sister.

You are in a fight with a friend because your friend is spending lots of time with the person he or she is dating.
What do you say to your friend?
Pick someone to play your friend.

✂ ···

Your parents have told you that you can't go to a party this Saturday. You don't agree with this and decide to talk to them.
What can you say to them?
Pick two people to play your parents.

You are angry because your friends
played basketball over the weekend
without telling you.
What can you to say to your friends?
Pick someone to play your friends.

✂ ....

You want to ask your mom or dad if you
can go out with friends.
How do you do it?
**_Pick someone to play your mom
or dad._**

You are upset because your teacher gave you a bad grade on an assignment. You want to talk to him or her about it.
What can you say?
Pick someone to play your teacher.

✂ ···

You just started at a new school and are trying to meet people. There is a nice person in your class who you want to talk to.
What can you say?
Pick someone to play your classmate.

A classmate has posted something about you online, and you are upset about it. You decide to talk to a friend for support.
What can you say?
Pick someone to play your friend.

✂ ⋯⋯⋯⋯⋯⋯⋯⋯⋯⋯⋯⋯⋯⋯⋯⋯⋯⋯⋯⋯⋯⋯

You are having trouble with one of your classes and want to ask your teacher for help.
What can you say?
Pick someone to play your teacher.

Communication Strategy
Cue Cards

STRIKE WHILE THE IRON IS COLD!

✁ ....

I STATEMENTS!

BE SPECIFIC!
(No "You always ..." or
"You never ...")

✂ ....

PUT YOURSELF IN THEIR SHOES!

HAVE A FEW SOLUTIONS IN MIND AND REMEMBER TO COMPROMISE!

✂ ....

DON'T GIVE UP!

STRIKE WHILE THE IRON IS COLD!

I STATEMENTS!

BE SPECIFIC!

(No "You always ... " or "You never ... ")

PUT YOURSELF IN THEIR SHOES!

HAVE A FEW SOLUTIONS IN MIND AND REMEMBER TO COMPROMISE!

DON'T GIVE UP!

Communication Strategy Descriptions

1. **Strike while the iron is cold**. Pick the right time to have a conversation. Having a conversation when upset often leads to saying things that you later regret. You can have a more constructive conversation once you have both calmed down. You also want to find a time when both of you are not busy or distracted by something else. To strike while the iron is cold, start by asking the other person if it is a good time to talk.

2. **I statements**. I statements tell the other person about how you feel (use a feeling word) without blaming the other person. Often, when we argue we say things that blame the other person. It is more effective to tell the other person how his or her behavior makes you feel: "I feel hurt when you interrupt me when I am talking to you." You can also use I statements to express positive feelings: "I am happy we got to spend time together. Let's do it again soon."

3. **Be specific**. Avoid saying things like "you always" or "you never." It is unlikely that someone always or never does something. It makes the other person feel defensive and makes him or her less likely to listen to what you are saying. Also, you should try to focus on the present situation rather than bringing up things that happened the past.

4. **Put yourself in their shoes**. Understanding another person's perspective, while acknowledging your own feelings, makes it easier to come to a compromise. Remember that just because you understand another person's perspective does not mean you agree. But, it is helpful to start a conversation positively by acknowledging how the other person feels. Putting yourself in someone's shoes involves (a) thinking about how the other person feels and (b) communicating that to the other person. It often starts with "I understand you . . ."

5. **Have a few solutions in mind and remember to compromise**. If you want to work something out, do a little prep work. Come up with a few possible compromises to resolve the conflict before having the conversation. It is also helpful to ask the other person during the conversation if he or she has any ideas about how to solve the problem. This shows that you are open to compromising.

6. **Don't give up**. Changing the way we communicate is not easy. But, if you keep working, you will see a difference. Don't give up does not mean you should keep fighting when things are heated. It means you should keep trying to use these communication strategies to improve your relationships even if it does not go well the first time.

CERTIFICATE
OF PARTICIPATION

Presented to

_____

for the successful
completion of the
IPT-AST Group

Signed _____

Date _____

References

Andrews, G., Sanderson, K., Corry, J., & Lapsley, H. (2000). Using epidemiological data to model efficiency in reducing the burden of depression. *The Journal of Mental Health Policy and Economics*, 3, 175–186.

Brent, D. A., McMakin, D. L., Kennard, B. D., Goldstein, T. R., Mayes, T. L., & Douaihy, A. B. (2013). Protecting adolescents from self-harm: A critical review of intervention studies. *Journal of the American Academy of Child and Adolescent Psychiatry*, 52, 1260–1271.

Brown, J. D., Wissow, L. S., Zachary, C., & Cook, B. L. (2007). Receiving advice about child mental health from a primary care provider: African American and Hispanic parent attitudes. *Medical Care*, 45, 1076–1082.

Clarke, G. N., Hornbrook, M., Lynch, F., Polen, M., Gale, J., Beardslee, W., . . . Seeley, J. (2001). A randomized trial of a group cognitive intervention for preventing depression in adolescent offspring of depressed parents. *Archives of General Psychiatry*, 58, 1127–1134.

Clarke, G. N., & Lewinsohn, P. M. (1995). *Instructor's manual for the adolescent coping skills course.* Unpublished manual, Oregon Health Sciences University, Portland.

Costello, E. J., He, J. P., Sampson, N. A., Kessler, R. C., & Merikangas, K. R. (2014). Services for adolescents with psychiatric disorders: 12-month data from the National Comorbidity Survey–Adolescent. *Psychiatric Services*, 65, 359–366.

Cuijpers, P., Geraedts, A. S., van Oppen, P., Andersson, G., Markowitz, J., & van Straten, A. (2011). Interpersonal psychotherapy for depression: A meta-analysis. *American Journal of Psychiatry*, 168, 581–592.

Cuijpers, P., Muñoz, R. F., Clarke, G. N., & Lewinsohn, P. L. (2009). Psychoeducational treatment and prevention of depression: The "coping with depression" course thirty years later. *Clinical Psychology Review*, 29, 449–458.

Cuijpers, P., van Straten, A., Smit, F., Mihalopoulos, C., & Beekman, A. (2008). Preventing the onset of depressive disorders: A meta-analytic review of psychological interventions. *American Journal of Psychiatry*, 165, 1272–80.

Durlak, J. A., Weissberg, R. P., Dymnicki, A. B., Taylor, R. D., & Schellinger, K. B. (2011). The impact of enhancing students' social and emotional learning: A meta-analysis of school-based universal interventions. *Child Development*, 82, 405–432.

Fergusson, D. M., Horwood, J., Ridder, E. M., & Beautrais, A. L. (2005). Subthreshold depression in adolescence and mental health outcomes in adulthood. *Archives of General Psychiatry*, 62, 66–72.

Foster, S., Rollefson, M., Doksum, T., Noonan, D., Robinson, G., & Teich, J. (2005). *School mental health services in the United States, 2002–2003* (DHHS Pub. No. [SMA] 05-4068. Rockville, MD: Center for Mental Health Services, Substance Abuse and Mental Health Services Administration.

Gillham, J. E., Reivich, K. J., Freres, D. R., Chaplin, T. M., Shatté, A. J., Samuels, B., . . . Seligman, M. E. (2007). School-based prevention of depressive symptoms: A randomized controlled study of the effectiveness and specificity of the Penn Resiliency Program. *Journal of Consulting and Clinical Psychology*, 75, 9–19.

Gillham, J. E., Shatté, A. J., & Reivich, K. J. (2001). Needed for prevention research: Long-term follow-up and the evaluation of mediators, moderators, and lay providers. *Prevention & Treatment, 4*, Article 9.

Gould, M. S., Marrocco, F. A., Kleinman, M., Thomas, J. G., Mostkoff, K., Cote, J., & Davies, M. (2005). Evaluating iatrogenic risk of youth suicide screening programs: A randomized controlled trial. *The Journal of the American Medical Association, 293*, 1635–1643.

Hine, C., Howell, H., & Yonkers, K. (2008). Integration of medical and psychological treatment within the primary health care setting. *Social Work in Health Care, 47*, 122–134.

Horowitz, J. L., & Garber, J. (2006). The prevention of depressive symptoms in children and adolescents: A meta-analytic review. *Journal of Consulting and Clinical Psychology, 74*, 401–415.

Horowitz, J. L., Garber, J., Ciesla, J. A., Young, J., & Mufson, L. (2007). Prevention of depressive symptoms in adolescents: A randomized trial of cognitive-behavioral and interpersonal prevention programs. *Journal of Consulting and Clinical Psychology, 75*, 693–706.

Jaycox, L. H., Reivich, K. J., Gillham, J., & Seligman, M. E. P. (1994). Prevention of depressive symptoms in school children. *Behaviour Research and Therapy, 32*, 801–816.

Joiner, T. & Coyne, J. (1999). *The interactional nature of depression: Advances in interpersonal approaches.* Washington, DC: American Psychological Association.

Keenan, K., Hipwell, A., Feng, X., Babinski, D., Hinze, A., Rischall, M., & Henneberger, A. (2008). Subthreshold symptoms of depression in preadolescent girls are stable and predictive of depressive disorders. *Journal of the American Academy of Child and Adolescent Psychiatry, 47*, 1433–1442.

Knapp, P. K., & Foy, J. M. (2012). Translations: Integrating mental health care into pediatric primary care settings. *Journal of the American Academy of Child and Adolescent Psychiatry, 51*, 982–984.

Kovacs, M. (2003). *Children's Depression Inventory: Technical manual.* Toronto: Multi-Health Systems.

Lewinsohn, P. M., Solomon, A., Seeley, J. R., & Zeiss, A. (2000). Clinical implications of "subthreshold" depressive symptoms. *Journal of Abnormal Psychology, 109*, 345–351.

Masia-Warner, C., Nangle, D. W., & Hansen, D. J. (2006). Bringing evidence-based child mental health services to the schools: General issues and specific populations. *Education and Treatment of Children, 29*, 165–172.

Merikangas, K. R., He, J., Burstein, M., Swanson, S. A., Avenevoli, S., Cui, L., . . . Swendsen, J. (2010). Lifetime prevalence of mental disorders in US adolescents: Results from the National Comorbidity Survey Replication–Adolescent Supplement (NCS-A). *Journal of the American Academy of Child and Adolescent Psychiatry, 49*, 980–989.

Merry, S. N. (2007). Prevention and early intervention for depression in young people: A practical possibility? *Current Opinions in Psychiatry, 20*, 325–329.

Merry, S. N., Hetrick, S. E., Cox, G. R., Brudevold-Iverson, T., Bir, J. J., & McDowell, H. (2011). Psychological and educational interventions for preventing depression in children and adolescents. *Evidence-Based Child Health: A Cochrane Review Journal, 7*, 1409–1685.

Mihalopoulos, C., Vos, T., Pirkis, J., & Carter, R. (2012). The population cost-effectiveness of interventions designed to prevent childhood depression. *Pediatrics, 129*, e723–e730.

Mufson, L., Dorta, K. P., Moreau, D., & Weissman, M. M. (2004). *Interpersonal psychotherapy for depressed adolescents* (2nd ed.). New York: Guilford Press.

Mufson, L., Dorta, K. P., Wickramaratne, P., Nomura, Y., Olfson, M., & Weissman, M. M. (2004). A randomized effectiveness trial of interpersonal psychotherapy for depressed adolescents. *Archives of General Psychiatry, 63*, 577–584.

Mufson, L., Moreau, D., Weissman, M. M., Wickramaratne, P., Martin, J., & Samoilov, A. (1994). The modification of interpersonal psychotherapy with depressed adolescents IPT-A: Phase I and Phase II studies. *Journal of the American Academy of Child and Adolescent Psychiatry, 33*, 695–705.

Mufson, L., Weissman, M. M., Moreau, D., & Garfinkel, R. (1999). Efficacy of interpersonal psychotherapy for depressed adolescents. *Archives of General Psychiatry, 56*, 573–579.

Muñoz, R. F., Cuijpers, P., Smit, F., Barrera, A. Z., & Leykin, Y. (2010). Prevention of major depression. *Annual Review of Clinical Psychology, 6*, 181–212.

National Association of Pediatric Nurse Practitioners (NAPNAP). (2013). NAPNAP position statement on the integration of mental health care in pediatric primary care settings. *Journal of Pediatric Healthcare, 27*, 15A–16A.

Radloff, L. S. (1977). The CES-D scale: A self-report depression scale for research in the general population. *Applied Psychological Measurement, 1,* 385–401.

Reynolds, W. M. (2002). *Reynolds Adolescent Depression Scale* (2nd ed.). Port Huron, MI: Sigma Assessment Systems.

Rice, F. (2010). Genetics of childhood and adolescent depression: Insights into etiological heterogeneity and challenges for future genomic research. *Genome Medicine, 2,* 68–73.

Ryan, N. D. (2003). Child and adolescent depression: Short-term treatment effectiveness and long-term opportunities. *International Journal of Methods in Psychiatric Research, 12,* 44–53.

Stice, E., Shaw, H., Bohon, C., Marti, C. N., & Rohde, P. (2009). A meta-analytic review of depression prevention programs for children and adolescents: Factors that predict magnitude of intervention effects. *Journal of Consulting and Clinical Psychology, 77,* 486–503.

Tanofsky-Kraff, M., Shomaker, L., Wilfley, D. E., Young, J. F., Sbrocco, T., Stephens, M., ... Yanovsky, J. A. (2014). Targeted prevention of excess weight gain and eating disorders in high-risk adolescent girls: A randomized, controlled trial. *The American Journal of Clinical Nutrition, 100,* 110–118.

Tanofsky-Kraff, M., Wilfley, D. E., Young, J. F., Mufson, L., Yanovski, S. Z., Glasofer, D., & Salaita, C. G. (2007). Targeting binge eating for the prevention of excessive weight gain: Interpersonal psychotherapy for adolescents at high-risk for adult obesity. *Obesity, 15,* 1345–1355.

Tanofsky-Kraff, M., Wilfley, D. E., Young, J. F., Mufson, L., Yanovski, S. Z., Glasofer, D. R., ... & Schvey, N. A. (2010). A pilot study of interpersonal psychotherapy for preventing excess weight gain in adolescent girls at-risk for obesity. *International Journal of Eating Disorders, 43,* 701–706.

Tram, J. & Cole, D. A. (2006). A multimethod examination of the stability of depressive symptoms in childhood and adolescence. *Journal of Abnormal Psychology, 115,* 674–686.

US Department of Health and Human Services. (2010). *Healthy People 2020.* Retrieved from https://www.healthypeople.gov/.

Vogel, M. E., Malcore, S. A., Illes, R. C., & Kirkpatrick, H. A. (2014). Integrated primary care: Why you should care and how to get started. *Journal of Mental Health Counseling, 36,* 130–144.

Weare, K., & Nind, M. (2011). Mental health promotion and problem prevention in schools: What does the evidence say? *Health Promotion International, 26,* i29–i69.

Weissman, M. M., Markowitz, J. C., & Klerman, G. L. (2000). *Comprehensive guide to interpersonal psychotherapy.* New York: Basic Books.

Weist, M. D., Rubin, M., Moore, E., Adelsheim, S., & Wrobel, G. (2007). Mental health screening in schools. *Journal of School Health, 77,* 53–58.

Wilfley, D. E., MacKenzie, K. R., Welch, R. R., Ayres, V. E., Weissman, M. M. (2000). *Interpersonal psychotherapy for group.* New York: Basic Books.

World Health Organization. (2008). *The global burden of disease: 2004 update.* Geneva, Switzerland: WHO Press.

Young, J. F., Benas, J. S., Schueler, C. M., Gallop, R., Gillham, J. E., & Mufson, L. (2015). A randomized depression prevention trial comparing IPT-AST to group counseling in schools. *Prevention Science.* Advance online publication, December 5. doi:10.1007/s11121-015-0620-5.

Young, J. F., Gallop, R., & Mufson, L. (2009). Mother-child conflict and its moderating effects on depression outcomes in a preventive intervention for adolescent depression. *Journal of Clinical Child and Adolescent Psychology, 38,* 696–704.

Young, J. F., Kranzler, A., Gallop, R., & Mufson, L. (2012). Interpersonal Psychotherapy–Adolescent Skills Training: Effects on school and social functioning. *School Mental Health, 4,* 254–264.

Young, J. F., Makover, H. B., Cohen, J. R., Mufson, L., Gallop, R., & Benas, J. S. (2012). Interpersonal Psychotherapy–Adolescent Skills Training: Anxiety outcomes and impact of comorbidity. *Journal of Clinical Child and Adolescent Psychology, 41,* 640–653.

Young, J. F., Mufson, L., & Davies, M. (2006). Efficacy of Interpersonal Psychotherapy–Adolescent Skills Training: An indicated preventive intervention for depression. *Journal of Child Psychology and Psychiatry, 47,* 1254–1262.

Young, J. F., Mufson, L., & Gallop, R. (2010). Preventing depression: A randomized trial of Interpersonal Psychotherapy–Adolescent Skills Training. *Depression and Anxiety, 27,* 426–433.

About the Authors

Jami F. Young, Ph.D., is an associate professor of clinical psychology at Rutgers University. Dr. Young developed Interpersonal Psychotherapy – Adolescent Skills Training (IPT-AST), a depression prevention program for adolescents. She has conducted three randomized controlled trials of IPT-AST, with a fourth under way. Dr. Young has trained and supervised clinicians in IPT-AST, as well as in interpersonal psychotherapy for the treatment of depression. Her research examines the efficacy of depression prevention programs and risk and protective factors for youth depression.

Laura Mufson, Ph.D., is a professor of medical psychology in psychiatry at Columbia University Medical Center (CUMC), and director of the Department of Clinical Psychology at New York State Psychiatric Institute. In addition, she is director of clinical child psychology in child psychiatry at Columbia University College of Physicians and Surgeons. She is the developer of Interpersonal Psychotherapy for Depressed Adolescents (IPT-A) and has published extensively on interpersonal psychotherapy and its adaptations for treating youth in diverse settings.

Christie M. Schueler, Ph.D., is a clinical psychologist who has served as a group leader and project coordinator at Rutgers University for two studies of IPT-AST funded by the National Institute of Mental Health. She has worked in academic and hospital settings with children, adolescents, and adults diagnosed with depression as well as a variety of other disorders. Dr. Schueler has extensive experience running IPT-AST groups and has provided IPT-AST training and supervision to psychology graduate students and community clinicians.

Index

academic performance, 137
adaptations of IPT-AST, 171
adolescent depression, 17–22, 44–47
affect. *See* feelings and mood
aggression, 21, 154–157
anhedonia, assessment of, 18, 27, 127
anxiety
    assessment of, 20–21
    effects of IPT-AST on, 167–168, 170
    group process and, 153–154
appetite disturbances, assessment of, 18, 28, 127
assessment. *See also* depression symptoms and
        monitoring depression symptoms
    of abuse, 21, 162–163
    instruments for, 16, 140, 192
    interpersonal inventory as, 12, 29–33, 34–38
    of self-harm and suicidality, 19–20, 161–162
    of suitability for IPT-AST, 17–22, 140–141
attendance
    discussion about, 38, 42, 97–98, 100–101
    missed sessions and, 151–153
    research findings and, 170–171
    in school settings, 143

booster sessions
    attendance and, 152, 170
    coleaders and, 24
    engagement and, 155
    outline of, 189
    overview of, 11, 125–126, 135
    rationale for, 11, 125, 168
    reviewing progress in, 127–129
    skill review in, 130–132
    work at home and, 133
bullying, 21, 160–161

CBT. *See* cognitive-behavioral prevention
        programs
Center for Epidemiological Studies Depression Scale,
        16, 140
Child Depression Inventory, 16, 140
clinical interview, 17–22. *See also* assessment
closeness circle
    example of, 30
    overview of, 12, 29
    template for, 190
cognitive-behavioral prevention programs
    compared to IPT-AST, 4–5, 165
    Coping With Stress, 4, 165
    Penn Resiliency Program, 4
coleaders, 15, 24, 64, 71–72, 150
communication, psychoeducation about, 50–56
communication analysis
    examples of, 55–56, 77–78, 92–93
    in booster sessions, 129
    in middle phase, 70–71, 76–78, 92
    overview of, 13, 54–55, 58
    in termination phase, 110
communication note cards
    templates of, 198–203
    use of, 52–53
communication strategies
    application of, 78–85, 129–132
    barriers to use of, 112–114
    cue cards of, 215–224
    descriptions of, 13–14, 58–63, 225
    examples of, 65–67, 79–81, 83–84, 131–132
    maintenance of, 121
    review of, 74, 111–112, 130–132
    teaching of, 58–63
comorbidity, 20–21, 154, 170

concentration difficulties, assessment of, 19, 28, 127
confidentiality
    discussing with adolescent and parent, 17, 24–25
    discussing with group, 41
    issues related to, 157–158
conflict, interpersonal, 21–22, 48, 76, 165, 169, 172
course of IPT-AST, 10–11
crises
    disclosure of suspected abuse, 162–163
    self-harm and suicidality, 161–162
culture, 6, 169

decision analysis
    in booster sessions, 129–130
    examples of, 86–87
    in middle phase, 85–87, 93
    in mid-group session, 104
    overview of, 14, 70–71, 85–87
    sensitive topics and, 160
    in termination phase, 113
depression symptoms
    assessment of, 16–20, 27–28, 127
    checklist of, 192
    monitoring of, 40, 49–50, 57, 72–74, 90, 109,
        115–116
    prevalence of, 2–3
    psychoeducation about, 44–47, 115–118
    vignettes of, 193–197
development of IPT-AST, ix-x, 3–4, 5, 9, 144, 164
diagnosis. See assessment

education. See psychoeducation
efficacy of IPT-AST, 164–169
emotions. See feelings and mood
empirical evidence for IPT-AST, 164–173
engagement of adolescents. See also attendance and
        satisfaction with IPT-AST
    in initial phase, 39, 40–41, 49
    in pre-group sessions, 24–27, 154–155
    reluctant teens and, 153–154
    in school settings, 141–142

family involvement. See parent involvement
fatigue, assessment of, 18, 28, 127
feelings
    assessment of, 18–19, 27–28, 127
    expression of, 59–61

goals of IPT-AST, 9. See also individual goal setting
grief, 13, 21–22, 48
group composition, 5, 6, 22–23
group dynamics, management of, 15, 153–157
group format, benefits of, 9
group rules, 41–43

guilt, assessment of, 19, 28, 127

homework. See work at home.

individual goal setting, 12–13, 36–38, 98–99
individual sessions. See pre-group sessions, mid-group
        session, booster sessions
initial phase of IPT-AST
    communication analysis in, 54–56, 58
    communication strategies in, 58–67
    engagement and, 39–44
    group rules, establishing in, 41–43
    outlines of, 179–181
    overview of, 10, 39–40, 69
    psychoeducation in, 11–12, 44–47, 50–56
interpersonal inventory
    examples of, 32–33, 34–35, 36
    overview of, 12, 29–33, 34–36
    questions to ask during, 35, 191
interpersonal problem areas, 13, 21–22, 48
interpersonal psychotherapy, 3–4, 9, 11–14, 21, 171
interpersonal scenario notecards
    templates of, 204–214
    use of, 53–56, 57–58
interpersonal skill building, 3, 4, 10, 13–14
IPT. See interpersonal psychotherapy
IPT-A. See interpersonal psychotherapy
irritability, assessment of, 18, 27, 127

major depressive disorder. See depression symptoms
middle phase of IPT-AST
    communication analysis in, 76–78, 92–93
    communication strategies in, 78–85
    decision analysis in, 85–87, 93
    mood ratings aloud in, 73–74, 90
    outlines of, 182, 185–186
    overview of, 10, 70–72, 95
    role play in, 81–84
    work at home in, 87–88, 91–93
mid-group session
    attendance and, 152, 166, 170
    coleaders and, 24, 150
    discussion with adolescents about, 27, 68,
        89–91
    engagement and, 155
    outlines of, 183–184
    overview of, 10, 71–72, 96–97, 106–107
    parents and, 17, 27, 99–104, 159
    scheduling and, 71–72
    sensitive topics and, 160
missed sessions, 151–153
monitoring depression symptoms
    via depression checklist, 12, 19–20, 40, 49–50, 57,
        72, 90, 109, 114, 141

in individual sessions, 27–28, 127
overview of, 12
self-monitoring of, 115–118
mood
assessment of, 18, 27–29
ratings of, 12, 28–29, 33, 40, 49–50, 57, 73–74, 90, 109, 127
and relationships, 3, 10–12, 26–27, 50–51, 73–74
review of changes in, 115–116

nonsuicidal self-injury, 20, 161–162
NSSI. *See* nonsuicidal self-injury

parent involvement
in mid-group session of IPT-AST, 99–104
in pre-group session of IPT-AST, 24–27
issues regarding, 141–142, 158–159
pre-group sessions
coleaders and, 24, 150
engagement and, 24–27, 154–155
goal setting and, 12–13, 36–37
interpersonal inventory and, 10, 12, 29–33, 34–36
outlines of, 177–178
parent involvement in, 24–27
psychoeducation in, 25–27
prevention
concept of, 11, 25–26
implementation of, 7–8, 139–143, 147–150
levels of risk and, 5–6, 144–147
public health impact of, 1–2
rationale for, 1–4, 136–137
psychoeducation
about communication, 50–56
about depression, 26–27, 44–47
overview of, 11–12
about prevention, 25–27, 43–44
psychomotor agitation/retardation, assessment of, 18, 27, 127

relationships
assessment of. *See* interpersonal inventory
and goal setting, 12–13
and IPT-AST, 3–5, 9
and mood, 3, 10, 11–12, 26–27, 50–51, 73–74
research, *See also* empirical evidence for IPT-AST
on adaptations of IPT-AST, 171
current and future directions in, 172–173
on efficacy of IPT-AST, 164–169
on moderators of efficacy of IPT-AST, 169–170
on satisfaction with IPT-AST, 170–171
Reynolds Adolescent Depression Scale, 16, 140
risk factors for depression
elevated symptom of depression as, 3, 140
empirical research and, 3–4, 165, 169, 172–173

interpersonal risk factors, 3–4
levels of prevention and, 4–6, 140–141
role of group members, 43–44
role of group leader, 15, 43–44
role play
example of, 65–67, 83–84
overview of, 14
for application of communication strategies, 63–67
for illustration of impact of communication on others, 53–54, 57–58

sadness, assessment of, 18, 27, 127. *See also* depression symptoms
satisfaction with IPT-AST, 170–171
school settings
identification of participants and, 16, 140–141
implementation of IPT-AST in, 137–143, 163
logistical considerations and, 142–143
rationale for prevention in, x, 7, 136–137
research on IPT-AST in, 164–171
scripting, 14, 70–71, 78–81, 104–105, 129–130
self-harm. *See* nonsuicidal self-injury
self-report instruments, 16, 140, 192. *See also* assessment
settings for IPT-AST implementation
community, 7–8, 148–149
mental health, 8, 148
primary care, 7–8, 147–148
school, 7, 136–143
sexuality, issues related to, 160
sleep disturbances, assessment of, 18, 27, 127
structure of IPT-AST, 10–11
subthreshold depression, ix, 45
suicidality, assessment of, 19–20, 28, 127, 138, 161–162. *See also* depression symptoms
suitability for IPT-AST, determining, 16–23
symptoms. *See* depression symptoms

techniques of IPT-AST, 11–15. *See also* communication analysis, decision analysis, psychoeducation, monitoring depression symptoms, individual goal setting, interpersonal inventory, interpersonal skill building, role play, scripting, work at home
termination phase of IPT-AST
maintaining skills and, 121
need for further services and, 108
outlines of, 187–188
overview of, 11, 108, 124
review of changes in mood in, 115–116
review of changes in relationships in, 119–121
review of communication strategies in, 111–114
warning symptoms and, 116–118

training of group leaders, 15
treatment of adolescent depression, 1, 3–4, 9

weight gain/loss, assessment of. *See* appetite
    disturbances, assessment of

work at home
    assignment of, 87–88, 95, 105, 114, 133
    example of, 88
    overview of, 14–15, 87–88
    review of, 91–93, 110